SHAKESPEARE
ON STAGE AND OFF

SHAKESPEARE
ON STAGE AND OFF

Edited by
Kenneth Graham and Alysia Kolentsis

McGill-Queen's University Press
Montreal & Kingston • London • Chicago

ISBN 978-0-7735-5924-0 (cloth)
ISBN 978-0-7735-5925-7 (paper)
ISBN 978-0-2280-0006-8 (ePDF)
ISBN 978-0-2280-0007-5 (ePUB)

Legal deposit fourth quarter 2019
Bibliothèque nationale du Québec

Printed in Canada on acid-free paper that is 100% ancient forest free (100% post-consumer recycled), processed chlorine free

This book has been published with the help of a grant from the Stratford Festival.

Funded by the Government of Canada | Financé par le gouvernement du Canada | Canada | Canada Council for the Arts | Conseil des arts du Canada

We acknowledge the support of the Canada Council for the Arts.
Nous remercions le Conseil des arts du Canada de son soutien.

Library and Archives Canada Cataloguing in Publication

Title: Shakespeare on stage and off / edited by Kenneth Graham and Alysia Kolentsis.
Names: Graham, Kenneth J. E. (Kenneth John Emerson), 1960– editor. | Kolentsis, Alysia, 1976– editor.
Description: Includes bibliographical references and index.
Identifiers: Canadiana (print) 20190161507 | Canadiana (ebook) 20190161531 | ISBN 9780773559240 (cloth) | ISBN 9780773559257 (paper) | ISBN 9780228000068 (ePDF) | ISBN 9780228000075 (ePUB)
Subjects: LCSH: Shakespeare, William, 1564–1616—Dramatic production. | LCSH: Shakespeare, William, 1564–1616—Stage history. | LCSH: Shakespeare, William, 1564–1616—Adaptation. | LCSH: Shakespeare, William, 1564–1616—Criticism and interpretation.
Classification: LCC PR3091 .S33 2019 | DDC 822.3/3—dc23

This book was typeset in 10.5/13 Sabon.

For Josephine Harris
and in memory of Dr Jules Harris

CONTENTS

FIGURES

ACKNOWLEDGMENTS

Many of the essays in this volume were presented in June 2017 at the second Shakespearean Theatre Conference, "Shakespeare 401: What's Next?" in Stratford, Ontario. Two others were presented in 2015 at the inaugural Shakespearean Theatre Conference, "Language in Text and Performance." We would like to thank everyone involved in both conferences, including our institutional sponsors, the Stratford Festival, the University of Waterloo, and St Jerome's University. We are especially grateful to Dr Jules and Josephine Harris for their generous financial support of the conferences, as well as of this book. Mark Abley, Jonathan Crago, Kathleen Fraser, and the rest of the team at McGill-Queen's University Press believed in this project from the beginning and provided expert guidance, while the insights of the press's anonymous readers significantly strengthened the result. Finally, we would like to thank our families, Beth and Jimmy Graham and Mike, Lucia, and Anna Crosby, for the love, encouragement, and joy they give us.

SHAKESPEARE
ON STAGE AND OFF

INTRODUCTION

KENNETH GRAHAM AND ALYSIA KOLENTSIS

Shakespeare On Stage and Off is dedicated to the proposition that Shakespeare's enormous prestige as poet, playwright, and popular culture phenomenon both enriches our culture and provides an occasion to reflect upon developments within it. The book's three parts, "Playing with Shakespeare," "Working with Shakespeare," and "Living with Shakespeare," explore contemporary stagings of Shakespeare's plays, propose a new approach to those plays through the work we do every day, and probe Shakespeare's persistent and adaptive presence in life beyond the stage. Together they portray a Shakespeare who animates conversations about such apparent oppositions as work and play, tradition and experiment, performance and identity, unity and diversity, similarity and difference, reader and text, and audience and artist. This Shakespeare is inescapable, but he is also malleable, subject to constant redefinition and new understandings. He speaks to us only as much as he is spoken to by us. What we are is inseparable from what he is, or, to put it differently, we understand him partly by understanding ourselves, and vice versa.

The idea for this volume emerged from "Shakespeare 401: What's Next?," the second Shakespearean Theatre Conference, held in Stratford, Ontario, in June 2017, and the majority of the chapters that follow were first presented there. Written for an audience both of specialists and of general readers with a special interest in Shakespeare, the nineteen chapters showcase the variety and vitality of Shakespeare's interaction with contemporary life and culture. Their subjects include stage productions of Shakespeare in London, Stratford-upon-Avon, Edinburgh, New York, Minneapolis, Los

Angeles, Toronto, and Stratford, Ontario; live theatre broadcasts from London and Stratford-upon-Avon (as watched in Austin, Texas, and South Bend, Indiana); films from India and the United Kingdom; and television shows from the United Kingdom and the United States. There are also chapters on reading stage directions and modernizing Shakespeare's language, and a cluster of chapters proposing a new multidisciplinary approach to the plays that emphasizes their relationship to professional and personal forms of knowledge. Regrettably, there are limits to what a volume such as this can cover. Readers will find no consideration of graphic and manga Shakespeare (especially popular among students familiar with these formats), web series such as *Nothing Much to Do* (also aimed at a young audience), or novelistic rewritings of Shakespeare (e.g., the Hogarth Shakespeare); and, apart from Amrita Sen's chapter on Vishal Bhardwaj's Shakespeare films, they will find no sustained discussion of Shakespeare's presence outside North America and the United Kingdom. What they *will* find is a set of lively and readable contributions in several written modes, from close readings to personal reflections, from careful analysis of staging practices to an account of a dinner party. All, we hope, are provocations to further thought about our relationship to Shakespeare, wherever we encounter him.

PLAYING WITH SHAKESPEARE

As Antoni Cimolino begins this section by pointing out, the text of *Hamlet* is a script that can be performed on stage in multiple ways. Playing Shakespeare entails a process of playing with Shakespeare's script, a process of invention and discovery in which some possibilities are tried and rejected, others are tried and adopted, and many more are never attempted at all. Initially, the director faces major decisions about performance style: for example, Christie Carson shows that a production of *Two Gentlemen of Verona* might aim for psychological realism and believable characters, or it might opt for a less naturalistic, more self-consciously "theatrical" effect. As the process approaches its goal of performance, it becomes more and more specific by virtue of the choices it embodies. Hamlet, for example, may wear black tights or blue jeans; he may appear to be melancholy or mad; and he may be played by a man or a woman. Together, the accumulated performance choices of live theatre create new meanings for the play in its historical moment: this is not some universal idea of *Hamlet* that we are witnessing, but a particular production of the play – one that, as the company continues to play and experiment with it, may be different tomorrow.

Because playing Shakespeare necessarily moves from the words on the page toward their physical embodiment on the stage, the essays in this section raise questions about the nature and significance of language. Shakespeare, Cimolino notes, sometimes thematizes the power of words. But which words? In performance, the choice of language can be critically important, as it is in much world literature today. Will Shakespeare's English be used, or will the play be translated, as it was in the Shona-language production of *Two Gentlemen of Verona* that Carson examines? What is the significance of such a choice in a multicultural, linguistically rich environment? Roderick McKeown finds a different example of translation in a bilingual production of *Hamlet*, which spoke to the deaf by using American Sign Language. Here the very idea of language expands from something spoken to something performed, the eloquence of action that is another of Shakespeare's themes. Although words were as central to his theatre as they have been to any theatre in history, the Shakespearean stage nevertheless abounded in non-verbal elements, not the least of which was the actor's body. Contemporary theatre continues to explore not only the potential of Shakespeare's words but also the potential of bodies on stage to create and express meaning. Along these lines, Linda McJannet investigates the trend toward "physical theatre." While some movements and gestures – whether those of ASL or of ordinary body language – carry a set meaning upon which theatre of many kinds can draw, physical theatre invents movements that attempt to serve an expressive function. Can actors convey, for example, the shattering force of a tempest through synchronized movements on stage? And why might such an endeavour be appealing at the current moment?

Perhaps no theatrical practice does more to shape the meanings of Shakespeare's plays on today's stage than the casting choices known as colour-blind and cross-gender casting. In some ways, playing Shakespeare resembles a laboratory experiment in which a slight change in the chemicals mixed can significantly alter the reaction that takes place. What new meanings are produced when a black Iago seduces Othello, as in the Royal Shakespeare Company production examined by Christina Luckyj? Is the reaction the same,

Lauren Eriks Cline asks, when a black Julius Caesar is assassinated in Obama-era Minneapolis as when a white Caesar is stabbed in Trump-era New York? What is precipitated by the female performances of Hamlet and *All's Well That Ends Well*'s Lavatch that McKeown studies in recent Toronto productions? Such casting choices shake things up: colour-blind casting, Luckyj writes, "complicates assumptions about the relation of race to character." The point may be broadened. Many casting and performance decisions complicate not only the relationship of race to character, but the relationship of gender and sexuality to character, of ethnicity to character, of nationality to character, or religion to character, or education to character, and so on. Race and gender don't exist in isolation, or as simple, binary oppositions (black and white, male and female), and the various components of character mix together in complex ways to produce hybrid identities that, Luckyj reminds us, may be the site of internal conflict and division. The complexity of the identities that these performances create – performance itself being, as Carson implies, at least partly a language used to create identity – reflects the complexity of contemporary identities. They make differences visible, but they also present new opportunities for connection.

Of course, the most important connection live theatre makes is with its audience, whose members are too often thought of as passive recipients of the creative discoveries made by the artists on and behind the stage. Shakespeare, who sometimes called explicitly on his audience to contribute imaginatively or sympathetically to the performance, knew better. While "Playing with Shakespeare" as a whole shows an awareness of the audience's active role, two of the chapters pay particular attention to the challenges new trends in Shakespearean performance present to audiences. McJannet suggests that the audience's role in interpreting the visual images and kinetic metaphors of physical theatre is so important that they should be considered "co-creators" of what they see. Eriks Cline goes further, drawing on reception studies to conceptualize spectators as helping to write, rather than simply to record or to observe, the meanings of race in the performances they attend. Live theatre, after all, is a form of interaction in which an audience responds to the performers, who in turn may respond during the performance to the audience's response. The two groups play off, and with, each other.

WORKING WITH SHAKESPEARE

Just as "Playing with Shakespeare" explores the ways that audiences are called upon to help make meanings in performance, and encourages us to understand performance as an interactive and often reciprocal process, "Working with Shakespeare" invites us to consider how active and encompassing the work of Shakespeare can be in contexts beyond the theatre. Traditional literary scholarship often presents literature as a lens through which to view the world (that is, we may study Shakespeare in part to understand something of what it means to be human) or focuses on its artistic properties with meanings to be gleaned through interpretation and analysis. The contributors to the "Working with Shakespeare" section of this volume seek to expand – sometimes radically – our understanding of what literature is for, what it may do, and how it intersects and interacts with areas of expertise that may at first glance appear profoundly removed from the literary and the theatrical. They share an interest in Shakespeare's utility, but not in a customary or a dogmatic sense. When Julia Lupton draws on the field of social work to analyze *Twelfth Night*, her interpretive goal is not to arrive at a new set of meanings inherent in or limited to the play. Rather, she asks how the expertise and perspectives of social workers might expand our understanding of the play's concerns more generally. How are the acts of succour dramatized in *Twelfth Night* sustained and experienced across communities and cultures? How might the play help us locate and understand "rhythms of duress, capacity, and repair" that recur in a variety of circumstances, geographical locations, and historical periods? In Lupton's view, social workers like those she interviews are not remote experts whose insights may be of incidental use to literary scholars; they are, instead, wonderfully imagined as "knowledge partners" whose perspectives best exist in vibrant dialogue with our own.

Lupton's vision of a convivial reading circle of knowledge partners is shared by Russell Bodi, who argues for the value of reciprocal exchange between representations of physical conflict in Shakespeare and the lived experience of street fighters. The laconic, imprisoned street fighter featured in Bodi's study possesses a tacit and embodied knowledge of conflict that grants him a singular perspective into the skirmishes represented in Shakespeare's works. Bodi, like Lupton, suggests that this sort of expertise is useful both to an understanding of Shakespeare – the ways in which Shakespeare's conflicts often demonstrate unexpected elements of collaboration and respect, for example – and to broader notions of conflict. What do Shakespeare's fights and the experiences of Bobby the Street Fighter tell us about the relationships between conflict and volition, collaboration and defiance? What might the improvised choreography of a street fight tell us about the movement of bodies in performance, and bodies in the world?

Another shared aspect of the chapters in "Working with Shakespeare" is the animation and promise awakened by a broader understanding of "applied" Shakespeare. Working with Shakespeare need not be work at all; if anything, we work best when we allow ourselves to play. These chapters brim with excitement about new opportunities for encounters with Shakespeare, perhaps most evidently in David Goldstein's account of cooking through Shakespeare. Goldstein offers a test case in extreme experimentation with critical method. His team of knowledge partners – a group of food professionals including chefs, restaurateurs, and food critics – collaboratively design, cook, and eat a meal based on the feasts and foods of *Timon of Athens*. This experiment reconsiders the boundaries of research and criticism, inviting us to think of physical endeavour – the preparation of a meal, the act of eating itself – as a form of criticism. Criticism that is fundamentally embodied, research that is visceral and open to sensory reception and pleasure: such a model encourages an expansive revision of what it means to share knowledge with others. One of the insights about *Timon of Athens* that emerged during the meal, Goldstein notes, is the interactive, mutually dependent relationship of organic growth that is at odds with Timon's solipsism: "There is only reciprocity," Goldstein writes.

Jeffrey Wilson echoes Goldstein's maxim with the evocative term "interpretive reciprocity," which neatly captures the guiding principle of the "Working with Shakespeare" section. Wilson's chapter considers Prince Hal's famous "redeeming time" soliloquy in *1 Henry IV* alongside the theoretical lens of narrative criminology. Yet he envisions the tenets of this theory not merely as prized and borrowed tools transplanted onto Shakespearean criticism, but as porous concepts receptive to reciprocal insight. We may understand Hal's rationalization of his behaviour in this speech as reflective of "narratives of desistence" common to juvenile offenders, but we should also ask how Shakespearean examples can be used to build criminological theories.

In Wilson's account, private stories, lived experience, and traditions of criticism from disparate fields all play a role in interpretive processes, and we open ourselves up to rich and unexpected possibilities when we consider how Shakespeare need not be the starting nor the end point of critical inquiry. Partnership, collaboration, and mutual exchange are the guiding values of these chapters, each of which invents new avenues for our interactions with Shakespeare.

LIVING WITH SHAKESPEARE

What does it mean to live with Shakespeare today? Beyond the stage, how do the historical conditions with which we are so familiar – ubiquitous visual spectacle, relentless connectivity – inform our encounters with our most famous playwright? As the chapters in the final section of *Shakespeare On Stage and Off* suggest, living with Shakespeare now involves attending to the changed and expanded meanings that emerge when his works are repeatedly rewritten, reinvented, and remediated – that is, adapted for consumption in new and different media.

Film continues to be the favourite medium for offstage Shakespeare. Conventional critical wisdom holds that Shakespeare films highlight the aspects of the plays that seem most resonant and suggestive to the culture from which they emerge. Franco Zeffirelli's 1968 *Romeo and Juliet*, for example, captured the youthful exuberance that informed the vital socio-cultural shifts of the 1960s, while Baz Luhrmann's 1997 version united the language of Shakespeare with the kinetic visual trends of late-century media. "Living with Shakespeare" extends this critical legacy to show how certain plays seem particularly responsive to the concerns of our cultural moment. Hayley O'Malley's chapter on Ralph Fiennes's screen adaptation of *Coriolanus* illustrates how the conflicts of this tragedy, so dependent on deft social manoeuvring, are thrown into brilliant relief when filtered through the hyper-mediated, technology-dependent lens of current culture. New technologies, then, extend the parameters of adapted Shakespeare and act as reflections of themes within the plays, while at the same time opening possibilities for engagement with the world from which they emerge.

Live theatre broadcast Shakespeare, now broadly available in cinemas and arguably the most direct link between Shakespeare on stage and off, shares similar traits and concerns. When theatrical productions are filmed for wide release, the film director's vision is more vital and prominent than we might imagine, and may even conflict with the vision of the play's director. R.W. Jones's careful analysis shows that the camera does not capture the action on stage in a neutral or straightforward way, despite the "fly on the wall" illusion; instead, its effects work to build a distinct vision of the play. Peter Holland explores more generally the experience of livecast Shakespeare. Holland's personal account of watching productions on various London stages from the dark and distant seat of a cinema in South Bend, Indiana, isolates the stark differences between attending a live production and watching a "live" broadcast. That London performances may now easily be accessed elsewhere is a remarkable boon readily acknowledged by Holland. Yet, while the mediated Shakespeare encountered in theatre broadcast can reproduce "original" stage effects, what about the other sorts of effects – nostalgia, distance – that are simultaneously produced? In gaining broader access to Shakespeare, what is lost?

The chapters in "Living with Shakespeare" also contend with ways that revisions of Shakespeare subtly (and not so subtly) alter Shakespearean themes, even as those themes help to shape current cultural understandings. While the collision of the political and the personal is commonplace in Shakespeare's drama, particularly in representations of political conflict encroaching on domestic spaces, O'Malley and Amrita Sen ask how we utilize and rethink these Shakespearean representations in the context of current global politics. O'Malley explores the strategic use and conspicuous absence of children and youth in Fiennes's *Coriolanus*, while Sen shows how the domestic elements of *Macbeth*, *Othello*, and *Hamlet* are foregrounded in Vishal Bhardwaj's Indian Shakespeare trilogy, *Maqbool*, *Omkara*, and *Haider*. While these films draw on contemporary political contexts – the setting of *Haider*, for example, is disputed Kashmiri territory – the focus of each production remains resolutely personal. Tellingly, it is the female characters who consistently bear the harshest burdens of political turmoil.

Contemporary society also draws on and reshapes a Shakespearean thematics of sexual and cultural difference. Due to his canonical status, Shakespeare has been enlisted for centuries to stand for social norms such as heterosexual marriage and Christian religious belief, as well as for the superiority of the English language or of Western civilization as a whole, even as his works have also been seen to challenge or question these norms. As is often remarked, Shakespeare himself seems remarkably even-handed about such matters: the complex gender identities and sexuality of the sonnets and of comedies such as *As You Like It* and *Twelfth Night*, where cross-dressing and misrecognitions scramble patterns of desire, give way to heterosexual relationships and marriage; outsiders such as Shylock and Othello are scapegoated and stigmatized, but also rendered sympathetic. This apparent ambivalence has ensured that Shakespeare's writings – and the idea of "Shakespeare" more generally – have remained a key location for debates about a range of cultural questions. For example, Lisa Starks finds that the popular Shakespeare biopics are preoccupied with issues of gender and sexuality. Shakespeare's own disputed sexuality is treated gingerly. He is both aligned with and dissociated from the male-male desire expressed in the sonnets; such desire is instead typically displaced onto another canonical author, Christopher Marlowe, whose openly transgressive sexuality these biopics often portray favourably. A step further away from the plays, Brandon Christopher looks at *Star Trek*'s long-standing engagement with Shakespeare. In the *Star Trek* universe, Christopher argues, Shakespeare represents the superiority of an anthropocentric, Anglo-American world view. His authority is appropriated to underwrite a number of plot lines that celebrate assimilation to this world view. Both Starks and Christopher explore how Shakespeare continues to shape and be shaped by the conversations taking place in and through the forms of popular culture.

Audiences, which are so important to the stage performances studied in "Playing with Shakespeare," provide a crucial bridge between the forms of culture where Shakespeare is adapted, remediated, and transformed and the everyday lives where he is experienced and absorbed. The chapters in "Living with Shakespeare" consider audiences in many ways. While Jones and especially Holland show how the experience of a play's audience differs from that of a film's viewers, Jones and O'Malley question the idea that film audiences are less active interpreters than their counterparts in the theatre. Today's audiences are savvy readers of the language of film, instinctively recognizing the significance of a close-up shot, a juxtaposition of images, and what is left out of the frame. Moreover, by exercising such knowledge and skills, film engages in what Lupton calls "capacity building": the visual images and media technologies highlighted in Fiennes's *Coriolanus*, for example, can help audiences build their capacity for an important kind of media literacy. A very different type of audience interaction appears in *Sleep No More*, an adaptation of *Macbeth* that Jacob Claflin characterizes as "an immersive performance event." *Sleep No More* is interactive, and so openly grants its audience some ability to determine the performance's meaning. But the audience's apparent control is strictly limited. Claflin shows that this immersive but restricted audience experience in some ways resembles playing a video game. Probably the most active audience experience considered in these pages is the culture of fandom that surrounds the Shakespeare biopics. Starks demonstrates how fan websites allow audiences to have their say by writing sequels and parallel fanfiction of their own. These websites bring into view one of the fundamental facts of Shakespeare's movement from the play on stage to the life off it: the performance or the adaptation may come to an end, but its interaction with our lives does not stop.

The final few chapters in this volume return us to the question of language with which we began. While O'Malley is particularly attentive to film's tendency to substitute images for words, Claflin documents the copious imagery in *Sleep No More*, which contains not one word of *Macbeth*. With *Sleep No More*'s replacement of words entirely with material objects, we may have reached the maximal distance from Shakespeare's language. But of course we still read Shakespeare. How, then, shall we approach his words on the page? Are we properly equipped to do so, or should we – or the words – change? Gina Hausknecht proposes one way in which we can become better readers of Shakespeare – by paying more attention to the stage directions in our editions of his plays, while also understanding the editorial history and conventions of these texts. If we do so, she contends, we will be able to read both more critically and more imaginatively, staging the plays in our minds. In the final chapter, Eric Spencer provocatively argues not that we should modernize Shakespeare's language, but that it is time that we seriously considered whether we should do so. Spencer brings sober consideration to bear on a topic often discussed with more heat than light and, while leaving the question open, invites the reader to think in a similarly productive manner. Both Hausknecht and Spencer do what this volume as a whole does – challenge the reverence and awe that leave Shakespeare static and unchanging, unable to speak to life today. They encourage instead an active engagement that wrestles the Shakespearean angel until he blesses us, both on stage and off.

PART ONE

PLAYING WITH SHAKESPEARE

I

THE PLAY'S NOT THE ONLY THING

ANTONI CIMOLINO

In the theatre, there's no such thing as Shakespeare's *Hamlet.* Or Shakespeare's *King Lear.* Or Shakespeare's *Antony and Cleopatra.* Or any of the other plays in the canon. At least not in the same way that there's a novel by Charles Dickens called *Great Expectations* or a painting by Leonardo da Vinci called the *Mona Lisa.* Shakespeare left us no work of *theatrical* art called *Hamlet.* All he left us was a *script*: an instruction manual, if you like, for making a seemingly infinite variety of possible theatrical *Hamlet*s.

When we read Shakespeare's manual for *Hamlet*, all those possibilities remain open to us. We can imagine the scenes in as much, or as little, detail as we like. And what we mentally see or hear in one scene need not be consistent with what we hear or see in the next. In our mind's eye, we can envisage both a dashingly Byronic romantic hero *and* a fat thirty-year-old who still hasn't finished school. In our mind's ear, we can hear a whole chorus of the various inflections and emphases that could be given to a single line. We can simultaneously entertain two or more different meanings for the same word, line, or speech, savouring the ambiguity. For that matter, we needn't stage the play in our minds at all. We can focus on it solely as text, pondering the differences between folio and quarto versions, for instance, with no particular thought as to how they might look or sound.

But in the theatre, we can't keep our options so open. We have to make choices, beginning with the text. Folio? Quarto? Most likely, a conflation. But *whose* conflation? Or do we compile our own? And then what lines do we cut? We have to bring the performance in under three hours, otherwise the overtime budget will be seriously out of joint. How far do we go in clarifying the text? Do we let Hamlet say, "I'll make a ghost of him that lets me" (1.4.85)[1] and hope that tennis fans, at least, will understand the word *lets* in the sense of obstruction, not permission, or do we look for some metrically acceptable substitute, such as *stops* or *stays*?

What kind of world do we create on stage? Even a completely bare platform takes on a particular meaning when you put the play onto it. What kinds of people are the characters going to be? We have to make specific choices about which actors to hire, what we're going to give them to wear, and how they're going to comport themselves on stage. Is Polonius a doddering old fool, a sinister spymaster, or a loving father doing his best to deal with difficult situations? Shakespeare's words allow all these possibilities, and more. How will we present the Ghost? White makeup? Smoke and mirrors? A hologram? How raunchy will Ophelia get in her mad scene? How Oedipal will Hamlet get in the closet scene? Each of our myriad choices – some made in advance by the director and the designers, others emerging from rehearsal – contributes to a unique theatrical experience called *Hamlet*, with its own distinct meaning and its own distinct emotional impact.

Our choices are guided by the ideas, themes, and language we find in the text – and those findings can vary wildly from production to production. This became vividly apparent in the Stratford Festival's 2014 season, when we presented two versions of *A Midsummer Night's Dream* – one picking up on the idea of the play as a nuptial celebration, the other a radical distillation of the text that focused on the surprising amount of cruelty embodied in its language. The two productions could not have been more different.

Several things in the text of *Hamlet* struck me when I was preparing to direct it for the 2015 Stratford Festival season. One that particularly influenced my thinking is found in the graveyard scene. We all know that death is a major theme in this play, but we might not pay close attention to the First Gravedigger's remark that he took up his trade on the same day Hamlet was born. But to me, that line has an incredible resonance: a baby was born on the very day that the man who (we assume) is eventually going to bury him started his grave-digging work. It's like *Waiting for Godot*: "They give birth astride of a grave, the light gleams an instant, then it's night once more" (Beckett 1954, 57). That was one reason why I decided to set the play in a graveyard.

Our set consisted of an array of black slabs, made to look like polished granite, evoking both tombstones and war memorials

Figure 1.1 | Ophelia's burial, showing the slabs as tombstones.

– specifically, the memorial in Berlin for the murdered Jews of Europe. The slabs were different sizes and could be moved around to delineate different spaces: a bedroom, a throne room, a chapel. So everywhere we went in the play, we were in the midst of death.

The text makes references to night, to sleeping, to dreaming. "In that sleep of death, what dreams may come" (3.1.66). The whole play feels dreamlike; there are logical inconsistencies in it that are revealed in the cold light of reason. And time in *Hamlet* seems oddly fluid: we're never quite sure how long has elapsed between events. So in my production, we didn't adhere to a strictly naturalistic time frame. We began in the period of the First World War, though the Ghost (who, despite having died relatively recently, really belongs to a former era) wore medieval armour. As the action progressed, more modern elements began to appear, culminating in the arrival of another new regime in the person of Young Fortinbras, whose troops wore modern flak jackets.

About that Ghost: there's a question about his identity that seems to me to be crucial to Hamlet's dilemma, and thus to the whole meaning of the play. And it's a question that, in my view, goes to the heart of Shakespeare's art itself. *Hamlet*, as we all know, is full of references to performance, to acting, to the theatre. It also, I would argue, invites us to think about "words, words, words" (2.2.192) as themselves a subject for dramatic investigation. I'll try to explain what I mean in the following roundabout fashion.

The play begins with demands for identification. The opening words – "Who's there?" – are met with a counter-challenge: "Nay, answer me. Stand and unfold yourself." And that in turn is answered by what sounds like a password: "Long live the King!" (1.1.1–3). There are two ways of unfolding yourself, of expressing who you are: what you *say* and what you *do*. Word and action. Text and performance. And both can be ambiguous, misleading, or downright deceitful.

When the Ghost appears, the immediate response of the witnesses is to demand speech from it – and they perceive that speech is what it wants from them. But is this apparition really what it seems to be – the spirit of the late king, come from purgatory – or is it a "goblin damned" (1.4.40), a devil in disguise wanting to drag the credulous down to hell? These soldiers, with their careful reliance on passwords, know the dangers of saying the wrong thing. In this case, the wrong words could have consequences for their immortal souls, and they don't want to take any chances. So they ask Horatio to do the talking: "Thou art a scholar; speak to it" (1.1.42).

Now, I'm not sure that a postsecondary education is actually a prerequisite for conversing with a ghost, but it doesn't matter anyway, because it's not Horatio with whom the Ghost wants to exchange words. Perhaps "thou that usurp'st this time of night" isn't the most tactful way to address a freshly usurped and murdered monarch, but at any rate the Ghost gets huffy: "It is offended ... See, it stalks away!" (1.1.46, 50). So, right at the beginning of the play, we've been introduced to the idea of the power of words: the need to say the right thing to open a door to action – and the risks of opening the *wrong* door.

The Ghost, too, wants to know who's there. It's looking for Hamlet. So in my production, the Ghost carried a lantern, sweeping its beam across the stage and into the auditorium, both probing and blinding the audience (figure 1.2). By thus hindering the audience from properly *seeing* the Ghost, I left room for doubts about its true identity.

The idea of the power – and unreliability – of words continues to resonate through the play. In Claudius's court, the first thing Hamlet utters is a play on words: "A little more than kin, and less than kind." The next thing he says is also a pun: "I am too much in the sun." Words can have veiled meanings. Even actions can be suspect:

Figure 1.2 | The Ghost (Geraint Wyn Davies) shines his lantern at Horatio (Tim Campbell).

"Seems, madam? Nay, it is. I know not 'seems.'" And a couple of lines later: "These indeed seem, / For they are actions that a man might play" (1.2.65, 67, 76, 83–4).

Heartfelt words, though, can offer release. As soon as he's alone, Hamlet goes into his first soliloquy, venting all his pent-up emotions. And when he has to shut up, the pressure starts to build again: "But break my heart, for I must hold my tongue" (1.2.159). At the same time, he seems to despise himself for merely *saying* when he should be *slaying*: "This is most brave, / That I ... / Must like a whore unpack my heart with words" (2.2.521–4).

It's not just spoken words Shakespeare invites us to consider; it's also words committed to paper. Hamlet seems to do a lot of reading after he sees the Ghost. "What do you read, my lord?" asks Polonius (2.2.191). And *why* does he read? Is it just for show, like the book that Polonius puts in Ophelia's hand when he sets her up as a honey trap? Or is Hamlet actually looking to printed words for answers?

References to the written word seem to dovetail with the elusive quality of memory in this play. "My tables – meet it is I set it down" (1.5.107): On the face of it, that's a curious thing to say. Note to self: don't forget to avenge father's murder. "Remember me," urges the Ghost (1.591). And, from the cellarage, he repeatedly demands that Hamlet's companions swear to secrecy, as if saying it once weren't enough to lock it in. Hamlet struggles to recall the Player's speech about Hecuba – and there's that very curious moment with Reynaldo when, for no apparent reason, Polonius forgets what he's going to say next. Words in Hamlet's world seem to be hard to retain in memory. Maybe you *do* need to write things down.

At any rate, written words play key roles in the story. Hamlet writes a poem to Ophelia and a letter to Claudius. Claudius gives letters to his ambassadors, charging them to do no more than is written therein. And, crucially, Hamlet writes a play script, or at least a fragment of one: "a speech of some dozen or sixteen lines" (2.2.480). This is his master stroke: the device by which he can assure himself of the Ghost's veracity. The idea comes to him from witnessing a performance. Noting the emotional impact of the Player's Hecuba speech, Hamlet realizes that the power of language is such that it can make an audience betray their own feelings: "For murder, though it have no tongue, will speak / With most miraculous organ" (2.2.532–3).

As a theatre artist, I love the idea that putting on a play is a way to make audiences painfully aware of issues in their own lives. But the reason it's so important to Hamlet is that it offers him a way to resolve the doubt with which he's struggling. Even though he keeps talking about revenge, it seems clear to me that what Hamlet really wants is something far better than that: justice. Grasp that fact, and the mystery of his so-called delay evaporates. People say Hamlet dithers. But think about it. You see a ghost and you run out and kill somebody based on its say-so? That way institutional confinement lies.

In order to act justly, not psychotically, Hamlet needs empirical evidence to back up the Ghost's allegations. And he gets it by putting on a play. The stakes riding on that performance are huge. That's why he gives such detailed advice to the players on how to hold the mirror up to nature. Don't mouth it. Don't saw the air too much. Don't *under*play it, either. Make it *real*. It's vital to him that they get it right.

It's vital for the same reason that it's vital to the sentries in that opening scene to get it right when they confront the Ghost. Because on the Ghost's true nature depend two very different world views. As a society we no longer bother much about whether purgatory exists or not. But for Shakespeare's audience, this was a burning issue – literally. To a Catholic, believing in purgatory, the Ghost could be credible. But to a Protestant, there's only heaven and hell – and people don't come back from hell. In that scenario, the Ghost must be a demon.

Hamlet is clearly conflicted in his beliefs. Even after declaring, "It is an honest ghost," he admits, "The spirit that I have seen / May be a devil" (1.5.138; 2.2.537–8). And in "To be or not to be," he specifically says people don't come back from the dead. So, if Claudius starts like a guilty creature at the play, then Hamlet will know which version of the universe he's living in, and he'll know what course is just.

To me, religion is clearly central to the play; the text is steeped in it, from Marcellus's reference to the season of our Saviour's birth to Hamlet's observation about a divinity that shapes our ends. But because we don't share the same religious context in which Shakespeare wrote, audiences today may not take seriously Hamlet's doubts about the Ghost. So in my production, I tried to make that context visible by finding ways to manifest what is implicit in the text. For instance, I made Polonius a Lutheran minister. That choice not only brought together church and state in the spirit of Cardinal Richelieu, it also provided the key to Polonius's tendency to sermonize and offer sententious advice.

Also, the text tells us that Elsinore has a chapel – so we created one on stage, arranging the black slabs like pews, with a giant illuminated crucifix on the back wall (figure 1.3). By making that the place where Polonius sets Ophelia out to wait for Hamlet, with book in hand, I was able to have the "To be or not to be" speech – a contemplation of letting go the struggle in this world in favour of the next, and realizing that the next is not assured – take place in a house of worship. By suiting the action on stage to the references in the text (even seemingly incidental ones like Ophelia teasing her brother about "ungracious pastors" [1.3.46]), we sought to make the idea of the afterlife – and its importance to Hamlet – more immediate, more available, to today's audience.

Once Hamlet's mousetrap has snapped shut on Claudius, and guilt is proven, there should be nothing further to stand in his way. But again religion proves a stumbling block, and again I sought to make that clear by having Hamlet's encounter with Claudius take place in that same chapel, under the crucifix. This wasn't an arbitrary choice. It reinforced my view that Hamlet's decision not to act at that point is entirely logical. Here was Claudius seemingly (though *only* seemingly, as it turns out) deep in conversation with God, in God's house. Hamlet has just had clear confirmation that

Figure 1.3 | Claudius (Geraint Wyn Davies) prepares to pray; the slabs now serve as pews.

the Ghost is real, which in turn means that purgatory exists. And Hamlet doesn't want Claudius to go to purgatory. He wants him to go to hell. So he stays his hand.

The point at which Hamlet does really blow it comes in the next scene, when he abandons logic for passion and kills Polonius. This is the turning point of the play. It's like Romeo's killing of Tybalt: it forever changes his ability to do what he needs to do. For Hamlet at this point, everything changes. He realizes that, to borrow the words of *Lear*'s Albany, "Striving to better, oft we mar what's well" (1.4.344). Striving to better – to substitute justice for revenge – has been Hamlet's challenge all along. He has been so meticulous in trying to deal justly with Claudius, rather than vengefully, that he hasn't been able to act. But then, in a moment of passion, he commits an unjust murder of his own.

With that, he realizes that, in this world, you can't achieve perfect action. However carefully you try to orchestrate events, they keep spinning out of your control. Life isn't like a play: you can't direct or stage manage it. In trying to do better, you mar what's well. From that point on, Hamlet accepts the need for action, however imperfect, because to keep waiting for all the ducks to align in a perfect row is likely going to mean further deaths. His words become very different, less concerned with scruple: "from this time forth, / My thoughts be bloody, or be nothing worth!" (4.4.65–6). In his hands, words on paper now become lethal instruments. He rewrites Claudius's warrant for his death, consigning Rosencrantz and Guildenstern to their untimely ends.

Eventually, his language reflects his comparatively serene acceptance of the fact that he's going to have to settle for revenge after all, and that he himself is probably going to die in the attempt. To be or not to be is no longer really the question; we've all got to die sometime. The readiness is all.

So, to recap: every theatrical production makes decisions about how the words on the page translate into action on the stage, and each of those choices will create a different theatrical experience. That's why we can still make discoveries about these plays four centuries after they were written. But the larger point I've been circling around is that working on this play reinforced for me something I had long thought: that there is a fundamental ambivalence in Shakespeare's attitude to words, the very elements of his art.

"He words me, girls, he words me" (5.2.192), says Cleopatra, and Shakespeare's canon is full of characters skilled in the manipulative use of words. He seems to take a somewhat jaundiced view of the power of language, even as he revels in it. Henry V, for instance, is a brilliant orator, but his motives are murky, to say the least. Richard III, Iago, Edmund: all are master manipulators, brilliant actors, using language and performance to deadly ends. As an artist in words and stagecraft, Shakespeare was himself a master manipulator. So he was well aware that, in life, discerning true motive is very difficult. He seems very suspicious of good actors, because – unlike the plain speakers like Kent or Enobarbus, who dare to say what everyone else is thinking – their art consists of speaking what they don't feel. As a result, you can never be quite sure who's really there. I think he was working through that in *Hamlet*. I think that play's investigation of the power of words and performance reflects his own questions about the playwright's responsibility.

At the end of *Love's Labour's Lost*, when Shakespeare casts the shadow of death over his comedy, Rosaline challenges Berowne's use of words, his "gibing spirit," his propensity for sarcasm: "The world's large tongue / Proclaims you for a man replete with mocks, / Full of comparisons and wounding flouts" (5.2.842, 826–8). She tells him to go to a hospital and try, with his jokes, to get the terminally ill to laugh. If he can do that, then there will be some reason for his humour, beyond making fun of other people or showing himself off like a peacock. And though Berowne protests that this is too great a challenge for comedy – "Mirth cannot move a soul in agony" (5.2.841) – I do wonder if this isn't Shakespeare himself wondering about the intent of comedy and calling for a reformation of its use. It's almost as if he's looking at his own role as a playwright and wondering, "Why am I doing this? What *good* is this doing?" And so I find it interesting to see him, half a dozen years later, in the play within the play in *Hamlet*, showing his tragic hero trying to use theatre to achieve justice and thereby to do good in the world. And, unfortunately, failing.

There is no clear lesson to be learned from all of this: Shakespeare isn't the kind of playwright who teaches us lessons. Rather, what I see in *Hamlet* is a kind of circular exploration of the power of words, and of the responsibility that comes with that power. In *Hamlet*, Shakespeare constantly draws our attention to the manipulative uses we make of words; to the deceptive yet potentially truth-revealing art of the theatre; to the illusions and dreams that are our alternate realities. Even as he holds his own art of deception to its highest standards, taking it to its loftiest levels of accomplishment, he is drawing our attention to that art's dangers and its limitations.

Words, words, words: how do we read them, how do we use them, what do they tell us about ourselves? The play isn't the *whole* thing; full of potential as they are, the words on the page are just the starting point. It's the living theatre we make out of them that catches the consciences of us all and forces us to confront that overwhelming question: Who's there?

NOTE

1 All references to Shakespeare's plays are to Shakespeare (2002). The version of *Lear* cited is *King Lear: A Conflated Text*.

REFERENCES

Beckett, Samuel. 1954. *Waiting for Godot*. New York: Grove Press.

Shakespeare, William. 2002. *The Complete Works*. Edited by Stephen Orgel and A.R. Braunmuller. New York: Penguin.

2

GLOBAL *OTHELLO*, THEN AND NOW

The 2015 Royal Shakespeare Company Production in Context

CHRISTINA LUCKYJ

The perfect emblem of the 2015 Royal Shakespeare Company (RSC) production of *Othello* may well be its handkerchief. As in other productions, the precious napkin is dropped, snatched, thrown, lost, and memorialized; unlike other productions, in this one the handkerchief is *black*. In his groundbreaking essay, "Othello's Black Handkerchief," Ian Smith (2013) challenged the dominant reading practices that assume the handkerchief's whiteness and identify it as an emblem of Desdemona's body; in a rare example of critical influence on performance, the RSC production not only stages Smith's radical challenge to convention but extends it by reimagining Iago as black as well. According to Michael Coveney (2015), this bold move "makes you see the play anew." Indeed, when Dominic Cavendish (2015) writes that "history is being made" with this casting of a black Iago, challenging the "apartheid mode of whites-only," we might consider that the same might be said of black actors playing Othello. Heralded as a "landmark in the company's history" (Newman-O'Connor 2015, 58), the production directed by Iqbal Khan featured a multi-ethnic cast that, in addition to the British-Tanzanian actor Lucian Msamati as Iago, included the Ghanian-born British actor Hugh Quarshie as Othello, the British-Indian actor Ayesha Dharker as a Muslim Emilia, black British actor David Ajao as Montano, and a multi-racial company of soldiers. I want to explore the new interpretive possibilities that this staging opened up, not only for contemporary productions of *Othello* but also for our understanding of the play in its early modern global contexts.

At first glance, the notion of a black Iago seems puzzling, even troubling. After all, Iago himself boasts in soliloquy, "When devils will the blackest sins put on / They do suggest at first with heavenly shows" (2.3.336–7), a speech that suggests his black sins are belied by his appearance.[1] Many critics emphasize Shakespeare's inversion of the moral coding attached to colour: for them, the white Iago behaves, ironically, more like Aaron, the scheming black villain in *Titus Andronicus*, while Othello, with his descent from "men of royal siege," arouses first admiration and then sympathy as a victimized colonial subject (Hunter 1968, 150–1; Orkin 1987, 170). For other critics, however, the play *confirms* Iago's racist insinuations by revealing Othello as Emilia's "blacker devil" (5.2.131), a barbarous murderer who reverts to racial or religious origins; for them, Iago's normative whiteness is essential to Shakespeare's racism (Neill 2006, 138–47; Loomba 2002, 95).

Yet both these positions in the notoriously polarized atmosphere of *Othello* criticism rely on anachronistic notions of "race" associated with the later history of slavery with its pseudo-scientific racial divisions rather than the more fluid conceptions circulating in Tudor England. In early modern England, "race" denoted not the pseudo-scientific classification with which we are familiar but rather family lineage, nation, or even "the whole race of mankind" (*Timon of Athens* 4.1.40); systemized, institutionalized "racism" as we know it had not yet fully developed. Modern conceptions of "race" are inevitably bound up with the historical exploitation of black bodies as commodities in the real slave trade that developed later in the seventeenth century. In Shakespeare's time "Moor" could signify the persecuted Moorish population of Spain, the powerful inhabitants of North Africa (including Barbary, Morocco, or Mauritania), Africans in general, any dark-skinned people (including Indians), or – since religious faith was often a more significant difference than skin colour – Muslims of any colour, either of Africa or the Ottoman Empire (Neill 1998).

In the past few decades, *Othello* critics have reread Moors as "rich and powerful peoples close to the heart of civilization" (Skura 2008, 299), as key political allies to the English Crown (Bak 1996), and as hybrid figures who represented "the intersection of European and non-European cultures" (Bartels 2008, 187). Their nuanced historical readings suggest that Othello would have been perceived as far from the "erring barbarian" that Iago claims he is (1.3.348–9). Indeed, some have recognized (though usually only in passing) that Iago is equally a cultural outsider in Venice (Bartels 2008, 14; Loomba 2002, 104). In the Italian novella by Geraldo Cinthio that served as Shakespeare's source material, the evil Ensign is unnamed. By christening him Iago, Shakespeare hints at his country of origin: Spain, England's most powerful, hated enemy, whose patron saint, St Iago, was also known as the Moor-killer. In Shakespeare's time, Spanish Moors had become a persecuted minority, soon (in 1609) to be expelled from their country; the English were more likely to see themselves, like the Moors, as victims of Spanish persecution (Griffin 1998, 84). As Vanessa Corredera (2016, 30) remarks, "early moderns constructed alterity in inconsistent and varied ways." By representing the protagonist as an assimilated Moor and his antagonist as a figure of more profound difference, the 2015 RSC production tapped into different forms of otherness accessible in Shakespeare's original play.

Every contemporary production must situate itself within the play's racialized stage history, for, as Nigerian writer Ben Okri once remarked, "if [*Othello*] did not begin as a play about race, then its history has made it one" (quoted in Neill 2006, 113). In the past twenty-five years, that history has been moving in two different directions: toward colour-based casting on the one hand and colour-blind casting on the other. The problematic history of blackface impersonation (incarnated in Laurence Olivier's 1964 performance) has now made the role of Othello exclusively the property of black actors, with the happy result that "more black actors get pay cheques because of *Othello*" (Thompson 2015). And, beginning with Paul Robeson, many black actors have identified deeply with Othello: Ray Fearon, who played the part in 1999 for the RSC, remarked simply, "Because I'm black, I know how he feels" (Bate 2009, 165). Yet such colour-based casting, with its potential conflation of role and reality, has troubled some black actors, such as Hugh Quarshie, who claims that "of all the parts in the canon, perhaps Othello is the one which should most definitely not be played by a black actor," because of the "risk [of] making racial stereotypes seem legitimate and even true" (1999, 5). At the same time, the ubiquity of colour-blind casting in contemporary theatre has meant that Othello is rarely an isolated black presence on the stage: Bianca, Emilia, and some of the soldiers are often played by black actors, and this diversity tends to diminish race as a primary factor in the play's dynamic. Indeed, today's audiences are so accustomed to colour-blind casting that "coloured casting [can] become as blinding as colour-blind casting" (Hankey 2005, 105); audiences new to the play may wonder if they should even notice Othello's blackness.

Although theatre-goers may never be entirely blind to the actor's race, colour-blind casting certainly complicates assumptions about the relation of race to character. Msamati's Iago combined the advantages of both colour-based and colour-blind casting, suggesting Iago's otherness through the actor's body while diminishing Othello's isolation on the stage. As an instance of "non-traditional casting" in which, as Ayanna Thompson notes, "actors of color cast in roles not traditionally associated with race, color or ethnicity [are used to] make a socio-political statement about the character's subjection, outsider status" (2006, 7), the RSC's black Iago was immediately marked as a "stranger" (1.1.135), much like the Moor himself. For, despite the "contemporary, culturally diverse world" surrounding both characters, in this production "racism still simmer[ed] below the surface" (Taylor 2015). In Act 2, for example, tensions exploded among the racially diverse company of soldiers: in an invented rap contest, a white Cassio tells the black Montano that it is "rare to see a black man on the right side of the law," while Montano derides Cassio by suggesting he's "taking orders from a Moor." Such moments signalled a diffuse, systemic racism rather than the simple white-over-black paradigm that has dominated *Othello*'s theatrical history. In this way, the production communicated – in Kyle Grady's words – "the inherent complexity that accompanies interethnic relations" (2016, 76).

Having himself co-directed the 1989 Greenwich production in which both Othello and Iago were played by black actors, Quarshie finally agreed to take on the role of Othello under similar conditions for the RSC. Yet, unlike both the Greenwich and the 1990 Folger productions in which a lighter-skinned black Iago brought down a blacker (and more emotional) Othello (Potter 2002, 171), Quarshie's lighter skin advertised his assimilation, and he took a restrained, intellectual approach, his clipped delivery and greying hair communicating Obama-like authority. If Msamati's janitor-like Iago often swept the stage with a large broom, Quarshie's Othello donned silk and velvet and drank champagne. This Othello, "far more fair than black"

(1.3.288), recalled Charles Marowitz's 1972 rewriting of the play, *An Othello* (1974), in which a black Iago denounced Othello as "a house Nigger who knows when to nod" (265). In Quarshie's RSC performance, Othello's violence, when it emerged, was not innate but rather a product of the ruthless Venetian military culture that had made him into a professional brutalist, capable of waterboarding prisoners and of turning what is, in Shakepeare's text, his *own* racial self-loathing onto Iago. "My name ... is now begrimed and black / As *thine* own face," he tells the blacker man after subjecting him to torture, altering the wording of the original text's "*mine* own face" (3.3.388–90, emphasis added). As Iago used racist epithets to damage Othello in the opening scene, so Othello here turned them back on Iago.

A black Iago clearly allowed Quarshie to play against racist stereotypes of the gullible, excitable Moor. As he put it, "There was no possibility of suggesting that a clever and cunning white man could easily dupe a credulous black man because, in our production, both Othello and Iago were black" (2016). Strengthening the military bond between the two men was their shared cultural history, providing a plausible context for Othello's trust in his ensign. "I know *our* country disposition well," Iago insinuates. "In *Venice* they do let God see the pranks / They dare not show their husbands" (3.3.204–6, emphasis added). Quarshie's Othello is disarmed not by Iago's insider knowledge as a Venetian (as is so often assumed), but by his ability to compare their common cultural background with Desdemona's doubly alien "country forms" (3.3.241). As Cavendish (2015) remarks, "At a stroke we move beyond black-and-white ideas of racism as a motivator for Iago, and racial difference as the reason for Othello's ruinous suggestibility. In this version they're both outsiders." Othello and Iago were here not only deeply connected by an ethnic bond that intensified Iago's resentment at being overlooked in favor of the snobbish white Cassio, they were also profoundly *alike*. As Paul Prescott (2015) remarks in the program notes, "According to Emilia, another man has done to Iago what Iago does to Othello. From this perspective, both Othello and Iago are insecure, gullible and violent." Indeed, this production reinforced such analogies between the two men: as Othello was psychologically tortured by Iago, so Iago was physically tortured by Othello; both men inflicted and suffered violence.

The risk, of course, was that the affinities between the two men would be ascribed to stereotypes of race: of brutal black men and black-on-black violence. That the production avoided doing so can be attributed not only to Quarshie's carefully controlled, cerebral Othello but also to Msamati's charismatic Iago. Indeed, one might go so far as to say that Iago occupied the position not taken up by Othello in this production – that of vulnerable, abject stranger whose actions were rooted in anguish rather than malice and whose rapport with the audience engendered profound sympathy and delight. A victim of racism himself, he turned racist discourse against the man he sardonically calls "the Moor." Nowhere was this clearer than in the opening scene, where Iago, in response to Roderigo's racist slur on Othello as the "thick-lips" (1.1.66), paused, furious, before turning the remark into a massive joke, blowing raspberries to exaggerate the size of his own lips. Later, just before inciting the drunken brawl in Cyprus, Iago launched into a mournful Zimbabwean folk song that conveyed his deep sense of loss and isolation. Michael Billington (2015) noted that Iago, "more than Othello, is the play's outsider, who resents both assumed white superiority and Othello's integrationist tactics." Yet, though clearly shaped by racist discourse in the world he inhabits, this Iago was not defined or explained by it; Msamati (2016) himself declared that "I don't believe that what drives Iago is racial at all. There is something deeper, much more dangerous." Observing the world from its margins, this Iago acted to make other men know what marginalization feels like. "Ironically, in making my Iago black," reflects Iqbal Khan (2016), "I made the play less about the black-and-white race issue and perhaps more about betrayal and other things. I liberated the more complex powers within that play." Freed from his usual position as mouthpiece for white culture, this Iago became the outsider whose experience of exclusion transcended race, winning the trust and sympathy of the audience.

Theatre is a collaborative form in which a play is made new with each production; it need not be faithful to some illusory original. Iago is not black in *Othello*. Yet I want to suggest briefly that, by moving us beyond black/white oppositions, this production can also remind us of the global politics of Shakespeare's play. Khan's *Othello* speaks to a contemporary world that is increasingly multi-racial and global; Shakespeare's *Othello*, as Emily Bartels argues, similarly emerged at a time when "the English needed to figure out the politics and parameters of a new globally oriented environment ... to decode and encode an expansive network of cultural identities and differences" (2008, 17). And if, as Ian Smith has recently pointed out, "in

[our] color-conscious society, blackness often functions too easily as the mark of unassailable difference" (2016, 108), in Shakespeare's world, nation and religion were arguably a far more important measure of that difference. Recent critics have recognized this by pursuing Othello's alleged association with Islam (Vitkus 2003), but they often overlook the more obvious difference present from the beginning, in Iago.

In Cinthio's novella, the unnamed Ensign's status as a stranger is suggested by his eventual return to "his own country" (Neill 2006, 443). In creating Iago, Shakespeare gives Cinthio's hint a local habitation and a name. Spaniards, like Italians, were often associated with a poisonous inwardness and Machiavellianism, and Iago is true to type. "I am not what I am," he declares (1.1.65), and his personal god is Janus, the two-faced deity (1.2.33). But this Spaniard, like his namesake, St Iago, also has a special relation to the Moor. As Barbara Everett suggests, "Iago came into the play because of Othello – the Moor-killer along with the Moor" (2000, 67). By giving Iago a Spanish name, Shakespeare associates him with a hostile European power whose obsession with purity of blood and excluding strangers made it the antithesis of multicultural Venice. Yet, even if Iago claims kinship with him as a cultural outsider, the play refuses to pin down Othello's ethnicity in the same way. In early modern England, Moors more often appeared as hybrid, cross-cultural figures such as Leo Africanus, author of the *Geographical Historie of Africa* (1526; translated into English in 1600), "by descent a More, borne in Spain, in religion a Mahumetan, and afterward a Christian" (Pory 1600), or as political allies, like the Moorish ambassador who visited London in 1600 to try to forge a military alliance with England against Spain (Harris 2000). Brabantio may associate the Moor with "bondslaves and pagans" (1.2.99), but Othello is not only descended from "men of royal siege," he is a Christian – perhaps even a Protestant (Pechter 1999, 41) – who confesses his sins "truly ... to heaven" (1.2.22, 1.3.122). It is Iago who erodes his faith by trading in false images, as Protestants accused Catholics of doing. For an early modern audience, a Spanish Iago might well initially seem stranger – and certainly more threatening – than his well-assimilated general.

Yet if Iago's name – coupled with his Spanish oath, "Diabolo, ho!" (2.3.142) – raises the spectre of the Spaniard, his otherness is complicated by the close bond he forges with the English audience.

One might even argue that the first stranger to whom Shakespeare requires us to extend our imaginative empathy is Iago. "Abhor me," "Despise me," Iago challenges Roderigo – and by implication the audience (1.1.6, 8) – but the play's dynamic is carefully calibrated to thwart Iago's invitation. For English audiences, "honest Iago" becomes exactly what he pretends to be with others, as he breaches the boundaries of theatrical illusion, engaging them directly in his schemes, speaking a prose packed with their English proverbs and singing their English drinking songs. From dangerous stranger, Iago in Shakespeare's play becomes compelling ally. The play's powerful impact is fuelled by this complicity with Iago, and by the conflicting allegiances it fosters. With his heavily accented English and black skin, Msamati's Iago also began the play as an outsider (albeit a more sympathetic one than Shakespeare's Spaniard), yet he soon became – in the words of a reviewer – a "highly engaging figure who develops a cheeky rapport with the audience" (Taylor 2015). Director Khan (2015) remarked that the Stratford audience "had never felt so much of a connection with Iago." And, as with Othello, that connection is forged across a barrier of difference. Dennis Britton observes that "English racial, religious and national politics become all the more difficult to navigate when they confront two equally problematic figures of difference, the Moor and the Spaniard. *Othello* stages a particularly English conundrum: which of these figures needs to be more different, and how and when for the sake of religion, nation, and empire should certain kinds of difference be obscured while others made visible?" (2011, 45). By making Iago's difference more visible than Othello's, Iqbal Khan's 2015 RSC production challenged the simple opposition that has dogged the play's critical and theatrical history, while reminding us of theatre's extraordinary power to forge both creative and destructive alliances.

NOTE

1 All references to *Othello* are to Neill (2006).

REFERENCES

Bak, Greg. 1996. "Different Differences: Locating Moorishness in Early Modern English Culture." *Dalhousie Review* 76: 197–216.

Bartels, Emily C. 2008. *Speaking of the Moor: From Alcazar to Othello*. Philadelphia: University of Pennsylvania Press.

Bate, Jonathan. 2009. "Introduction." *Othello*. London: Macmillan.

Billington, Michael. 2015. "*Othello* Review: History Is Made with RSC's Fresh Take on the Tragedy." Review of *Othello*, Royal Shakespeare Company, Stratford-upon-Avon. *Guardian*, 12 June. https://www.theguardian.com/stage/2015/jun/12/othello-rsc-stratford-hugh-quarshie-lucian-msamati-joanna-vanderham.

Britton, Dennis Austin. 2011. "Re-'turning' Othello: Transformative and Restorative Romance." *English Literary History* 78 (1): 27–50.

Cavendish, Dominic. 2015. "Electrifying." Review of *Othello*, Royal Shakespeare Company, Stratford-upon-Avon. *Telegraph*, 12 June. https://www.telegraph.co.uk/culture/theatre/theatre-reviews/11663749/Othello-RSC-Stratford-review-electrifying.html.

Corredera, Vanessa. 2016. "'Not a Moor Exactly': Shakespeare, Serial and Modern Constructions of Race." *Shakespeare Quarterly* 67 (1): 30–50.

Coveney, Michael. 2015. Review of *Othello*, Royal Shakespeare Company, Stratford-upon-Avon. *What's On Stage.com*, 22 June. https://www.whatsonstage.com/stratford-upon-avon-theatre/reviews/othello-royal-shakespeare-company_38030.html.

Everett, Barbara. 2000. "'Spanish' Othello: The Making of Shakespeare's Moor." In *Shakespeare and Race*, edited by Catherine M.S. Alexander and Stanley Wells, 64–81. Cambridge: Cambridge University Press.

Grady, Kyle. 2016. "*Othello*, Colin Powell and Post-Racial Anachronism." *Shakespeare Quarterly* 67 (1): 68–83.

Griffin, Eric. 1998. "Un-Sainting James: Or, *Othello* and the 'Spanish Spirits' of Shakespeare's Globe." *Representations* 62: 58–99.

Hankey, Julie. 2005. *Shakespeare in Production: Othello*. Cambridge: Cambridge University Press.

Harris, Bernard. 2000. "A Portrait of a Moor." In *Shakespeare and Race*, edited by Catherine M.S. Alexander and Stanley Wells, 22–36. Cambridge: Cambridge University Press.

Hunter, G.K. 1968. "*Othello* and Colour Prejudice." *Proceedings of the British Academy* 53: 139–63.

Khan, Iqbal. 2015. "Director's Commentary." *Othello*. RSCLive. DVD.

– 2016. "Iqbal Khan: 'I Want Shakespeare to Speak Urgently in a 21st-Century Context.'" *The Stage*, 28 June. https://www.thestage.co.uk/features/interviews/2016/iqbal-khan-want-shakespeare-speak-urgently-21st-century-context/.

Loomba, Ania. 2002. *Shakespeare, Race and Colonialism*. Oxford: Oxford University Press.

Marowitz, Charles. 1974. "An *Othello*." In *Open Space Plays*, edited by Charles Marowitz. Harmondsworth, UK: Penguin.

Msamati, Lucian. 2016. "Interview." *Othello*. RSCLive. DVD.

Neill, Michael. 1998. "'Mulattos,' 'Blacks,' and 'Indian Moors': *Othello* and Early Modern Constructions of Human Difference." *Shakespeare Quarterly* 49 (4): 361–74.

– ed. 2006. *Othello*. Oxford: Oxford University Press.

Newman-O'Connor, Kelly. 2015. Review of *Othello*, Royal Shakespeare Company, Stratford-upon-Avon. *Shakespeare Newsletter* 65 (1): 58–9.

Orkin, Martin. 1987. "*Othello* and the 'Plain Face' of Racism." *Shakespeare Quarterly* 38 (2): 166–88.

Pechter, Edward. 1999. *Othello and Interpretive Traditions*. Iowa City: University of Iowa Press.

Pory, John. 1600. "To the Reader." *A Geographical Historie of Africa, Written in Arabicke and Italian by John Leo a More*. London.

Potter, Lois. 2002. *Shakespeare in Performance: Othello*. Manchester: Manchester University Press.

Prescott, Paul. 2015. "Whose Play Is It?" *Othello: William Shakespeare*. Royal Shakespeare Company program.

Quarshie, Hugh. 1999. "Second Thoughts about Othello." International Shakespeare Association Occasional Paper No. 7. Chipping Campden, UK.

– 2016. "Playing Othello." *Discovering Literature: Shakespeare and Renaissance Writers*. British Library (website). https://www.bl.uk/shakespeare/articles/playing-othello.

Skura, Meredith Anne. 2008. "Reading Othello's Skin: Contexts and Pretexts." *Philological Quarterly* 87 (3–4): 299–334.

Smith, Ian. 2013. "Shakespeare's Black Handkerchief." *Shakespeare Quarterly* 64 (1): 1–25.

– 2016. "We Are Othello: Speaking of Race in Early Modern Studies." *Shakespeare Quarterly* 67 (1): 104–24.

Taylor, Paul. 2015. "Racism Still Simmers in Black Iago Production." Review of *Othello*, Royal Shakespeare Company, Stratford-upon-Avon. *Independent*, 15 June. https://www.independent.co.uk/arts-entertainment/theatre-dance/reviews/othello-rsc-stratford-upon-avon-review-racism-still-simmers-in-black-iago-production-10320449.html.

Thompson, Ayanna. 2006. "Practicing a Theory/Theorizing a Practice: An Introduction to Shakespearean Colorblind Casting." *Colorblind*

Shakespeare: New Perspectives on Race and Performance, edited by Thompson, 1–26. London: Routledge.

– 2015. "I Am Not What I Am." *Othello: William Shakespeare*. Royal Shakespeare Company program.

Vitkus, Daniel J. 2003. *Turning Turk: English Theater and the Multicultural Mediterranean, 1570–1630*. London: Palgrave.

3

SHAKESPEARE, SPECTATORS, AND THE MEANING OF RACE ON STAGE

LAUREN ERIKS CLINE

How do we know if an audience is seeing colour? If a director casts Shakespeare roles in racially "unconventional" ways – as in the productions explored by Christina Luckyj in the preceding chapter – how can critics know whether audiences saw those casting decisions as significant? Sometimes the answer to this question is clear, as spectators make their race-conscious reception explicit in the reviews, letters, or diaries, where they record their reactions to the performance. When the African-American actor Ira Aldridge played Othello at Covent Garden in 1831 (the first black actor, to our knowledge, to do so), some of his reviews reflected Victorian Britain's racist ideologies in horribly unambiguous terms. A reviewer for the *Figaro in London*, for example, objected to the idea that Aldridge would be qualified to play Othello just because "nature has supplied the man with a skin that renders soot and butter superfluous" (6 April 1833, 56). On Aldridge's tour of the European continent, some audience members wrote about race with equal frankness but greater complexity, as they imagined how Aldridge's experiences of anti-blackness in the United States might inform his interpretation of the Jewish character Shylock. As one Russian spectator wrote, "Ira Aldridge is a mulatto born in America and feels deeply the insults leveled at people of another color by people of a white color in the New World. In Shylock he does not see particularly a Jew, but a human being in general, oppressed by the age-old hatred shown towards people like him" (Lindfors 1999, 354). These spectators, it feels safe to conclude, saw the actor's race as significant – as a visible sign that affected the meaning of the play and its characters. Yet the record of reception is not always so clear. In 1833, the same year that Aldridge performed Othello in London, the actor-manager Charles Macready "browned up" the actress playing Cleopatra in his production of *Antony and Cleopatra*; but this racialized make-up choice, Celia Daileader writes, did not provoke a strong reaction from reviewers (2006, 209). Nor did the practice spread to other theatres, even though Edmund Kean's similar preference for "tawny face" make-up had set a trend for stage Othellos in 1814. Similarly, when Roger Livesey became the first known actor to "black up" to play Caliban at the Old Vic in 1934, his choice of makeup excited "virtually no critical comment" (Griffiths 1983, 175).

Such curious moments, when spectators seem incurious about the meaning of race, have posed problems for one of the dominant approaches to Shakespeare reception studies, which I think of as the "remaking Shakespeare in our own image" approach. This approach owes much to the theatre scholar Jan Kott, whose influential study *Shakespeare Our Contemporary* (1964) argued that each age sees in Shakespeare a reflection of its present-day concerns. While critics have since pushed back against the more universalizing tendencies in Kott's work, many scholars who study Shakespeare performance continue to operate on the basic premise proposed by *Shakespeare Our Contemporary*: when faced with a particular production, they ask how it is reinterpreting Shakespeare through the lens of contemporary ideologies. The underlying theory behind this approach is that there is a reflective relationship between cultural surroundings and theatrical performance. What happens offstage should register onstage, and the prevailing performance tradition of the moment should mirror its historical milieu. Anthony Dawson's thorough study of *Hamlet* in performance provides some examples of the insights that this reflective approach can generate. Dawson analyzes how Restoration actor David Garrick's "acting became both a *reflection* of, and a contribution to, his culture's construction of Shakespeare"; how Victorian actor-manager Henry Irving "*mirror[ed]* the time's interest in 'intensity'"; and thus how "the shifts from Garrick to Kean to Irving can … be used to trace the fitful trajectory of the human subject, at least in its European manifestations, over almost two centuries" (1995, 34, 59, 62–3; emphases added). This reflective theory has helped produce many important studies of Shakespeare performance, because it is good at making certain things more visible: namely, resemblances (places where the symbols, words, and images on stage seem similar to those being used in other cultural and political contexts), parallel trajectories (places where shifts in performance practice seem to happen in tandem with new historical or aesthetic developments), and confirmation of predicted measurements (places where spectator response seems to provide corroborating evidence for existing historical narratives).

Yet a reflective approach to performance history also makes other things harder to see, especially those places where a Shakespeare production doesn't seem to have affected spectators in quite the way that present-day critics think it should have. If scholars begin by looking for a correspondence between a theatre event and its historical moment, the performances that receive the most analysis will tend to be those that either comfortably fit or clearly contradict the historical narratives we expect to see mirrored on stage. If the reflection of social change looks incoherent or opaque, that production may receive less notice, as its racial meanings slip out of our line of sight. Or else it may end up having its strangeness flattened by analytical filters aimed at enhancing visibility and symmetry.

In this chapter, I aim to gather and briefly illustrate some ongoing conceptual shifts in Shakespeare performance history that I believe can help make sense of these opaque performances without trying to clear them up. While difficult to assimilate into traditional theatre histories, Shakespeare productions that provoke unexpected audience responses – that is, responses that do not match existing historical narratives – can offer privileged sites for analyzing a feature of stage Shakespeare that is itself often inconsistent and slippery: the meaning of race on stage. "The exact significance of an actor's race is perpetually in flux," Ayanna Thompson argues, "because we as a society have not been able to pinpoint a stable signification for race" (2006, 8). Given this instability and fluctuation, I would argue that a reflective approach might not always be the best tool for understanding the role of race in Shakespeare performance. Taking up Thompson's call to develop new methodologies that allow critics to address the intersection between reception studies and race studies, I want to track three shifts that have the potential to turn spots of imperfect visibility from an obstacle into an opportunity.

The first shift is from thinking about audience reception to thinking about spectator production. Shakespeare scholars have come increasingly to think of spectators as active agents in the performance, thanks in part to critics working in a subfield of performance studies devoted to analyzing theatrical audiences. Reception studies, in its early incarnations in the 1980s and 1890s, often articulated a desire to understand how spectators act as interpreters and readers of performance: Shakespeare performance scholars such as Barbara Hodgdon, for example, urged us to "situate spectators and their reading strategies as ... primary objects of investigation" (1998, 171). I think it is possible to push the activity of spectators even further by thinking of them not only as *readers* of performance processes but also as *writers* of performance meanings (Eriks Cline 2017). This conceptual shift draws on studies of audience reception by critics such as Hodgdon and Marvin Carlson, as well as on studies of theatre reviews and theatrical memoirs by scholars such as Paul Prescott and Charlotte Canning, in order to make the literary and textual strategies employed by historical spectators a central object of analysis. Approaching spectator narratives as a medium for shaping performance meaning – rather than as a descriptive record of a meaning that was produced by actors and directors – allows scholars to read audiences not as failing to see race, but as *using* incoherence, opacity, and indirection to construct racial meanings.

A second shift is from approaching stage productions and the audience responses they provoke as reflections of historical changes to analyzing spectator narratives of performance as refractions of those changes. Reflection (in which light or sound hits a surface and is thrown back into the medium from which it originated) assumes a certain directness of perception. Yet while some racial meanings circulate close enough to the surface of visibility to cast a clear reflection in the narratives produced by historical audiences, others – especially those racial ideologies that depend for their effectiveness on being unseen or unspoken – may not create an impression that is directly representable. Miriam Gilbert (2005), for example, has argued that the intensity of racial meaning in post-Holocaust productions of *The Merchant of Venice* led some directors and actors to employ strategies of deflection rather than reaction. Audiences at these performances might also articulate their understanding of race in roundabout ways, taking oblique angles of response that offer a less direct confrontation with charged memories and meanings. Refraction – which occurs when light or sound moves across media, slows down, and changes paths – accounts for these cases of indirect or redirected meaning. It enables critics to see how meaning passes from the medium of performance to the medium of narrative in slanted as well as symmetrical ways, so that spectator narratives can produce not only mirror-like descriptions of objects but also changes in the angle, speed, and density of meaning.

The third shift is from looking for race as a system of visible signs – as features clearly registered and marked by spectators – to seeing racial signifiers as produced through tensions between visibility and opacity. This shift brings the critical lenses for analyzing performance reception into better alignment with new frameworks for analyzing racial performance. Critics such as Ayanna Thompson (2006), Daphne Brooks (2006), and Kyle Grady (2016) have pointed out how the historical significance of blackness, for example, has often depended on complex interactions between hyper-visibility and colour-blindness – as well as strategic acts of "passing" in order to gain acceptance in a different racial or ethnic group. Studies by Vivian Huang (2016) and Carla Della Gatta (2016) similarly explore how Asian-American and Latinx performances are made meaningful not only through visibility but also through perceptions of inscrutability, or through the sounds of actors' voices. ("Latinx" is a gender-neutral term for Latin American cultural or racial identity.) Race, in other words, may often be produced as much by what spectators can't see or choose not to see as by what they do see.

By shifting toward spectator production, refraction, and (in) visibility, scholars will be able to bring such insights from critical race theory to bear not only on our analyses of dramatic texts or performance signifiers, but also on the representational techniques chosen by theatrical audiences when they record their responses. Taking a non-reflective approach to studying how audiences write race in Shakespeare performance, scholars may discover that what looks at first like a perceptual failure to see race is, in many cases, a rhetorical strategy for making race invisible.

In the rest of this chapter, I play out some implications of these wider shifts by examining a contemporary tale of two *Caesar*s: the Acting Company / Guthrie Theater's Obama-inspired production of *Julius Caesar* in Minneapolis in 2012 and the Trump-like tyrant at the Public Theater in New York City in 2017. The diptych provided by these productions of *Julius Caesar* is partially the creation of news media pundits, who asked why the Public's staged assassination of a presidential lookalike in 2017 had produced so much more backlash than the Guthrie's had in 2012. Indeed, the reception histories of these two productions of *Caesar* raise a number of fascinating questions about the changing conditions for producing political Shakespeare. In this chapter, I focus on one: how have critical reactions shaped the meaning of race and identity in these productions? By choosing to pose this question in response to performances of *Julius Caesar*, which is not normally thought of as one of Shakespeare's "race plays," I hope to demonstrate how the conceptual shifts I have outlined might open up new ways to think about how audiences receive and write racial meaning into Shakespeare performance.

So how did audiences at the joint Guthrie and Actors Theater performance of *Julius Caesar* represent the performance as about race or about Barack Obama? In terms of audiences' direct engagement with blackness, the stories told about Bjorn DuPaty's performance as Caesar are a mixed bag. While writers for the *Minneapolis–St Paul Magazine* ("Review" 2013) and a Shakespeare blog at the *American Conservative* (Millman 2012) explicitly mark DuPaty as black, reviews in the *New York Times* (Green 2017), the *Minneapolis Star Tribune* (Royce 2012), and the *Twin Cities Daily Planet* (Gabler 2012) paint a more opaque picture. The race of the lead actor is not mentioned directly but instead constructed obliquely, through indirect references to basketball, hip hop music, and what one reviewer describes as "one of those shake-it/grasp-it/pound-it handshakes typically encountered in made-for-TV movies about urban youth" (Gabler 2012). The writers of these reviews all frame the production as deliberately contemporary, but not all of them mention Barack Obama by name. The narratives register DuPaty as black but also obscure racial visibility by placing his appearance among a range of other contemporary signifiers, especially of class. The headlines in the *New York Times* and the *Star Tribune* – "Beware the Suited Men Wielding Letter Openers" (Grode 2012) and "Caesar Wears a Business Suit" (Royce 2012) – both suggest that DuPaty's performance is more prominently marked by costuming decisions that signal class status than it is by somatic markers of race.

But the blackness of DuPaty's performance took on a different significance in the context of the Public Theater's *Caesar* in 2017. On 11 June, the Fox News Insider ran the headline "NYC Play Appears to Depict Assassination of Trump" (2017). This initial story provoked a wave of new narratives – some as long as newspaper articles or blog posts and some as short as 140-character tweets – each competing to tell the story of what this "NYC Play" and its staged assassination meant. While there is much to say about these responses, what particularly fascinates me is the way that they frame the significance of race. Every narrative that I read constructs lead actor Gregg Henry's body as signifying Donald Trump. Fox News (as demonstrated by headlines like "'Assassination Porn': Activist Defends Disrupting NYC Trump Stabbing Play") goes so far as to claim that the actor's body references Trump more clearly than it references Julius Caesar, the character that Henry is ostensibly representing ("Assassination Porn" 2017). But the bodily and sartorial signifiers that spectators read as "Trump-like" are only inconsistently or indirectly linked to whiteness in these commentaries. While blondeness, which is described in almost all reviews of the production, bears a recognizable racial association (Cox 2017; Andrews 2017), the actor's signature red tie is more about shaping a recognizable, individual character than it is about marking his belonging to a particular racial category. A reference to Caesar's "Slavic wife" explicitly marks a category of race and ethnicity (S. Gilbert 2017; Green 2017), but Caesar's "petulance" points toward whiteness in less direct ways (Green 2017).

By contrast, blackness becomes more visible in the 2017 spectator narratives. First, Bjorn DuPaty's race takes on a new significance as his identification with Barack Obama becomes retrospectively more settled: in order to characterize the earlier production as a theatrical precedent for representing the assassination of a sitting president, defenders of the Public Theater production argue that DuPaty's body clearly and directly referenced Obama's. Those critical of the Public production make other forms of non-white racial representation more explicit as well. A number of spectators in 2017 cast the racial, ethnic, and gendered identities of Caesar's assassins as significant in a way that 2012 spectators of the Guthrie's production did not. Although the Guthrie production featured not only a black Julius Caesar but also a black Brutus (indeed, in a striking substitution, many of the 2017 articles looking back on the Guthrie's "Obama-inspired" production ran with a picture of black actor Will Sturdivant as Brutus rather than one of DuPaty as Julius Caesar), the spectators' initial responses in 2012 treat the blackness of one of Caesar's assassins incidentally if at all. Criticisms of the Public's production, on the other hand, often frame the attack on Trump-Caesar as explicitly or implicitly racialized. Not only did Fox News report that the performance "appears to depict President Trump being brutally stabbed to death by women and minorities," Fox writers repeatedly refer to the play itself as an "NYC Play" – a phrase that, when compared with "a Shakespeare play," is loaded with non-white racial and ethnic meaning ("NYC Play" 2017). The video that Fox News embeds beneath its "Assassination Porn" story (2017) further entrenches racial categories, as the white body of protestor/spectator Laura Loomer is shown pointing confrontationally at a group of actors of colour. The camera angle, which shows Loomer from the back and the actors playing the assassins from the front, invites the viewer to take up the perspective of the white spectator, faced with racialized antagonism. Whereas narratives of the Guthrie's production stay selectively colour-blind in a way that refracts racial meanings through the oblique angle of class, many responses to the Public's *Caesar* either craft or contest the narrative of whiteness under threat, with conditions of hyper-visibility imposed on non-white bodies.

While one might feel tempted to dismiss outraged responses to the Public's performance as incoherent, ahistorical, and inconsistent, I linger with them, because incoherence, ahistoricism, and inconsistency are often precisely the discursive tools with which racial meanings are made. To see how such indirect tools work, however, scholars may sometimes need to shift our conceptual approach to Shakespeare performance to focus on spectator production, narrative refraction of meaning, and techniques of invisibility and opacity as well as visibility. In the trajectory of recent productions of *Julius Caesar*, for example, it is clear that reviews are not just records of what an audience member saw or failed to see but also active interventions, intended to affect how others will see the performance. Representations of the productions do not simply reflect what would have been visible on stage but refract it through ideological, visual, and narrative lenses in order to fashion claims about when and how race matters on stage. Such claims, moreover, are not all operating above the threshold of visibility. What spectators decide not to note about the bodies of actors such as DuPaty or Henry – or what they decide to represent only obliquely – is often just as significant as what they do describe. If we want to understand when and how spectators see Shakespeare in colour, then, we will need analytical tools designed to register colour-blindness, not only as a casting technique but also as a spectator strategy.

NOTE

A version of this essay appears in *Shakespeare Studies* 47 (2019).

REFERENCES

Andrews, Travis. 2017. "Trump-like 'Julius Caesar' Assassinated in New York Play. Delta, Bank of America Pull Funding." Review of *Julius Caesar*, Public Theater, New York. *Washington Post*, 12 June. https://www.washingtonpost.com/news/morning-mix/wp/2017/06/12/trump-like-julius-caesar-assassinated-in-new-york-play-delta-bank-of-america-pull-funding/?utm_term=.c273183c28f6.

"'Assassination Porn': Activist Defends Disrupting NYC Trump Stabbing Play." 2017. Fox News Insider. 19 June. http://insider.foxnews.com/2017/06/19/donald-trump-assassination-play-julius-caesar-shakespeare-new-york-laura-loomer-hannity.

Brooks, Daphne. 2006. *Bodies in Dissent: Spectacular Performances of Race and Freedom, 1850–1910*. Durham, NC: Duke University Press.

Canning, Charlotte. 1993. "Constructing Experience: Theorizing a Feminist Theatre History." *Theatre Journal* 45 (4): 529–40.

Carlson, Marvin. 1989. "Theater Audiences and the Reading of Performance." In *Interpreting the Theatrical Past: Essays in the Historiography of Performance*, edited by Thomas Postlewait and Bruce A. McConachie, 82–98. Iowa City: University of Iowa Press.

Cox, Gordon. 2017. "Controversial 'Julius Caesar' Play Opens to Standing Ovation in Central Park." Review of *Julius Caesar*, Public Theater, New York. *Variety*, 12 June. http://variety.com/2017/legit/news/julius-caesar-opening-trump-like-play-1202463844/.

Daileader, Celia R. 2006. "The Cleopatra Complex: White Actresses on the Interracial 'Classic' Stage." In *Colorblind Shakespeare: New Perspectives on Race and Performance*, edited by Ayanna Thompson, 205–20. London: Routledge.

Dawson, Anthony. 1995. *Hamlet: Shakespeare in Performance*. Manchester: Manchester University Press.

Della Gatta, Carla. 2016. "From West Side Story to Hamlet, Prince of Cuba: Shakespeare and Latinidad in the United States." *Shakespeare Studies* 44: 151–6.

Eriks Cline, Lauren. 2017. "'Mere Lookers-On at Life': Point of View and Spectator Narrative." *Nineteenth Century Theatre and Film* 44 (2): 154–72.

Gabler, Jay. 2012. "Acting Company and Guthrie Theater Bring 'Julius Caesar' Awkwardly into the 21st Century." Review of *Julius Caesar*, Acting Company / Guthrie Theater, Minneapolis. *Twin Cities Daily Planet*, 21 January. https://www.tcdailyplanet.net/julius-caesar-guthrie-theater-acting-company-review/.

Gilbert, Miriam. 2005. "Performance as Deflection." In *A Companion to Shakespeare and Performance*, edited by Barbara Hodgdon and W.B. Worthen, 319–34. Malden, MA: Blackwell Publishing.

Gilbert, Sophie. 2017. "The Misplaced Outrage over a Trumpian *Julius Caesar*." *Atlantic*, 12 June. https://www.theatlantic.com/entertainment/archive/2017/06/the-misplaced-outrage-over-a-trumpian-julius-caesar/530037/.

Grady, Kyle. 2016. "Othello, Colin Powell, and Post-Racial Anachronisms." *Shakespeare Quarterly* 67 (1): 68–83.

Green, Jesse. 2017. "Can Trump Survive in Caesar's Palace." Review of *Julius Caesar*, Public Theater, New York. *New York Times*, 9 June. https://www.nytimes.com/2017/06/09/theater/review-julius-caesar-delacorte-theater-donald-trump.html.

Griffiths, Trevor. 1983. "'This Island's Mine': Caliban and Colonialism." *Yearbook of English Studies* 13: 159–80.

Grode, Eric. 2012. "Beware the Suited Men Wielding Letter Openers: The Acting Company's Version of 'Julius Caesar.'" Review of *Julius Caesar*, Acting Company / Guthrie Theater, Minneapolis. *New York Times*, 22 April. http://www.nytimes.com/2012/04/18/theater/reviews/the-acting-companys-version-of-julius-caesar.html.

Hodgdon, Barbara. 1998. *The Shakespeare Trade: Performances and Appropriations*. Philadelphia: University of Pennsylvania Press.

Huang, Vivian L. 2016. "Some Island Unknown to the Rest of the World: Inscrutability, Asian Americanness, Performance." PhD diss., New York University. ProQuest (10139647).

Kott, Jan. 1964. *Shakespeare Our Contemporary*. Translated by Boleslaw Taborski. Garden City, NY: Doubleday.

Lindfors, Bernth. 1999. "'Mislike Me Not for My Complexion …': Ira Aldridge in Whiteface." *African American Review* 33 (2): 347–54.

Millman, Noah. 2012. "Obama's Ides Of March: The Acting Company Production of Julius Caesar." Review of *Julius Caesar*, Acting Company / Guthrie Theater, Minneapolis. *Millman's Shakesblog*. In *American Conservative*, 21 May. http://www.theamericanconservative.com/shakesblog/obamas-ides-of-march/.

"NYC Play Appears to Depict Assassination of Trump." 2017. *Fox New*

Insider. 11 June. http://insider.foxnews.com/2017/06/11/donald-trump-julius-caesar-stabbed-death-women-minorities-shakespeare-central-park.

Prescott, Paul. 2013. *Reviewing Shakespeare: Journalism and Performance from the Eighteenth Century to the Present*. Cambridge: Cambridge University Press.

"Review: *Julius Caesar* @ the Guthrie Theater." 2013. *Minneapolis–St Paul Magazine*. 19 December. http://mspmag.com/arts-and-culture/the-morning-after/review_julius_caesar_the_guthr/.

Royce, Graydon. 2012. "Caesar Wears a Business Suit." Review of *Julius Caesar*, Acting Company / Guthrie Theater, Minneapolis. *Minneapolis Star Tribune*, 20 January. http://www.startribune.com/caesar-wears-a-business-suit/137759458/.

Thompson, Ayanna. 2006. "Practicing a Theory / Theorizing a Practice: An Introduction to Shakespearean Colorblind Casting." In *Colorblind Shakespeare: New Perspectives on Race and Performance*, edited by Thompson, 1–26. London: Routledge.

4

"THE SLUTTY CLOWN SPEAKS THE PROLOGUE"

Cross-Gender Casting on the Toronto Stage

RODERICK H. MCKEOWN

The past few years have seen a remarkable proliferation of cross-gender casting in southern Ontario productions of Shakespeare. This is not always programmatic: the logistics of mounting plays in repertory mean that cross-casting supporting roles is frequently merely a matter of pragmatism, but it can be a strategic choice on the part of the director – and seems increasingly to be so. To take a single example of each from the same season of the Canadian Stage's Shakespeare in High Park, Toronto, Jan Alexandra Smith played both an expediently female Marcus in Keira Loughran's 2014 *Titus Andronicus* and a deliberately female Jaques, modelled on Simone de Beauvoir, in Nigel Shawn Williams's concurrent *As You Like It.*

Cross-casting *major* roles has been rarer in Canadian mountings of Shakespeare's plays but is becoming more common. Since 2011, the Stratford Festival alone has seen Seana McKenna as Richard III and as Jaques in 2016's *As You Like It*, while Chris Abraham's 2014 *Midsummer Night's Dream* offered Tara Rosling as Lysander, one-half of a fugitive lesbian pair, with Evan Buliung and Jonathan Goad alternating in the roles of Oberon and Titania – fairy queen in drag one night, and king the next. In 2018, Stratford doubled down, casting Seana McKenna in the title role in *Julius Caesar* and Martha Henry as Prospero in *The Tempest. The Comedy of Errors*, too, had one male and one female performer in lead roles as a pair of identical twins. In Toronto, Philip McKee's 2013 *Lear* at Harbourfront presented Claire Coulter in the title role. In 2017 alone, Toronto audiences saw Lucy Peacock as the Duchess rather than the Duke in Groundling

Theatre Company's *Measure for Measure*, and in the summer they had the opportunity to see Diane D'Aquila as a female Lear for the Canadian Stage Company, before McKenna, too, played the role in 2018 for Groundling. In between, Christine Horne earned a Dora Mavor Moore award nomination for her performance as Hamlet in Ravi Jain's production of *Prince Hamlet* – please note: not Princess.

This chapter examines the growing trend of cross-casting roles in southern Ontario productions of Shakespeare. I focus on two productions with very different reasons for cross-casting, achieving very different effects: ted witzel's 2016 *All's Well That Ends Well*, staged as part of the Canadian Stage Company's Shakespeare in High Park, and Ravi Jain's *Prince Hamlet,* staged in March of 2017 by Why Not Theatre in collaboration with Toronto's Soulpepper Theatre Company.

I have chosen these two productions partly out of expediency, but they also illuminate each other quite nicely through their contrasts. The directors took markedly different approaches to developing their shows and reached the decision to cross-cast characters at different stages in the creative process. What I find significant is that *Prince Hamlet*'s cross-casting of every role but Gertrude and Claudius managed to deliver a production that, although innovative on any number of fronts, and very free with the gender of its cast, delivered an interpretation of the gender of its characters that was remarkably conservative. In contrast, witzel's cross-casting was in part driven by the pragmatic need to double his cast with that of Birgit Schreyer Duarte's production of *Hamlet*. Despite this, and despite the fact that his main piece of cross-casting was the minor role of the Clown, Lavatch, that small change in casting had far more extensive ramifications for the play's exploration of gender and sexuality, an exploration far more radical than the gender-blind – or, as Ravi Jain would no doubt correct me, gender-conscious – casting of *Prince Hamlet.*

PRINCE HAMLET

Ravi Jain and Christine Horne's *Prince Hamlet* was billed as a remount of Jain's 2007 *The Prince Hamlet*, which found a novel approach in intercutting scenes of narrative dialogue with the earlier scenes they narrate, whether those scenes appear in the play or not. In Act 3, Scene 1, for example, Rosencrantz and Guildenstern's report to Claudius and Gertrude of their conversation with Hamlet was intercut with the actual conversation in Act 2, Scene 2, while Ophelia's report in Act 2, Scene 1 of her encounter with the distracted Hamlet was intercut with that exchange, which does not appear in Shakespeare's play (Citron 2007). This concern for narrative and control of the flow of information was preserved in the 2017 production, but *The Prince Hamlet* featured Philip Graeme as the Prince, so the 2017 revival's casting of Horne as Hamlet was an innovation. Interviewed by Carly Maga (2017) for the *Toronto Star*, Jain drew attention to the gender-conscious casting, stating that in 2007 "the out-of-the-box casting was young people playing old people. But women played women, men played men and, for the most part, everyone was homogenous." Despite those comments, Jain was more interested in Horne as an actor than in her sex or gender. As Horne relates, "It wasn't actually 'I want to have a female Hamlet ... so what female should I pick?' It was just me as an actor in this play he wanted to look at again."[1]

This attitude was picked up by the critics, in both positive and negative terms. Taylor Long (2017), writing for *Broadway World*, praised Horne, noting that "gender becomes inconsequential in her portrayal of the pensive prince. Horne's Hamlet is hopeful in his plans for revenge, and devastated in his uncertainty. Her piercing eyes swell with tears, veins pulsing in her neck as her Hamlet strains to understand his mortality." Where Long praised that inconsequentiality, though, Wayne Leung's take on the role gender played – or didn't play – in this production was that an opportunity was missed, and, although voicing his support for "an inclusive approach to casting the classics," he wished that the production had taken on all the "implications and questions raised by a female Hamlet" (2017).

I tend to split the difference between the two, particularly as I take issue with Leung's use of the term "a female Hamlet." As he himself notes, "the role isn't really gender reversed; the character still reads as male (or he is at least referred to throughout with male pronouns)." In other words, despite the fact that the actor playing Hamlet is a woman, the character is gendered as male by language (those pronouns) and plot. Horne was a woman playing a Prince, not Princess, Hamlet.

Jain and Horne both describe a casting and rehearsal process that might have led to a production that engaged with questions of gender more thoroughly. But the production shifted away from directly considering gender as a result of the same casting ethos that prompted Jain to cast Horne in the first place. In casting a woman as Hamlet, he was explicitly trying to open up more pinnacle roles – Hamlet, Lear, and so on – to performers who would not, in traditional productions, have access to them. Horne, he told me, is a "phenomenal actor and deserves to be playing roles like this all the time and isn't."[2] His decision to engage in gender-conscious casting was thus born partly out of a simple wish to work with artists he admires, and partly out of a strong desire to open up roles to a more diverse range of performers, to "challenge race … [and] gender, and challenge our pre-conceived notions of who we thought these characters are, in order to create space to discover them anew." Then, at a conference on diversity and inclusion in the theatre, Jain's eyes were opened to another form of exclusion: (dis)ability. In his words, "someone at that conference said, 'You know, if anyone's thinking about casting, I want them to consider people of different abilities.' And I'm someone so progressive, so left-leaning – I would never have thought of that." And so, returning to Canada, Jain cast Dawn Jani-Birnley, a profoundly deaf actor, in the pivotal role of Horatio, and the focus of the production moved away from gender.

Instead, the production redoubled its intense focus on narrative, access to information, and the control of historical memory. As in the 2007 mounting, the production begins and ends with Horatio narrating the story: the whole show is an extended flashback. Jain also featured odd shifts of perspective – we are with Polonius behind the arras when he is stabbed, for instance, rather than witnessing the closet scene from a perspective close to Hamlet's. As the onstage narrator, Jani-Birnley was an almost continuous stage presence. She signed her own dialogue, signed narration of scenes in which she was sidelined, and engaged with Horne's Hamlet at other points, frantically signing – what? The play, then, was effectively bilingual, in English and in American Sign Language. As I do not understand ASL, when Jani-Birnley signed during Hamlet's heated exchanges with other characters, I could never be sure whether she was narrating, commenting, or egging Hamlet on. Jain and Jani-Birnley's interview with the *Toronto Star* makes it clear that, as the rehearsal process continued, Jani-Birnley's role grew, as Jain realized that to have only small parts of the play signed would render it as inaccessible to deaf audience members as any other production of *Hamlet.* The bilingualism of the production therefore became the focus of much rehearsal time and directorial effort. The result was that the

Figure 4.1 | Promotional photo of Christine Horne in *Prince Hamlet*.

experience of hearing audience members who did not know ASL mirrored the experience of deaf audience members: each group understood only the language the other did not.

Two photos illustrate the production's shift in focus during rehearsal from the gender of its award-winning lead to its themes of memory, narration, and epistemology. A promotional photo, taken early in the production's development (figure 4.1), makes much of Horne's femininity: she is carefully coiffed, and impeccably made up. She stares out of the photograph, challenging her audience with a direct gaze. The look is provocative, emphasizing Horne's femininity, while challenging traditional assumptions that women are looked at – seen, rather than seeing. Figure 4.2, taken late in the rehearsal period or in previews, better reflects Horne's actual appearance in the production. In this photo she is unglamorous, her hair in disarray, her make-up minimal. Her posture and affect in performance, too, were so casual as to be flippant: Horne's sardonic prince slouched through the role, delivering barbs in a gravelly tone reminiscent of a rebellious teenager. Neither the glamazon of the initial photo, nor a thigh-slapping pantomime principal boy, this Hamlet was a man who could be played by a person of any gender or sex. For Horne, gender simply was not a focus in rehearsal: "the binary became

Figure 4.2 | Christine Horne in *Prince Hamlet*.

who's hearing and who's not hearing, not who's a man and who's a woman. Even coming here to meet you, I was like, 'I'm not going to have anything to say!' because we didn't talk about it."

Jain's narrative of the play's rehearsal process is somewhat more complex than Horne's. Looking back to an early workshop of the play, he recalls that gender was definitely discussed, as he and his creative partners asked, "'Okay, so let's talk through what it would be. Do we have to change pronouns, and genders, and what's the statement?' We kind of batted it around a bit, but I always remember Christine saying we could *not* have a spin on it, and just do the play." In Jain's recollection, though, gender was not off the table in rehearsal, it was simply considered in a very pragmatic way by the performers: "We talked about it a lot in the room: 'Am I a man? Am I a woman? We haven't changed the pronouns – who am I?' And I always said – frustrating to some actors – you're you. Be you. Your essence is that character, and you will find the lining up of that in the playing of that." Jain's insistence on character as independent of gender was not, therefore, a refusal to consider gender in mounting the play; rather, it was way of thinking about gender that refused to prioritize it as central to identity. That refusal was itself a conceptual choice, not an avoidance of choice.

As Antoni Cimolino observes in Chapter 1, no production can mine every single element of *Hamlet*, in which Shakespeare plays so actively with so many concepts that any attempt to underscore every big idea would result in anarchy. Consequently, I do not join Leung (2017) in wishing for a play devoted to exploring gender simply because its lead is cross-cast: not all opportunities passed up should be described as missed. From my interview with Horne, it was very clear that, while she thought of her character as male, she wasn't thinking of the role in terms of "now I have to play a man." The script called for the cast to use male pronouns for Hamlet throughout, and according to both Jain and Horne the cast seldom slipped up.

The easy fluidity of gender that marked Horne's turn as Hamlet did not seem, on the night I saw the performance, to be equally true of all other cast members. The seven artists who did not double roles can be divided into three groups. Claudius and Gertrude were played by actors whose gender matched the characters. Among the cross-cast characters, the second group consisted of Horne and Jani-Birnley. Horne, as we have seen, was often coded as male by the pronouns used. Jani-Birnley's Edwardian tweeds marked her Horatio as male, but the lack of any vocal cues and the frenetic physicality of her signing meant that there was no room for a real performance of gender. In contrast, the performances of the third group, Ophelia, Polonius, and Laertes, who were also cross-cast, foregrounded the gender of their characters. Khadijah Roberts-Abdullah was a highly effective Laertes, but she struck me at the time as self-consciously macho; Jeffrey Ho's compelling Ophelia was soft-spoken, with a relatively high-pitched voice, and his body language was tentative, projecting a receptivity and timidity that seemed stereotypically feminine. Ho interacted with other performers with his weight on the balls of his feet, leaning into the other performers, with arms demurely down and angled slightly back; the image was bird-like, featherweight. Maria Vacratsis, as Polonius, also seemed to layer a self-conscious performance of masculinity on top of her performance of her character. Amusingly, J. Kelly Nestruck (2017), writing for Toronto's *Globe and Mail*, characterized Vacratsis as a "short and short-tempered Polonius [who] is an officious lackey who sits halfway between White House press secretary Sean Spicer and Melissa McCarthy's popular parody of him." Nestruck here picks up on the element of not just playing a character as being one gender, but playing that gender itself as another layer. If drag involves a layer of knowing, of camp, then at least Vacratsis and Roberts-Abdullah had hints of camp in their performance, sly deconstructions of conventional masculinity and hypermasculinity that drew attention to their performance of maleness.[3]

Why did some performers effectively read as gender-neutral (Horne, Jani-Birnley) and others (Roberts-Abdullah, Vacratsis, and, more arguably, Ho) read as self-consciously playing "drag"? In Horne's take on the rehearsal process and performances, the artists were not self-consciously performing the gender of their characters but rather including gender as only part of an overall character shaped by multiple identities: gender, familial bond, status. "The relationships were what they were. And I think that he [Jain] cast it well enough that they still had those qualities. If you put Khadijah and Jeff together, she is more stereotypically the big brother, and he is the little sister." Jain, too, saw the relationship between Laertes and Ophelia presented in the final production as growing organically out of the personalities of the two artists, saying that Roberts-Abdullah "had a more male energy, and Jeffrey had a very female energy. And I think again those were parts of themselves that they were able to connect to the characters they were playing."

But this articulation of the process downplays the extent to which Jain pre-determined that "energy"; his method of seeing what happens in rehearsal allows only for performance choices that have not already been cut off by casting choices. I half-playfully asked Jain whether he would ever have considered creating a butch Ophelia: "It would have depended on the actor I was working with. A lot of the way I work is dependent on who is in the room. I don't come in necessarily with a preconceived notion of 'Ophelia needs to be feminine' or 'Ophelia needs to be butch …' If Kawa [that is, Kawa Ada, an early casting choice] had played the role, it would have been different. I didn't have an idea of what I wanted the role to be." Yet despite Jain's openness to the idea of an Ophelia who does not conform to old-fashioned equations of femininity and frailty, it is hard not to feel that, to at least some extent, Ho was cast as a woman for his conventionally feminine qualities, just as Roberts-Abdullah was cast as a man for her more stereotypically masculine presentation. The portrayal of Ophelia is thus feminist in one sense, as it depicts a helpless woman chewed up by the patriarchal power politics of the royal court, and decries that treatment. But that very helplessness, tied to a heavily gendered portrayal of Ophelia, even if that gender is at odds with Ho's, in some ways reduces her death to the inevitable outcome of her gender.

The production, as a result, harkened back to stereotypical nineteenth- and twentieth-century generalizations about Hamlet being the universal human, accessible to all – Shakespeare's transcendent depiction of human consciousness. A woman can play Hamlet with no need to play "male" because *Hamlet*, in this formulation, is universally accessible to all, since Hamlet so universally reflects all. This sense of Hamlet as universal and Ophelia as particular enacts the dynamic Simone de Beauvoir enunciates in *The Second Sex*, of man as normal, and woman as other: "A man never begins by presenting himself as a certain sex; it goes without saying that he is a man" (1968, xv). Jain's progressive choices in casting (opening roles to performers who would, traditionally, have been barred from them) and dramaturgy (translating much of the play into ASL, and giving Gertrude more agency by importing lines from the first quarto) were thus in tension with other aspects of the production that seemingly bought into very traditional understandings of gender, and echoed very traditional critical readings of *Hamlet*.

THE SLUTTY CLOWN SPEAKS THE PROLOGUE

The same was not true of ted witzel's gloriously tasteless *All's Well*. Helen's disguise when she cures the King was a contemporary "slutty nurse" Hallowe'en costume; her cure involved using a power drill with a butt plug as a drill bit to extract a lost jewelled ring from the King's rectum. This explains when the King gave Helen a ring (it's not mentioned in the original text), but not how it got to where she found it. Parolles, the parasite who flatters Helen's intended, is outed as gay when the old count Lafeu finds his porn stash, then bashed as a closet case, before finally being accepted in the closing scene as he shimmies out in a sequined sheath dress.

Like Jain, witzel cross-casts in part to work with artists he admires, but he also sees it as a priority, in contrast to Jain's stated preference to cast talented actors, regardless of sex or gender. For witzel, it is an explicit item on his to-do list. "Whenever you give me a text by a dead white male, I go through and mark off every character who could be re-cast as woman. They just weren't writing a lot of parts for ladies, and I like working with actresses."[4]

In mounting his production of *All's Well*, witzel was also constrained by the necessity of doubling roles with the parallel production of *Hamlet*: "I knew that we were going to have a Gertrude who needed to double, so we had to have someone of the parental generation who would be female, and it could be Lavatch (the Dowager Countess's clown) or Lafeu." When I commented to him that Lafeu's role as defender of the established order made him a less than obvious choice, the response was blunt: "That's why the idea of gender-fucking Lafeu lasted about thirty seconds." Left with Lavatch, witzel initially "didn't realize how important La Vache would become at that point. The monologues I created hadn't been written then. I loved the idea of a slutty clown in a cow print dress."

witzel's decision to rewrite Lavatch as La Vache – the slutty clown in the cow print dress, who delivers three choric monologues – was thus prompted by a number of different pressures, including the need to match casting with another play, a wish to create roles for female collaborators, and a determination to subvert the gender norms of a character. There was also, on witzel's part, a wish to create an arc for the character of the Clown, who in the original text "exists to tell dick jokes and deliver a letter that serves no dramaturgical purpose." The arc witzel created reimagined Lavatch as the dead Count's bereaved mistress. In Shakespeare's text, the Countess's dubbing Lavatch as "knave" can be affectionate or exasperated; in witzel's adaptation, the word is slut. This is entirely in keeping with his intent to probe "toxic masculinity" and the complex interplay between social status and sexual difference. La Vache – played by a wonderfully blowsy Rachel Jones – delivered an opening monologue about love, and how it leads people to act in ways they regret. Beside her, the whole cast stood at attention, in tight formation as mourners at the old Count's funeral (figure 4.3). But one by one, starting with Helen, they clutched their chests as though their hearts were bursting out, then mimed holding them, beating, in their hands. First Helen, pining for Bertram, then Parolles, who very explicitly shared her interest in Bertram, then Lafeu, in love with the Countess, then the Countess, missing her husband, and then finally La Vache – who promptly dropped hers. She visually disrupted the scene, never joining the ranks of the others, dressed in cow-print and hot pink while the others are dressed for a funeral. Thematically, too, she undercut the romantic longing of others in the cast: while their beating hearts,

Figure 4.3 | At the funeral, *All's Well That Ends Well.*

cradled in their hands, were metaphorical representations of pain, hers was emphatically organic, messy, and slippery.

Given witzel's explicit interest in gender and sexuality, there was predictably more in this production than I can discuss in this chapter. But for my purposes, two effects of his production choices stand out. The first is the effect of promoting Lavatch from a tertiary male character, whose sexuality can be brought out for a joke and then safely retired, to a secondary female character, whose sexual history is of much greater consequence. In the original text, when Lavatch wishes to marry Isbel, he seeks the blessing of his mistress, the Dowager Countess. The exchange is the excuse for some jokes, and provides oblique commentary on the erotic travails of the younger generation. In witzel's reimagining, La Vache wishes to marry Derek, but her request for permission to marry comes as a cruel reminder to the Countess that she has twice lost her husband, once to a mistress – La Vache – and once to death, and that the mistress still has options. In Shakespeare's text, the Countess and Lafeu act as choric characters, priming the audience to approve of Helen's endeavours. In witzel's script, La Vache becomes the most important choric character, offering not only indirect but also very explicit commentary on the action of the play. Jones played La Vache, Diana's mother, and a Chorus who spoke and sang in the gaps between the three movements of the edited text.[5] This promotion of a tertiary character to secondary and the explicit sexualization of La Vache's relationship with the dead Count had striking effects on the relationships between many other characters in the play.

For example, in Shakespeare's text, the older generation is concerned solely with the sexual relations of its children. Any flickers of desire in the King or Lafeu for Helen are either part of a miraculous cure or largely vicarious; the Countess is concerned with protecting her bloodline, but by setting Bertram up with a suitable wife, not by taking a second husband. La Vache's prior sexual relationship with the Count draws the older generation into the sexual morass that witzel wishes to explore as, in this version, Lafeu openly courts the Countess, who enthusiastically accepts. Loosely speaking, when sexuality does not match up to normative standards of sex or gender identity, we can use the term *queer*. What do we use when the normative standard violated is a matter of age? Given how rarely we see depictions of sexuality in older characters, sexualizing the older generation seems almost more subversive than casting a woman as Hamlet.

The second, unexpected, knock-on effect is how the re-casting of La Vache affects our understanding of Parolles's ultimate position in the social hierarchy of the play. I have mentioned the tight formation of characters in the opening scene, but the same formation was repeated in the final scene of witzel's production. The formation, in the closing scene, became mobile, as the whole court moved as one, emphasizing the collusion of a range of disparate characters enforcing the normative standards of heterosexual marriage and pursuing answers from Bertram and Diana. The French courtiers, in tight formation, as in the opening funeral scene, moved swiftly, forcing first one witness and then another into physical retreat. What was striking about this production was that – contrary to tradition – Parolles was fully integrated into this choreography of social conformity. As in Shakespeare's text, a broken Parolles appeals to Lafeu and to Lavatch / La Vache for support, and Lafeu agrees to take him on as a fool. In witzel's terms, this means that he "has moved himself into a similar place as La Vache in terms of being a clown, which is historically a safe place to put queer men – you can stand on the side and make bitchy comments and be seen as a sad clown, and be that kind of Nathan Lane figure." Here I take issue with witzel, though, because La Vache is, as the Countess's hostility shows, not safe at all. To me, Lafeu's acceptance of a newly uncloseted Parolles, dressed in one of La Vache's cast-off dresses, opened up a whole new range of interpretive possibilities. If La Vache was mistress to the old Count, why should we not assume that Parolles, in drag, might now serve as master/mistress to Lafeu? Nathan Lane, after all, is not beyond sexual relationships, and if one clown can be lover to an aristocrat, why should another be presumed safe and neutered? While witzel confirmed that this was not his intention, his casting choices opened a Pandora's box of additional questions. One change of gender for a relatively minor character, although apparently less radical than casting a woman as Hamlet, thus opened up endless avenues for slippage in gender and sexual identity in a production that was geared to explore those concepts.

CONCLUSION

In comparing these two productions' engagements with gender and sexuality based on their casting practices, I have no wish to sell either production short. Each produced novel readings of a very old text, and each has become my mental benchmark for the play-text produced. After all, Jain's refusal to delve into gender is as much a theoretical and philosophical statement about gender as a more explicitly theorized formulation. Again, a *Prince Hamlet* that maintained its planned focus on gender could not have accommodated such an expansive engagement with questions of narration, mediation, epistemology, and embodiment. Yet it is worth considering the effects of cross-casting in light of the laws of unintended consequences. witzel never intended Lafeu to be read as bisexual, but the wild card of casting Jones as La Vache set off a chain of interpretive possibilities. Nor did Jain intend that his progressive casting choices should reinforce traditional readings of Ophelia, or render masculinity the default gender. As witzel pithily phrased it in conversation, "You just throw an image up there, and people project onto it from all directions." Yet the openness of response to his heavily cut staging suggests that Jain's more generous understanding of audience interpretation is closer to what actually takes place in the theatre: "I think if you pick it up" as being in the performance, "it is."

NOTES

1 Christine Horne, private conversation with the author, June 2017. Unless otherwise attributed, all subsequent quotations from Horne are from this conversation.

2 Ravi Jain, private conversation with the author, January 2018. Unless otherwise attributed, all subsequent quotations from Jain are from this conversation.

3 Ho's performance never seemed to shade into a parody of femininity, so the term "camp" does not apply.

4 ted witzel, private conversation with the author, June 2017. Unless otherwise attributed, all subsequent quotations from witzel are from this conversation.

5 witzel penned three monologues in contemporary language for La Vache as the play opened, as Helen travelled to France, and as she returned.

REFERENCES

de Beauvoir, Simone. 1968. *The Second Sex*. Edited and translated by H.M. Parshley. New York: Knopf.

Citron, Paula. 2007. "Something Fresh in the State of Denmark." Review of *The Prince Hamlet*, Why Not Theatre, Toronto. *Globe and Mail*, 25 September.

Leung, Wayne. 2017. Review of *Prince Hamlet*, Why Not Theatre / Soulpepper, Toronto. *Mooney on Theatre*, 20 April. https://www.mooneyontheatre.com/2017/04/20/review-prince-hamlet-why-not-theatresoulpepper/.

Long, Taylor. 2017. "Shakespeare's Reflection on Humanity Is Powerfully Human in Why Not Theatre's *Prince Hamlet*." Review of *Prince Hamlet*, Why Not Theatre / Soulpepper, Toronto. *Broadway World* (Toronto), 22 April. https://www.broadwayworld.com/toronto/article/BWW-Review-Shakespeares-Reflection-on-Humanity-is-Powerfully-Human-in-Why-Not-Theatres-PRINCE-HAMLET-20170422.

Maga, Carly. 2017. "Hamlet as Told by Why Not Theatre Is Full of Sound and Silence." *Toronto Star*, 19 April.

Nestruck, J. Kelly. 2017. "Signing Narrator Adds Sensational Layer to Ravi Jain's *Prince Hamlet*." Review of *Prince Hamlet*, Why Not Theatre / Soulpepper, Toronto. *Globe and Mail*, 20 April.

5

TWO PRODUCTIONS OF *THE TWO GENTS*

From the Globe Stage to the Royal Shakespeare Company, 2012–2014

CHRISTIE CARSON

> What kind of staging and acting conventions produce emotion and affect in the theatre? British theatre, in much of its Shakespeare production, tends to answer: realism.
>
> Escolme, "Decentring Shakespeare"

The Globe to Globe Festival of 2012 highlighted the fact that, while realism has become the standard for performances of Shakespeare in Britain, other theatre traditions outside the United Kingdom prefer their Shakespeare to come in a non-realist performance package. In this chapter, I would like to look at two productions of *The Two Gentleman of Verona,* which come out of two years of Shakespeare celebration in the United Kingdom. Using *The Two Gentlemen of Verona* as a case study, I hope to offer an example of what can be gained critically by having available to a wider audience a variety of approaches to the plays. But I will also acknowledge that audiences may feel resistant to unfamiliar presentations of these plays, seeing them more as a novelty than as a substantive shift toward a more inclusive, visually oriented presentation style that moves the emphasis away from Shakespeare's text.

The two productions under examination approached this play from either end of the non-realist (global-intercultural) / realist (local-Anglo-American) spectrum of performance. Each brought the play to its audience in a way that revealed unexpected moments of tenderness and power; each was part of a national celebration, the World Shakespeare Festival (WSF), which formed part of the Cultural Olympics of 2012, in one case, and the celebration of the 450th anniversary of the playwright's birth in Stratford in 2014, in the other. The first production, as part of the Globe to Globe Festival (which was the Globe Theatre's contribution to the WSF and which staged all thirty-seven Shakespeare plays, each one in a different national language, over six weeks), was aimed at an urban, multicultural audience, well versed in a variety of non-naturalistic performance styles. The second production was part of a celebration that, inevitably, looked at Shakespeare's town of origin and therefore focused on the nation's foremost producer of his work, the Royal Shakespeare Company (RSC), known for its tradition of realist presentation of characters and setting. The parallels between Shakespeare's own journey between Stratford and London and the characters' journey from Verona to Milan were impossible to overlook and seemed to catch the audience's imagination. Rather than fighting against this vision, these two productions embraced the youthful energy of the idea of new beginnings and played into, as well as with, audience expectations of the play performed in a celebration year. Each of these productions elicited an engaged audience response but in distinctly different ways: the first was exaggerated, funny, and filled with irony, while the second was endearing in its earnestness and innocence.

These two productions – the first performed by Denton Chikura and Tonderai Munyevu of the Two Gents Productions, directed by Arne Pohlmeier, and presented on 9–10 May 2012 at the Globe Theatre in London, and the second by the Royal Shakespeare Company, directed by Simon Godwin, and performed throughout the summer season of 2014 at the Royal Shakespeare Theatre in Stratford-upon-Avon – reflect the division in the play between cosmopolitan sophistication and rural honesty. From two men (and no dog) on the bare-bones Globe stage to a fully produced mainstage production in Shakespeare's home town, this play was performed to critical success in both venues. The Two Gents production, performed in Shona, was meant to represent Zimbabwe in the Globe to Globe Festival, despite the fact that the two actors and director are all UK-based and the production had formerly toured the United Kingdom and internationally in English. Despite, or perhaps because of, this somewhat unconventional interaction with the festival's proposed structure of inviting international guests to perform in London, this production helped to articulate the importance, or lack thereof, of language in this play. Bridget Escolme remarks in her summary of this festival on the importance of the overt theatricality that so many of the visiting companies brought to the stage: "The huge variety of non-realist forms offered by the Globe to Globe productions, so highly appropriate to this consciously theatrical, presentational space, allowed politics and emotion, and the politics of emotion, onto the stage in ways that are rarely seen in Shakespearean production here, despite assumptions that his are the most politically astute and emotionally heightened plays in our theatre history" (2013, 311). The RSC production, by contrast, chose a performance style that bordered on the didactic, emphasizing each character and situation in this early play that might remind an audience of similar elements later in the Shakespearean canon. This production highlighted the authentic (in the sense of the playwright's origins) and authoritative position, as well as the educational remit, of the RSC for its Stratford audiences of tourists and locals, whose expectations were clearly of psychological realism of character, as well as believability of setting and relationships.

If these two productions can be seen to illustrate two ends of the global/local performance spectrum, then it is not a surprise that one was created by two actors playing all the roles and the other was presented in a full production. The fact that one was in Shona and the other in Elizabethan English, and that one had just two performances, as part of a festival, and the other was part of the RSC season on the mainstage all form part of their individual contextual circumstances. However, what I would like to highlight here is that both productions successfully focused on the language of performance, above the articulation of the text, and saw the production as an opportunity to reconceptualize the play for a new audience. The first focused on the virtuoso performances of the two actors playing every part. The second approached the play as if it were new writing, making its action understandable in contemporary terms. So, while the Globe performance relied on the audience's imaginative engagement and suspension of disbelief, and the second relied on psychological realism, they both imbued the play with life and vitality through developing an engaged audience. In both cases, the clarity of the approach and the earnest desire to communicate with the present audience made the play vital and fun.

Turning first to the Two Gents production, I would like to focus on the overt performativity of its actors and then move on to consider the implications of this intercultural performance style in London in a year, and in a theatre, that claimed to celebrate the cultural mix of British society. The German-born, African-raised, white director of the Two Gents production, Pohlmeier, notes "that Bertolt Brecht and the Berliner Ensemble had … a considerable influence on South African theatre in the second half of the twentieth century, either directly, as their work became renowned internationally, or via other theatre artists and practitioners, including Peter Brook, who favoured a presentational over a representational approach to theatre-making" (Massai 2013, 157). In discussing the production with Sonia Massai after the Globe performance, Pohlmeier describes the benefits that came from working so closely on this play in more than one language: "The visual or acoustic features in productions where the directors and the actors and their audiences share the same language can come across as redundant if they are not carefully thought through, but they are essential in productions conceived with touring or international festivals in mind" (Massai 2013, 158). This comment signals the way that a visual, performative language allowed the audience to make its own connections to the story that was unfolding. The power of the tale came from the fact that these two actors had to perform all of the roles, making gender, race, age, and even humanity (the dog was played convincingly by Munyevu) part of the performance. Therefore, this production of the play highlighted its performativity for an English-speaking audience that had to follow the action through gesture and character relationships. The Globe space also allowed for extensive interaction with the audience, including several audience "plants," which helped to push the boundaries of what was acceptable within the parameters of the Globe to Globe Festival. The audience was encouraged to experience and empathize with both the characters' and the actors' struggles simultaneously in this very representational but also political show.

The extraordinary flexibility of the actors in performing all of the parts pointed out the power of both cultural and gender stereotypes to provoke laughter when performed in an almost pantomime manner, at great speed. In this way, Chikura and Munyevu created a sense of a shared language of character relationships. These performers were very self-aware and obviously enjoyed the interaction they developed with their audience. Alex Needham's review demonstrates this: "Changes in character from male to female are signified by the wrapping of shawls around waists and the kind of

Figure 5.1 | Denton Chikura as Julia: poor theatre in action.

mincing that would floor Julian Clary" (2012). The idea that these two actors could out-camp one of Britain's biggest gay icons both dates and localizes the critic and the performance. Mincing as a sign of femininity is as dated as the Pantomime Dame but equally iconic in London. However, this knowing use of stereotypes was a gentle rebuke for the British audience, who were very aware of the history of this performance tradition and its homophobic undertones; these actors both knew the concerns of their audience and could anticipate their reactions to these representational tropes. Penelope Woods, in her review, points out how audience recognition and interaction formed an essential part of the storytelling of this production; the "sense of shared endeavour was very much at home on the wooden open-air stage of the Globe" (2013, 224). The reliance on stereotypes and stand-ins for some of the characters was a form of shared shorthand that helped to draw the audience into the project of making the play with few resources; it was poor theatre in action, which pointed out the need for inventiveness in the face of very little financial support (something that demonstrated nicely what was expected by the audience of African Shakespeare). However, the global financial crisis of 2008, and its impact on artists worldwide, also created in this audience a sense of an embattled cultural sector internationally, something that became a theme of the Globe to Globe Festival as a whole.

So, this production did not rely on its virtuosity of character portrayal just to delight and entertain the audience. Rather, the aim was to engage its audience in a debate about issues that cross over international boundaries in an increasingly integrated twenty-first-century world. The playful performances could quickly become serious in this production, which did not shy away from some of the more difficult moments in the story. In one telling moment, the attempted rape of Silvia, the strength of this company's approach stood out. By quickly changing characters and leaving some characters to be played symbolically through bits of costume, the actors demonstrated their own skills and the complexity of their political position; their quick shifts of perspective made the audience choose whether to move with them empathetically or not. At the same time, this rapid reassessment of each character within a scene required an attentive audience to note the sudden shift in the play from comedy to something much more serious. Needham (2012) points out the extent to which this production highlighted the play's tendency to combine genres, adding a bit of tragedy to the comedy. He writes: "Not everything is played for laughs – the horror of the attempted rape of Sylvia by Proteus is conveyed by Munyevu sinisterly licking the long white glove he has worn while playing her part. And the problematic ending – in which Valentine abruptly hands over Sylvia to Proteus before Julia reveals her true identity, and the original couples are reunited – is not glossed over either, with a finale that seems appropriately flat and cold." Woods conveys in detail the ingenious approach the actors took to this complicated scene: "As Proteus seized Silvia, in the person of Chikura, Chikura wriggled out of the glove to return as Valentine startling his friend in this moment of aggression and Munyevu was left assaulting the glove" (2013, 225). This production helped to highlight how entirely central to the play the mixing of genres is, in an extremely funny, relevant, and poignant way. "Wriggling" out of the position of the young woman being assaulted and assuming the position of the betrayed friend formed the meaning of the scene, as well as presenting a comment on Shakespeare's evasive moral tone. Woods found the attempted rape scene somewhat more problematic than Needham: "Silvia's sudden de-physicalization, in an instant becoming a limp and helpless shred of fabric, was poignant but potentially evasive or too neat to deal sufficiently with this uncomfortable moment" (2013, 225). But I would suggest that the point made by this production is that this scene can be seen from several angles when the actors change their own perspective within it "in an instant" without making it clear to the audience which vantage point it should adopt.

The complex responses that the Cultural Olympics garnered provide important context for the first of these productions. While Stanley Wells writes that accounts of the festival demonstrated "afresh the extent of Shakespeare's enduring and increasing global relevance" (2013, xxv), Erin Sullivan suggests that "2012 marked the most intensive investigation of Shakespeare's relevance to modern global culture that any of *us* has ever seen" (2013, 11; my emphasis). The Two Gents company was not new to this play, nor was their production new to British audiences, given that this representation of Zimbabwe in the festival was, in fact, prepared and presented by a London-based company. The joy of the production, however, lay in the irony that this knowledge engendered within the audience, at least in some quarters. The acknowledgment of a multicultural community within London was an aim of this festival, and this production provided a space for recognition of hybrid identity in the public sphere of middle-class entertainment, usually the preserve of a white, entitled population. Woods writes: "This was a performance about being caught between the horizon-expanding education offered by travel and multiculturalism and the tensions of local identity and love" (2013, 224). This production stood out because of its ability to challenge the established view of what Shakespeare performance in London could or should look like. The Two Gents company was well-versed in both the language and the cultural assumptions of the "home" country, as well as in the expectations of an international festival – they were presenting a showcase to the world of what might be expected from African Shakespeare while at the same time placing their presentation in quotation marks. The complexity of this knowing exchange was what made the production so much fun for its spectators, who were well placed to understand the multiple levels of irony at work.

The opening up of new horizons in this early play was another subject of concern in this production. Friendships lost, and familiarity left behind, the two characters at the centre of this play drift into amoral behaviour. The Two Gents did not shy away from indicating ambivalence toward urban freedoms and from pointing out

Figure 5.2 | Julia and Lucetta (Tonderai Munyevu) in Verona.

the audience's own ambivalence towards African Shakespeare. In the attempted rape scene, it was a black male aggressor who threatened Silvia, first performed by another black man and then by a white glove. The action was halted when the first black man, in his former leading role as Valentine, a representative from the "home" environment, entered the scene and expressed dismay at the behaviour of his friend. The idea that prejudice and preconceived ideas about the behaviour of "foreigners" in general and black male foreigners in particular can result in the enactment of the very fears that have been expressed was a strong underlying statement in this production. The audience was encouraged to laugh at the action but then was asked to examine its own reactions in a starkly Brechtian way.

The second production, at the RSC in 2014 during the celebrations of the 450th anniversary of Shakespeare's birth, seemed to have discovered through this play a renewed appreciation of youthful enthusiasm. Simon Godwin, as associate director of the Royal Court Theatre, was accustomed to working primarily with new writers, so his approach to the play at the Royal Shakespeare Company was deeply rooted in the psychological realist strand of the contemporary

Figure 5.3 | Proteus (Mark Arends) and Julia (Pearl Chanda), the small-town lovers.

British acting tradition. He says in his commentary on the DVD of this production that he asked the actors to write biographies for their characters (2014). While this is conventional acting practice, it stands in direct contrast to the Brechtian and African traditions of non-naturalistic storytelling used by the Two Gents actors. Unusually, in the RSC production, the youthful, tentative, and unauthoritative approach taken by the director challenged the idea of a top-down presentation of how things must be done that is often associated with the RSC and its position as national cultural authority. In this production, the local audience in Stratford, comprising both tourists and residents, was invited to explore Shakespeare's youthful venture in writing alongside the first-time RSC director and the two young protagonists. The reliance in the first production on audience knowledge of a performance tradition that, according to Massai, "draws from South African township theatre as much as from Shakespeare" (2013, 157) was replaced by an approach that looked for truth and realism in the play's action. However, in both of these cases, the result was a similar sense of pleasure in the play and its playfulness, although both were also tinged with sadness.

The shift within the play itself from a provincial town where things are simple (Verona) to a cosmopolitan centre where morals and loyalties are much more complex (Milan), with the characters travelling through a forest inhabited by dangerous outlaw bands composed of banished men, in some ways makes a mockery of the "happily ever after" endings of Shakespeare's better-known comedies. Taking this morally complex play and making it believable for a contemporary audience posed a serious challenge to local notions of Shakespearean romanticism. In the DVD commentary, Godwin describes the challenge in very practical terms. He puzzles about making the letter that Proteus sends to Julia before the play begins understandable for an audience that never uses pen and paper to send messages. He lights on the idea of Valentine's Day, when cards are still exchanged. Similarly, he describes the struggle to make the servant-master relationship between Julia and Lucetta believable by providing an environment in which Lucetta is in a service position as a waitress, her social position made clear by her Scottish accent. Both of these decisions could be seen to rely on stereotypes and the expectations of status that come out of Britain as a class-conscious country. The decision to translate the essence of the Italian setting as a place where people are of a hotter temperament than the English was well received by the audience. The equation of the Scottish temper with Italian hot-headedness is a prejudice that would have struck an ironic note in the Two Gents production in London, but in Stratford in this RSC production it was presented with absolute seriousness. For the local audience, the class associations presented were not given as a point of archaic reference but rather as an up-to-the-minute reassertion of current conflicts (particularly the Scottish independence referendum vote that took place in the same year). The early rumblings of the fundamental divide between rural and urban societies in Britain, which would be reflected in the Brexit vote two years later, could already be seen on stage in this production.

Godwin's emphasis on innocence and its loss through exposure to love and temptation made the plot of the play quite simple and its aims straightforward. His approach seemed to echo what Escolme describes as the attraction of the realist tradition in British Theatre: "To feel in the theatre is to feel empathy with a plausibly rounded, psychologically drawn 'character'" (2013, 310). Godwin's own inexperience in approaching Shakespeare's work generated a production that highlighted the playwright's approach to dramatic structure and language. As Godwin puts it, "the greatest drama lies in the greatest compression of events, the sense of urgency that propels the drama forward" (2016). So, the freshness of this production came from Godwin's approach to Shakespeare as a young regional writer still honing his craft, an approach that relied on the cast to provide the missing details in the characters' development and relationships. By treating the language as if it were unfamiliar, or at least new to the director, the actors, and the audience, Godwin shed new light on Shakespeare's love of dramatic action. Language in both of these productions was seen as subordinate to the action on stage. It was assumed in both cases that the audience might struggle with the spoken text, so the stage action would be required to fill in the gaps – in the second production through recognizable situations and class interactions.

Like the Two Gents production, the RSC interpretation employed exaggerated emotions, but this time as a sign of youthful enthusiasm and a desire to connect with a realistic vision of young love in Britain in the twenty-first century. In both cases, the downplaying of the verbal language in favour of action and emotion reinforced the power of Shakespeare's cultural reach, but in an ironic way. It was assumed that, when watching a lesser-known play (a full-scale production of *The Two Gentlemen of Verona* had not been seen on the RSC mainstage in forty-five years), even the RSC audience would need some help in understanding the text. In this case, the director relied on clichés surrounding romantic comedies, using Valentine's Day (with a not-so-subtle reference to the protagonist's name) and other popular cultural references to bridge the gap between a young contemporary audience and a four-hundred-year-old play. So, like the mincing steps in the Two Gents performance, the reliance on cultural stereotypes in the RSC production allowed the play's youthful exuberance and earnestness to shine through in a way that signalled the global reach of Shakespeare's influence on the romance industry.

To illustrate the kinds of directorial decisions that could have caused offence but that, in the end, charmed the audience with an innocence of their own, I refer to the presentation of the key characters who were enacted as realistic, angst-ridden young millennials. The first was Proteus himself, who was played with a breathless excitement by Mark Arends. Julia and Lucetta demonstrated a servant-and-master relationship that developed into a friendship, playing on assumptions that most women of a certain social position

Figure 5.4 | Proteus and Valentine (Michael Marcus) at a Verona café.

have staff in one form or another. The charm and parochial sentimentality of Verona was demonstrated through a traditional outdoor café on Valentine's Day (figure 5.4). This romantic environment was contrasted on stage by the steamy nightlife of Milan, in which the Duke showed his wealth and power, as well as his dominance over his daughter and her chosen partner. All of these environments relied on visual cues that drew on the conventions of film and television romance and that were expressed in the set and costumes as well as in the characterization by the actors. Movement in the production was carefully constructed, and the discovery of Silvia by Valentine mimicked the decadence of the party scene from Baz Luhrmann's film *Romeo + Juliet*, with the exception that Silvia was a woman, not a girl, and Valentine's interest was clearly sexual (figure 5.5). The audience was not expected to know Shakespeare's text or the placement of this play within the canon (although many did). What it was expected to be familiar with was popular culture interpretations of Shakespeare's life and work, such as the Luhrmann film and *Shakespeare in Love* (in which Henslowe describes the winning features of this early play). Born in 1978, Godwin was directing the play for audience members of his own generation. The young

Figure 5.5 | Silvia (Sarah MacRae) and Valentine dancing in Milan.

male protagonists were the focus of the play, and their journey to love through self-discovery was the central concern, although some key points about romantic love and its challenges in the twenty-first century were presented throughout.

In this production, the portrayal that was the most strikingly different from traditional popular romance films was that of Silvia, who was envisioned as a strong and independent urban woman. Here she was picture perfect, in her picture window – the balcony from *Romeo and Juliet* was re-imagined here as a display case for her father's jewel, and the fragility of Juliet's position was replaced by Silvia's calm assurance. Still, the restrictions on her choice of husband remain, anticipating those in later plays. Silvia, like Juliet, Jessica, and Desdemona, has to find a way to escape her father's rules and household, even in this modern retelling of the story. In this context, the attempted rape scene had to be played rather differently. The realism of this scene drew simultaneously on an awareness of Shakespeare's other forest environments, where court civilities do not apply, and on the local reality of increased poverty and violent crime in rural England. Silvia was very physically forward in defending her honour and protesting her love for Valentine. Julia, by contrast, was forced to reveal her bound breasts to be recognized by her former lover, something that features in two different American teen adaptations of Shakespeare's comedies (*10 Things I Hate About You* and *She's the Man*). However, these two young women did not secure their future happiness in the forest, and both stood dejected and disillusioned at the end of the play.

This production placed the protagonists in a glittering world of money and control that they struggled to make sense of in Milan and an old-fashioned world of honest labour and sexual repression in Verona. As a precursor to the debates surrounding Brexit and to the divide it has created between the cities and the country, it spoke volumes about the impossible nature of the quest to return to old ways of seeing the world when life was simpler and Britain was united. The earnest and psychologically real RSC performance made the play more convincing for a British audience schooled in realism, linking it to the other plays in the canon in a general way for a knowledgeable local audience, but more emphatically linking it to recent U.S. popular cultural appropriations of Shakespeare's work on film, which had more relevance to the struggle of young British men and women in the audience. To present Shakespeare's work today, it is impossible to escape his legacy as both a local and a global cultural icon.

These two productions, then, were divided by two years and one hundred miles and, more importantly, by two distinctive performance styles. The Globe production presented a non-realist form that made complex use of audience response and intercultural knowledge, while the RSC production took a believable realist approach that depended on local knowledge of Shakespeare's origins, as well as on his commercial global reach. The Two Gents company created a deeply engaged and thoughtful audience response through its presentational approach, which made spectators think as well as feel, in a very Brechtian way. The RSC production evoked stereotypes and older prejudices about romance and class but mixed these ideas with the context of learning and viewing Shakespeare in a world of international media adaptations. Both productions spoke in poignant ways to a present-day audience. Both productions also raised profound questions about gender, race, love, and friendship for young people in Britain today, while foregrounding the possibilities of an active debate about the power of live performance to inform as well as to entertain. Together, these two productions demonstrate the range of performance approaches to Shakespeare's work and to audience interaction in the United Kingdom in the celebration years of 2012 and 2014. Working at either end of the performance spectrum, they demonstrate the flexibility of the plays as well as the willingness of audiences to experience Shakespeare in a variety of ways in the twenty-first century.

REFERENCES

Escolme, Bridget. 2013. "Decentring Shakespeare: A Hope for Future Connections." In *Shakespeare Beyond English*, edited by Susan Bennett and Christie Carson, 308–12. Cambridge: Cambridge University Press.

Godwin, Simon. 2014. "Director's Commentary." *The Two Gentlemen of Verona*. RSCLive DVD.

Massai, Sonia. 2013. "*Two Gentlemen of Verona* for/by Zimbabwean Diasporic Communities." In *Shakespeare Beyond English*, edited by Susan Bennett and Christie Carson, 157–60. Cambridge: Cambridge University Press.

Needham, Alex. 2012. Review of *The Two Gentlemen of Verona*, Two Gents Productions, London. *Guardian*, 14 May. https://www.theguardian.com/stage/2012/may/14/the-two-gentlemen-of-verona-review.

Sullivan, Erin. 2013. "Olympic Performance in the Year of Shakespeare." In *A Year of Shakespeare: Re-living the World Shakespeare Festival*, edited by Paul Edmondson, Paul Prescott, and Erin Sullivan, 3–11. London: Arden Shakespeare.

Wells, Stanley. 2013. "Foreword." In *A Year of Shakespeare: Re-living the World Shakespeare Festival*, edited by Paul Edmondson, Paul Prescott, and Erin Sullivan, xxiii–xxv. London: Arden Shakespeare.

Woods, Penelope. 2013. "*The Two Gentlemen of Verona*: Directed by Arne Pohlmeier for the Two Gents Theatre Company (Harare, Zimbabwe and London, UK) at Shakespeare's Globe." In *A Year of Shakespeare: Re-living the World Shakespeare Festival*, edited by Paul Edmondson, Paul Prescott, and Erin Sullivan, 223–6. London: Arden Shakespeare.

The Productions Online

Globe to Globe production: https://globeplayer.tv/videos/the-two-gentlemen-of-verona.

RSC production: https://shop.rsc.org.uk/collections/dvd-1/products/two-gentlemen-of-verona-rsc-dvd-2014.

6

EMBODYING THE SEA

Shakespeare and Physical Theatre

LINDA MCJANNET

In 2003, just after the beginning of the Iraq War, the Royal Shakespeare Company (RSC) collaborated with Cardboard Citizens, Britain's only theatrical company for homeless people, to stage Shakespeare's *Pericles, Prince of Tyre*, in a London warehouse, with shipping containers for sets. Director Adrian Jackson saw *Pericles* as an epic story of wandering and loss that would speak to the contemporary disruptions of war. He sought to involve audience members – physically and emotionally – in the experience of asylum seekers and other marginalized people who are (at best) at the mercy of a bureaucracy and (at worst) at risk of drowning in overcrowded boats or of bombardment in a no-man's land. On arrival, one reviewer reported, audience members were "checked in, issued with tags ... shepherded into a vast hall ... [and] confronted by intimidatingly complex immigration forms"; if the actors interspersed among them tried to tell their stories, they were silenced (Billington 2003). During one of the play's storm scenes, as Jackson described it, the women performers "became waves hurling themselves against the outside of the container, in a poignant evocation both of the storm and [of] the shocking experiences of people seeking asylum and being met with steely indifference" (quoted in Sharpe and Wright 2012, 143). Jackson's involvement of the audience in creating the theatrical event, his creative use of the actors' bodies, and his choice of a political theme are hallmarks of what has come to be known as "physical theatre."

Physical theatre descends partly from mid-twentieth-century German *tanztheatre* (dance-theatre). Choreographers Pina Bausch,

Figure 6.1 | *Körper* (*Bodies*, 2000).

Sasha Waltz, and others responded to the devastation of two world wars and to the signing of the Universal Declaration of Human Rights (1948) by asserting in their work the sacredness of the individual human body (Sörgel 2015, xiii). Bausch's work often included *movement trouvé* (found movement), the activities of ordinary (peacetime) life such as "walking, ... carrying babies, caressing, kissing" – or gently brushing someone's hair (Shevtsova 2003, 9–10). Waltz's groundbreaking *Körper* (*Bodies,* 2000) celebrated the body's sculptural beauty even while acknowledging its susceptibility to objectification (figure 6.1). Breaking with what they viewed as the ethos and aesthetic of classical ballet, this generation of choreographers sought (as Merce Cunningham put it) "not to show off, but to show" (1997, 60).

Physical theatre also builds on the work of theatre directors such as Antonin Artaud, Jacques Lecoq, and Jerzy Grotowski, who, in the mid-twentieth century, drew on mime, Asian drama, and the *commedia dell'arte* tradition of "the actor as improviser/dancer/acrobat" to champion versions of "poor theatre" centred on the actor's body rather than on a pre-existing dramatic text (Callery 2001, 11). An American actor's memory of a workshop suggests the power of Grotowski's method. Ryszard Cieślak, his lead actor,

> stripped to his shorts ... [and] performed a series of headstands, rolls, and backbends, each flowing into the next ... His body seemed to be made of liquid muscle, enormously powerful, yet utterly soft and supple. He moved with the strength and precision of an accomplished gymnast, yet there was something in his face ... that removed the work entirely from the world of gymnastics. It was as if the enormous muscular energy we witnessed was merely the ... emanation of an even more intense inner life. (Wangh 2000, xix)

As this passage suggests, Grotowski aimed to use movement to enhance the actor's expressive power, not to showcase physical feats per se. He also advocated for the barest minimum of sets, costumes, sound, and other theatrical effects. Few physical theatre companies today follow Grotowski's ideals to the letter, but they all view the body as, in John Farmanesh-Bocca's phrase, a "story-telling machine" (quoted in Dunn 2008) and challenge the hegemony of the spoken word. Some companies devise their own texts, but several have turned to classic works. Of thirteen ensembles featured in a recent theatre journal (Wright 2014), six had produced one or more of Shakespeare's plays, and a seventh could be added that performs the plays on trapeze. (See the Appendix at the end of this chapter for a list of these seven ensembles.)

In what follows, I will argue that physical theatre productions of Shakespeare, and productions influenced by this body-centred approach, have a particular appeal in twenty-first-century anglophone culture, which is, for better and for worse, simultaneously intensely mediated and body-obsessed. According to Siân Williams (resident choreographer at Shakespeare's Globe since 1999) and John Farmanesh-Bocca (founding director-choreographer of the Not Man Apart Physical Theatre Ensemble), the energy, imagination, and physical risk inherent in such productions engage audiences who often spend working hours in front of computer screens and leisure time at the gym or yoga studio and/or watching professional sports, film, and television.[1] Participants in and fans of extreme sports, such as skydiving and rock climbing, may also connect with the element of risk in physical theatre. As celebrated Shakespearean director Peter Brook put it, "When a man flies over the audience's head on a rope, every aspect of the immediate is put in jeopardy" (1968, 52). In Brook's *Midsummer Night's Dream* (1970), arguably the first

Shakespearean example of physical theatre, the actors' willingness to master circus skills, such as trapeze and stilts, and to risk bodily injury energized the audience and earned the performers an extra measure of respect.

In addition to displaying prowess and embracing risk, physical theatre relies on suggestion rather than realistic depiction. It thus encourages – even requires – audience members to be more than usually active makers of meaning. It asks them to interpret kinetic metaphors, in which most people have little formal training, as well as verbal and visual images that are part of everyday language and mass media and are widely studied in academic curricula. As audiences watch the performers transform themselves from dancers to actors, actors to characters, and (sometimes) characters to inanimate objects, they become "co-creators of the performance" (Callery 2001, 5). A representative sample of these creative, body-centred approaches can be seen in scenes of sea voyaging and shipwreck – and indeed how the sea itself has been "embodied" – in recent productions of *Pericles, Prince of Tyre,* and *The Tempest.*

The boundary between body-centred and other types of theatre is by no means cut and dried. Grotowski's dictums notwithstanding, physical theatre companies today often use music, video, and even built sets, and, in all forms of theatre, the actor's body is inevitably and rightly an important locus of meaning. In most modern productions, the storm scenes in *The Tempest* and *Pericles* employ a combination of sound, lighting, visual images, and nautical props (model boats, spars, sails, and ropes), as well as choreography and blocking for the actors, who may sway or stumble side to side or fall and roll on the stage to simulate being on the heaving deck of a ship. Some directors and designers strive for maximum verisimilitude via recordings of thunder and lightning, video projections of waves, or life-sized boats on the set. A 1958 production of *Pericles* at the Stratford Memorial Theatre (prior to the formation of the RSC) went a long way toward spectacular realism. As described by the reviewer for the *Liverpool Daily Post*, "A hollow ship provided the base of the set, which rocked and swayed during ... [the] storm sequence: 'Rigging and trees toss[ed] about. Huge areas of the stage [rose] solidly in the air'" (quoted in Kirwan 2012, 119). The actual heaving of the stage floor seems never to have been replicated, but many productions, including Gregory Doran's *Tempest* with Simon Russell Beale at the RSC in 2016, continue to deploy the hull of

Figure 6.2 | Pericles (Wayne T. Carr) battles the waves.

life-sized boats as the basis of the set. Designers also use fabric to create spectacular waves. Disdaining simple undulating strips (as in Mary Zimmerman's 2004 production in Washington, DC), Joseph Haj's *Pericles* (at the Oregon Shakespeare Festival and the Folger Theatre in 2015) covered the stage with yards of billowing blue fabric (figure 6.2). Thanks to strategically placed slits in the cloth, the floundering Pericles could thrust his head and shoulders above the waves or be engulfed by them, so this design element also led to greater use of bodily movement. In my viewing experience, mariners increasingly not only haul on ropes but swing on them or tumble "overboard" to suggest the power of the storm.[2]

On the other hand, many productions (for both aesthetic and financial reasons) rely on symbolic details to suggest a sea storm rather than to approximate one. Rupert Goold's "arctic" *Tempest* (2006 at the RSC, with Patrick Stewart) gave us a scratchy marine-radio issuing an ominous storm warning and brief glimpses of mariners and metal scaffolding, rather than the storm itself. Trevor Nunn's 2016 production of *Pericles* emphasized the ubiquity of the sea by means of a giant "porthole" intermittently visible on the rear wall (figure 6.3).

Figure 6.3 | Gower (Raphael Nash Thompson) speaks in front of the "porthole" with a view of the horizon.

In the storm scenes, the horizon line tipped slowly and ominously side to side, economically suggesting what a passenger would see through a porthole as the boat was rocked by giant waves. For some viewers (including me), this visual shorthand (using a single porthole and the watery horizon to suggest the whole ship and the storm) had a remarkably visceral effect; it reproduced in the spectator's body a measure of the mariners' vertigo. Creative design elements can thus also engage the audience members' sense of kinesthesia.

Not all maritime props succeed, however. In Jeremy Herrin's 2013 production of *The Tempest* at Shakespeare's Globe in London, several actors carried a large model galleon – five or six feet long – on their shoulders through the audience and up onto the stage, where they rocked and tossed it before it "sank" down the stage stairs and back into the "sea" of groundlings. While the actors' bodies momentarily functioned as the sea (supporting the galleon), their movements mimed those of terrified passengers or anxious stagehands, rather than ocean waves. This rather awkward sequence may explain why small boats are more common than large ones. In Lenka Udovicki's *Tempest* at the Globe in 2000 (with Vanessa Redgrave),

Ariel manipulated a simple paper boat, whose movements cued the mariners' efforts to secure ropes to the stage pillars and to control the helm mounted above the trapdoor centre-stage.

While all these productions involved bodily movement as well as ingenious props and set design, physical theatre and physical theatre–inspired productions rely even more heavily on the actors' bodies to create the illusion and embody the meaning of the sea. In *Pericles Redux* (2008), John Farmanesh-Bocca and seven members of the Not Man Apart Physical Theatre Ensemble brought a new kind of Shakespeare to audiences in Carmel, California, and at the Edinburgh Fringe Festival. Farmanesh-Bocca uses the term "redux" with his Shakespeare productions to suggest a "reduction," a paring down of the play to its essence, as well as a "bringing back" or revival.[3] His versions of Shakespeare include a fairly full version of the spoken text integrated throughout with dance and other kinds of movement ranging from gymnastics to slapstick clowning. In *Pericles*, the storm scenes, which are narrated by the poet John Gower in the text, were enacted onstage with gusto. The choreography included somersaults, falls, mariners clinging to each other hand-to-foot to avoid being tossed "overboard," and shoulder-stands that levitated their bodies off the stage. In a calmer moment, the mariners climbed the "mast" by crawling directly toward the audience on the floor, which suddenly shifted our perspective, as if we were looking down on them from the clouds. Later, while standing on one foot, they circled their free legs so as to angle their bodies slowly left and then right, like sailboats tacking into the wind. Ultimately, they became the sea, mimicking the movement of waves and whitecaps with alternately synchronized and syncopated jumps. These kinetic sequences emphasized the theme of endurance by giving substance and stage time to Pericles's epic wanderings.[4] They also required an unusual degree of metatheatrical awareness from the spectators. Reading the movements of the actors as they shifted from mariners to boats to waves and whitecaps, I submit, requires a nimbler exercise of the imagination than reading billowy blue fabric as the sea.

Farmanesh-Bocca also created maritime moments that emphasized the theme of loss. We saw Pericles cast Thaisa's coffin into the sea "with [his own] arms," an event mentioned retrospectively at 5.2.20 but not staged in the text (Shakespeare 2012). The mariners solemnly stripped off their middies, cast them into the wings, and became the waves that carried off her body. This latter movement required careful coordination, as their crossed arms enabled them to suggest the complex movement of an object controlled by the waves, which not only rises and falls but spins in the eddies. This image of Pericles' desolation, as the trunk containing his wife's body drifted inexorably away, lingered in the mind's eye and viscerally communicated his grief. According to reviews of the performances in Carmel and Edinburgh and to audience comments, this form of physical theatre left audiences "elated and amazed" and with "a lot to think about."[5]

Eight years later, in his *Tempest Redux* at the Odyssey Theatre in Los Angeles (2016), Farmanesh-Bocca choreographed the opening storm scene to convey through movement what it might feel like to drown.[6] The actors had entered individually to Dinah Washington's haunting ballad "This Bitter Earth" and were seated in lotus position about the stage. Suddenly, the storm sequence from Vivaldi's *Four Seasons* exploded on the sound track, unexpected after the bluesy ballad. As Prospero and Ariel forced a model ship down into imaginary waves, the sound muted, the lighting shifted to blue; simultaneously, the actors fell on their backs and mimed in slow motion the panic of submersion, flailing their arms and legs in an attempt to reach the surface. When Ariel and Prospero brought the boat up, the music resumed full volume, the lighting returned to red, and the characters jumped upwards with loud gasps, desperate to fill their lungs before the next dive. The sequence repeated several times, vividly suggesting not only the terror of suffocation, but the loss of light and sound experienced when one is underwater. Spectators also witnessed Ferdinand's frantic leap from the ship, which is described by Ariel after the fact but not enacted in the text. Ferdinand dove headfirst from a platform and was caught by four cast members just inches from the stage floor. With an actor holding each extremity, the quartet tossed him up till his body arched high above the stage, cushioned his descent, and tossed him up again, as if he were being buffeted by twenty-foot waves. The skill of the ensemble and Ferdinand's expression evoked the terror – but also the ecstasy – of a near-death experience. Whereas the sea choreography in *Pericles Redux* tended to stress physical and emotional endurance, in *Tempest Redux* it emphasized the vulnerability of the human body to natural forces.

Like Farmanesh-Bocca, actor and director Kathryn Hunter is steeped in physical theatre. Her 2005 *Pericles* at the Globe, in

Figure 6.4 | Aerialists as waves batter Pericles's ship.

partnership with choreographer Éva Magyar and aerial captain Victoria McManus, embraced the circus arts. Six aerialists played up to five different roles each, often changing costumes onstage.[7] During the storm, the actors cowered inside a skeletal ship's prow while drums and gongs provided storm sounds, but the heart of the scene was the aerial work. At first the performers were the mariners climbing in the rigging, literally to the "Heavens" (the canopy over the Globe stage). Then some began to swing across the stage in huge (and dangerous) arcs and became the waves battering the ship (figure 6.4). Eventually, a few, entwined in blue silk, dangled limply *above* us, as if drowned in the depths, in which we were thus also momentarily situated, looking up at them. Finally, their seemingly lifeless bodies descended, unrolling slowly down their blue ribbons; some lay still upon the stage, while others moved like the surf, rocking Pericles's exhausted body back and forth on the shore.

As in Farmanesh-Bocca's *Pericles Redux*, Hunter and Magyar's actor/dancer/aerialists also suggested the sea in gentler and more atmospheric ways. Before Gower's prologue, the discovery space at the rear of the Globe stage opened, revealing massed figures in white shirts and black trousers. The actors moved slowly in unison, two steps forward and one step back, tilting their bodies slightly, with the front foot extended, advancing and ebbing like waves. The effect was hypnotic. Old Pericles (a character in this version) and Gower entered through the ensemble to take their positions downstage centre. Gradually, the actors fanned out across the stage, and their movements became more expansive, accompanied by drums and clarinet. This choreographed sequence thus framed the entire action. It established the physicality that would characterize this production, suggested the sea's importance in the plot, and provided a visual analogue for the ebb and flow of Pericles's fortunes. It was repeated just before the intermission, when the apparently widowed Pericles left his infant daughter Marina in Cleon's care, and it signalled the intermission's end when it resumed fifteen minutes later. The sequence was reprised for the last time after Pericles mourned Marina's supposed death and returned to sea. As Pericles's griefs multiplied, the group's movements grew larger, their arms more open, and their bodies tipping backwards more precariously.

I have been arguing that physical theatre productions of Shakespeare have a special appeal to audiences in the new millennium, both in the small venues where physical theater tends to thrive and in prestigious ones like the Globe and the RSC. In essence, they amplify the sensorium of theatrical experience by communicating kinesthetically as well as verbally, visually, and aurally. Some physical theatre practitioners question the need for a separate label for what they do. Kathryn Hunter (2009) asserts that "theatre is always physical." Scott Graham and Steven Hoggett, creators of Frantic Assembly's working-class *Othello* and of the much-admired movement sequences in *The Curious Incident of the Dog in the Nighttime*, put it succinctly: they don't want "audience[s] to be leaning back and [saying] 'Wow' at the physicality"; they want them "to be leaning forward ... to catch the meaning" (quoted in Gardner 2015). To some extent, as I have argued, the "wow factor" cannot and should not be ignored; the skill and creativity of the performers is an important part of the delight of such a production. However, as Grotowski maintained, physicality is not an end in itself; its goal is to spark particular pleasures and opportunities for meaning-making – both for the performers and for audiences. The meaning audiences make is, of course, contingent upon culture, identity, and social placement, but Graham and Hoggett (and Hunter and Farmanesh-Bocca) bring us to a frontier of meaning that has the body as its locus – not just the bodies of the performers but of the spectators as well. The theatrical emphasis on the actor's body that began after the Second World War advocates for the "precious nature of physical [existence and] experience" (Sörgel 2015, xiii).[8] In addition to celebrating the body's agility and expressive power, physical versions of Shakespeare often embody this ethic as well, which is as relevant today – to us and to Shakespeare's work – as it was then.

APPENDIX: PHYSICAL THEATRE PRODUCTIONS OF SHAKESPEARE PLAYS

Theatre Grottesco, Paris (founded 1983) and Santa Fe, NM (since 1996), John Flax and Didier Maucort
12th Night [*sic*], 2009

Zen Zen Zo, Brisbane, Australia, Lynne Bradley and Simon Woods (founded 1992)
Macbeth, 1992
Macbeth: As Told by the Weird Sisters, 1998, 2002
Romeo and Juliet, 2004
The Tempest, 2009

SITI, New York, Anne Bogart and Tadashi Suzuki (founded 1992)
A Midsummer Night's Dream (2004, 2006)
Radio Macbeth (2009)

Frantic Assembly, London, Scott Graham and Steven Hoggett (founded 1994)
Othello, 2008, revived 2015

Not Man Apart Physical Theatre Ensemble, Los Angeles, John Farmanesh-Bocca (founded 2004)
Pericles Redux, 2008, 2009
Titus Redux, 2010

New American Theatre Company and Odyssey Theatre, co-producers, Los Angeles, in partnership with John Farmanesh-Bocca, creator and director
Tempest Redux, 2016

Fight or Flight Theatre Company, New York, John Behlmann, Eileen Little, Steven Cole Hughes (founded 2008)
Richard II, 2010
Henry V, 2011 (with Burning Coal Theatre, Raleigh, NC)

NOTES

1 Siân Williams, interview with the author, London, 11 August 2016; John Farmanesh-Bocca (Mission and Vision 2015).

2 Rope-swinging was a feature of the storm scene in Trevor Nunn's 2015 production of *Pericles* in Brooklyn, NY, for example. In Lenka Udovicki's production of *The Tempest* at the Globe in 2000, mariners swung wildly from rope ladders attached to the gallery above the stage.

3 Farmanesh-Bocca, comments during the Q&A after a performance of *Tempest Redux*, Odyssey Theatre, Los Angeles, 7 April 2016.

4 As of this writing, the promotional trailer for the 2008 Edinburgh Fringe Festival performances can be found at https://www.youtube.com/watch?v=atDsb3mQf7Q. I am grateful to Jones Welsh Talmadge, former co-artistic director of Not Man Apart, for sharing with me an archival video of the original production, which debuted in Carmel, California, in June 2008. He also spoke with me on several occasions about the company and its work.

5 Audience member's comment, "Pericles Redux @ the Kirk Douglas Theatre" (2009). For sample reviews, see Vittes (2009) and McKenzie (2008). The work also earned a top-five ranking in fifteen surveys at the Edinburgh Fringe Festival.

6 My comments are based on my experience of performances at the Odyssey Theatre on 6 and 7 April 2016. I am grateful to John Farmanesh-Bocca, who kindly spoke with me after the performance on 7 April and by phone in October 2016.

7 My comments are based on my viewing of the DVD in the archives at Shakespeare's Globe.

8 Sanchez-Colberg (1996, 54) also emphasizes this aspect of physical theatre.

REFERENCES

Billington, Michael. 2003. Review of *Pericles*, Royal Shakespeare Company / Cardboard Citizens, London. *Guardian*, 28 July. https://www.theguardian.com/stage/2003/jul/28/theatre.artsfeatures.

Brook, Peter. 1968. *The Empty Space*. New York: Touchstone Books.

Callery, Dymphna. 2001. *Through the Body: A Practical Guide to Physical Theatre*. New York: Routledge.

Cunningham, Merce. 1997. "The Function of a Technique for Dance (1951)." In *Merce Cunningham: Fifty Years*. Edited by Melissa Harris. Chronology and commentary by David Vaughan, 60–6. New York: Aperture.

Dunn, Leslie. 2008. "Perils of Pericles." Review of *Pericles Redux*, Not Man Apart Physical Theatre Ensemble, Carmel, CA. *Monterey County Herald*, 12 June. https://www.montereyherald.com/2008/06/12/perils-of-pericles/.

Gardner, Lyn. 2015. Review of *Othello*, Frantic Assembly, London. *Guardian*, 6 January. http://theguardian.com/stage/2015/jan06/frantic-assemply-othello-scott-graham-steven-hoggett-interview.

Hunter, Kathryn. 2009. "The Body Tells a Story in Itself." *Guardian*, 9 May. https://www.theguardian.com/stage/2009/may/09/kathryn-hunter-physical-theatre.

Kirwan, Peter. 2012. "Four Centuries of *Pericles*: An Overview." In Shakespeare 2012, 113–24.

McKenzie, Kathryn (Kathryn Nichols). 2008. "Acclaimed *Pericles Redux* Returns." *Monterey County Herald*, 23 October. https://www.montereyherald.com/2008/10/23/acclaimed-pericles-redux-returns/.

Mission and Vision. 2015. Not Man Apart. http://notmanapart.com/the-company.

"Pericles Redux @ the Kirk Douglas Theatre." 2009. Not Man Apart. https://www.youtube.com/watch?v=UDOL5BlntkY&t=33s.

Sanchez-Colberg, Ana. 1996. "Altered States and Subliminal Spaces: Charting the Road towards Physical Theatre." *Performance Research* 1 (2): 40–56.

Shakespeare, William. 2012. *Pericles*. Edited by Jonathan Bate and Eric Rasmussen. RSC Shakespeare. New York: Modern Library.

Sharpe, Will, and Kevin Wright. 2012. "Director's Cut: Interviews with Adrian Noble, Adrian Jackson, and Dominic Cooke." In Shakespeare 2012, 137–52.

Shevtsova, Maria. 2003. "Performance, Embodiment, Voice: The Theatre/Dance Cross-overs of Dodin, Bausch, and Forsythe." *New Theatre Quarterly* 19 (1): 3–17.

Sörgel, Sabine. 2015. *Dance and the Body in Western Theatre: 1948 to the Present*. New York: Palgrave Macmillan.

Vittes, Laurence. 2009. Review of *Pericles Redux*, Kirk Douglas Theatre, Culver City, CA. *Hollywood Reporter*, 20 July. https://www.hollywoodreporter.com/review/pericles-redux-theater-review-93368.

Wangh, Stephen. 2000. *An Acrobat of the Heart: A Physical Approach to Acting Inspired by the Work of Jerzy Grotowski*. New York: Vintage Books.

Wright, K.C. 2014. "13 Innovative Physical Theater Companies." *Backstage*, 4 November. http://www.backstage.com/news/13-innovative-physical-theater-companies.

PART TWO

WORKING WITH SHAKESPEARE

JULIA REINHARD LUPTON

INTRODUCTION

This cluster of chapters by Russell Bodi, David Goldstein, Jeffrey Wilson, and myself is entitled "Working with Shakespeare." Each of us has read a work by Shakespeare in conversation with a very different knowledge practice: street fighting in *Romeo and Juliet*, social work in *Twelfth Night*, cooking in *Timon of Athens*, and criminal justice in *Henry IV*. By "working with Shakespeare," we mean both reading Shakespeare for scenes and habits of work and using Shakespearean drama to explore scripts of enskilment (the acquisition of knowledge through training, apprenticeship, and practice) across time, space, and vocations through participant observation. We hope this experimental enterprise will generate new outcomes for Shakespeare scholarship, Shakespeare pedagogy, and public humanities.

Collectively we have undertaken to test what philosopher of science Michael Polanyi calls "personal knowledge" as a resource for Shakespeare studies. All scientific knowledge is personal, Polanyi argues, because it involves the whole person – body, mind, and passions integrated in the fluency of skill. Skilled knowledge unfolds in a concrete situation that motivates inquiry and in a scene of conviviality built by shared standards and intellectual virtues. "Conviviality" is Polanyi's term, which he derives from observations of animal socialization; the relevance of conviviality to food ways and to theatre as entertainment and hospitality is striking.[1] Personal knowledge is animated by the directed yet improvisational flow of intentionality and commitment: "the pouring out of ourselves into the particulars given by experience so as to make sense of them for some purpose given by coherent context" ([1958] 2015, 60). Polanyi distinguishes the "personal" from the merely subjective: "personal" indicates that the knower's *personhood*, understood legally, ethically, and performatively (as persona), is constituted and disclosed through acts of spirited inquiry, in which shared criteria and common tools should lead to "a responsible act claiming universal validity" (vii; cf. 65). Richard Sennett, in *The Craftsman*, speaks similarly of "tacit knowledge" and "material consciousness," the routine intimacy with materials and techniques that comes from the practice of a craft. "In the higher stages of skill," writes Sennett, "there is a constant interplay between tacit knowledge and self-conscious awareness, the tacit knowledge serving as an anchor, the explicit knowledge serving as critique and corrective" (2008, 50).

In the following chapters, we explore a range of instances of personal and tacit knowledge, as employed by social workers, skilled fighters, chefs, and criminologists. What might these forms of work, ranging from highly credentialed and evidence-based social science to more informal kinds of craft and physical culture, teach us about the knowledge environments of Shakespearean drama? For example, interview-based explorations of expertise reframe those areas of embodied knowledge, muscle memory, and practical judgment that belong to theatre as an art but are often left out of literary analysis. The personal testimony of people who have mastered other bodies of knowledge can bring to light patterns of judgment, attention, cooperation, and adaptation exercised by Shakespeare's characters. Looking at forms of work, skill, and tacit knowledge in Shakespeare joins thematic and poetic aspects of the plays (the plays as literature) to their gestural, cooperative, distributed, social, and capacity-building dimensions.[2] For Shakespearean pedagogy, "working with Shakespeare" can promote conversations about employment and skill formation among our students, from non-majors to PhD candidates, and encourage the cultivation of skills, capacities, and virtues within English studies that have always been implicit in our work but often remain latent and unacknowledged.

"Working with Shakespeare" invites us as Shakespeareans and literary scholars to supplement the favoured outcome of humanistic pedagogy, "critical thinking," with what contributor Jeffrey Wilson calls "vocational thinking": not vocational training per se, but rather a concerted mindfulness with respect to the capacities and virtues developed in the reading of literature and their possible uses in various employment settings. Building pathways among theatre, literary studies, and other forms of knowledge can draw attention to the range of skills activated and transmitted by theatrical training and liberal education and relevant to all walks of life that involve communication, affective labour, empathy, judgment, and trust. We can enhance the capacity building that is native to our disciplines by becoming more intentional about the resources already in our possession and by welcoming other knowledge partners – once and future social workers, street fighters, chefs, and probation officers – into the conviviality of our reading circles.

NOTES

1 "Knowledge stemming from conviviality takes place when an animal shares in the intelligent effort which another animal is making in its presence" (Polanyi [1958] 2015, 218).

2 For enskilment in Shakespearean drama, see Tribble (2013).

REFERENCES

Polanyi, Michael. [1958] 2015. *Personal Knowledge*. Chicago: University of Chicago Press.

Sennett, Richard. 2008. *The Craftsman*. New Haven, CT: Yale University Press.

Tribble, Evelyn. 2013. "Skill." In *Early Modern Theatricality*, edited by Henry Turner, 173–88. Oxford: Oxford University Press.

7

SHAKESPEARE'S SOCIAL WORK

From Displacement to Placement in Twelfth Night

JULIA REINHARD LUPTON

SURFING WITH SHAKESPEARE

I begin with a dialogue, but not from Shakespeare:

JULIA LUPTON: I love this passage in *Twelfth Night* where the Captain describes the shipwrecked Sebastian tying himself to a broken mast "that lived upon the sea" in order to survive the shipwreck. What does that language evoke for you as a social worker?

ADEN MICHAEL: Actually, that's very close to an image we frequently use when working with clients in distress. Of course we don't talk about broken masts. We talk about *surfing*. Surfing involves the surfer, the surf board, and the sea. Surfing requires that you understand and frame limits, and also that you respond to your environment. The water can either drown you or push you to shore.[1]

I am sitting at a small table in my house with Aden Michael, who works in mental health crisis management for the City of Los Angeles. We are here to talk about *Twelfth Night*. I want to know how Aden's work and life experience might help me understand and identify survival and adaptation strategies in a play about real and emotional shipwreck, family separation, and the need to rely on others to forge new attachments and find supportable living and employment situations. In this chapter, I integrate close readings of *Twelfth Night* with insights gained from observing theatrical work, teaching Shakespeare in community settings, and interviewing non-theatrical specialists like Aden. From my observations of rehearsals and my work with actors at the University of California, Irvine, I have come to respect the ways that theatre performs a kind of "social work" by building disciplines of cooperation and imaginative co-creation for its practitioners while modelling habits of interdependence and responsive judgment for its audiences. These skills and capacities are also at stake in the plays themselves; for example, the dramatic situations of crisis, separation, and survival depicted in *Twelfth Night* reflect the efforts of human adaptation, cooperation, and care in situations of vulnerability and exposure managed by theatre as an art form. What is *Twelfth Night*'s "social work" – that is, how does the play work through acts of sustaining succor, individual and community enskilment, familial repair, and the search for meaningful placement after traumatic displacement? In this chapter, I bring my own expertise as a Shakespeare scholar into dialogue with the knowledges practised by people in other fields in order to better understand what existential life-skills literature and theatre reflect upon, evaluate, and transmit.

I capture this range of functions under the term *capacity building*, which I first encountered in my work running an under-resourced humanities centre. In the non-profit sector, capacity building fosters the skills and knowledges that allow for individuals, organizations, communities, or nations to flourish on their own terms.[2] Capacity-building techniques include skills inventories and assets mapping, focusing on questions such as what resources do you already have, who are your allies, and how can you work more effectively toward your goals using what is available to you? Capacity building refuses a deficit or pathologizing model by starting instead from "the viewpoint that all communities have assets, skills, and resources … [but that] people need assistance in the identification of strengths and interferences, and in being able to see how these are not idiosyncratic, but fit into wider patterns created by social forces" (Smyth 2011, 114). How might patterns of capacity building give us a new appreciation of the social work dramatized in works of art and performed by theatre as an institution? And how might we use such insights to build bridges between literary study and other forms of employment that could be meaningful and empowering to college students, colleagues in other fields, and community readers?

Aden Michael was my second interviewee about *Twelfth Night*. My inquiry into Shakespeare's social work began after a talk I gave on Shakespeare and Scripture for a local retirement community, where I had spoken on *King Lear* and the Ten Commandments. Afterwards, my host, Sharon Roszia, told me that, in her own long career as a social worker, author, and activist in the challenging field of open adoption, she had encountered similar problems around anger, injury, forgiveness, and acknowledgment, and had arrived at ways of working through these problems that resembled some of the moments I had analyzed in Shakespeare's play.[3] I was intrigued. Sharon had suddenly shifted in my relational portfolio from another community rep requesting a fun and informative Shakespeare talk to a colleague and professional with her own fund of knowledge, experience, and wisdom. We met for coffee a week later, and she agreed to set up a meeting with friends and colleagues involved in different aspects of adoption counselling. Together, we read scenes from *Twelfth Night* and *The Winter's Tale* in tandem with worksheets and resources from their professional work.[4] I went away not only with a wealth of insights into the social and familial dynamics of the plays, but also with a new commitment to seeking out opportunities to read Shakespeare with informants from other walks of life.

I later expanded my interview set to students in a summer bridge program to UC Irvine; these students were entering college for the first time and were participating in this co-curricular activity as a form of collective mentoring and skills building. I also interviewed Sam Nasstrom, a young transgender floral artist, who generously connected his experience as a queer designer in the gig economy to Viola's willow-cabin fantasia.[5] I interviewed actor-activist Lisa Wolpe in the context of her work as a capacity builder engaging with communities of women, gay, queer, and transgender actors. Finally, social worker Brynn Bodi read a draft of this chapter and made additional comments.[6] My hope is that, through these mutual exchanges of knowledge and insight among readers from different walks of life, we can disclose the plays' multidimensional cultivation of human capacities for attachment, invention, and care in response to abuse, betrayal, and exploitation.

SHIPWRECK WITH SOCIAL WORKERS

Act 1, Scene 2 of *Twelfth Night* launches the play's enterprise of capacity building. The scene lays out the uneven landscape of virtues in Illyria: the special challenges, talents, and needs of Viola; the virtuous mirror of her situation provided by Sebastian's surfing; and the role of the Captain in helping Viola survive and flourish while also drawing out the capacities of others to mend and patch their shared world. Ships and shipwrecks are always opportunities for Shakespeare to explore what anthropologist of design Tim Ingold (2000) calls a "taskscape," which frames the built environment as a congeries of affordances, traffic patterns, and networked communication. The opening of *The Tempest* explores the ship, and by extension the stage, as a taskscape, insofar as the different members of the crew interact with each other, the stacked and outfitted workspace of the ship, and the tidal challenges of the ocean in order to keep the journey on track. Watching the scene being blocked for our local Shakespeare festival reminded me of the cooperative rhythms required to create theatre. Our director, Eli Simon, was the pilot. He oversaw the work of his cast and looked for larger patterns to clarify the action, but he was also soliciting the actors' own improvisational skills. Rushing en masse from one side of the stage to the other to communicate the effects of a ship being tipped by massive waves; rolling along the floor to express the force of the pitching vessel; hanging onto a central mast that would soon be lowered in a great crash: all of this involved stage design, sound design, fight choreography, vocal work, and stage management. (See Linda McJannet's account in chapter 6 of the virtuoso ensemble work that practitioners of physical theatre have brought to stagings of *The Tempest*.) I was also fascinated to witness how blocking this key scene required the courage, attention, care, trust, and respect of everyone in the room, from the acting ensemble to stage management, who must work together to sustain the fiction of the playworld while keeping each other safe. Rehearsal, I realized, is a *mise en scène* of capacity building.

In the parallel scene in *Twelfth Night*, the storm has already occurred, and Viola and the crew find themselves on shore. There are only two speaking parts, and the choreographic and design requirements are far simpler than in *The Tempest*. Yet it too is a scene of struggle and survival. We might compare Viola's predicament to any number of situations in which capacity-building techniques might be employed by a mentor, advocate, or caseworker – in this case the Captain – helping a client or patient get back on her feet. Aden, herself a refugee from civil war in Eritrea, connected immediately with the image of Viola and Sebastian as young persons displaced and separated by family loss, abuse, deportation, or disaster.[7] Taking up less extreme cases of distress, we might think of Viola as a young person seeking an appropriate apprenticeship, like the boy actor who would have played Viola or like any number of aspiring and vulnerable young people, male and female, seeking service in noble households, as Shakespeare might have done in his lost years, or, to bring this into our own circles of advisement, as an English major or graduate student considering different forms of employment. Finally, we might consider casting Viola-Sebastian as a homeless transgender teen who is seeking their place in a world whose norms don't accommodate their sense of self.[8] In interviewee Sam Nasstrom's words, "I really get how Viola has to engage in queer world-building throughout the play, and how exposed he is when he first arrives in Illyria. I've been there." Orphan, refugee, apprentice, or gender outlier: each of these scenarios offers a possible framework for community staging and collective reading. The point is not to determine one as more fitting than another, but instead to begin to locate rhythms of duress, capacity, and repair that reverberate across a range of situations, vocations, and epochs.

The scene begins with Viola's sense of profound spatial and existential disorientation: "What country, friends, is this?" (Shakespeare 2008, 1.2.1).[9] In drama, but also in life, physical space is always also moral space, a term developed by Charles Taylor (1989, 29) to describe how the zones of human action are always alive with intentionality and a sense of direction as we struggle to make decisions about what matters and to move toward goals that promise meaning. The special space of theatre, in which everything that appears on stage is there by design and every action is fraught with consequence, calls attention to the moral dimension of all human space. Taylor's *moral space* is the ethical transcription of and supplement to Ingold's *taskscape*, inviting me to bring together design studies, philosophy, and social work in a virtues- and capacities-based approach to literature and drama. Viola wants to know where she is, geographically, but she is also seeking orientation and direction in an ethical sense. "What country, friends, is this?" means, what norms and customs apply here? How do they relate to my own history and values? Is this a place of "friends" and "friendship" – that is, will I be able to cultivate the social attachments I need to survive and flourish?

The Captain is her caseworker, or her mentor, or her godparent. He belongs to both ship and shore: "for I was bred and born / Not three hours travel from this very place" (1.2.20–1). She pays him a bit of money: he is not a guardian angel or a good Samaritan, but rather a capable working man who sees this noble girl's welfare as part of his larger responsibility to his downed ship and their common world. They consider the fate of Sebastian: she thinks he has died at sea ("What should I do in Illyria? / My brother, he is in Elysium" [1.2.2–3]), but then allows herself to hope: "Perchance he is not drowned. What think you sailors?" (4). The Captain responds, "It is perchance that you yourself were saved" (5), injecting the theological language of providence into the romance language of mere luck or fortune and giving just a little ballast to her faintly voiced expression of hope.

Virtue language abounds in the Captain's description of Sebastian's efforts in the sea:

> I saw your brother,
> Most provident in peril, bind himself –
> Courage and hope both teaching him the practice –
> To a strong mast that lived upon the sea. (1.2.10–13)

This is a powerful emblem of virtue: providence now shifts from that hint of divine supervision to an attribute of Sebastian himself, able to look out (*pro videre*) for his own survival. He is "taught the practice" by two linked virtues, courage and hope. Courage belongs to classical virtue ethics, where it is often depicted as the meta-virtue that enables all the others by promoting action, actualization, and self-disclosure.[10] Hope, on the other hand, hails from St Paul's three theological virtues, hope, faith, and charity. Aden Michael understood this immediately: "Hope feeds courage," she explained to me, "and together they allow other forms of knowledge that a person might have to become active in the world." In Aden's work with severely distressed households, hope and courage, she told me, "can make the difference between succumbing to social forces and managing their impact."

Coming from her decades of experience working in adoption and foster care, Sharon Roszia was struck by Shakespeare's canny emphasis on the bond between brother and sister in this scene. In families that have been sundered and reconfigured by adoption, the search for birth siblings is much stronger than the search for birth parents, because these lost brothers and sisters attract less anger and resentment and are thus more available as conduits of hope and courage. The reality, however, as social worker Brynn Bodi commented, can lead to more pain: reunions with siblings "often end in great disappointment and further questions of identity because in many cases, the birth siblings are still with the birth parents." *Twelfth Night* investigates the fantasy structure of the family romance, and indicates some of its fault lines, but remains within what social workers, borrowing from anthropology and psychoanalysis, call "magical thinking."[11] The problems Shakespeare poses are very real, but the solutions he provides are less so.

Shakespeare typically melds classical and religious virtues into a composite unity that looks both outwards to the social plane of human effectivity and upwards to a framework for value that, however authored or authorized, is not simply manufactured by human beings but at once sustains and transcends them by beckoning beyond them. (Is it hope for Viola's survival that buoys Sebastian up among the waves?) Courage and hope, the Captain tells us, taught Sebastian to bind himself to the mast. In this image stretching back to Odysseus and forward to Aden Michael's urban surfers, Sebastian uses practical reason (prudence, *phronesis*) to harness affordances in the environment that supplement his physical strength. (When Viola refers to her own wit later in the exchange [line 57], she means *phronesis*, not a sense of humour.) Like "Arion on the dolphin's back," Sebastian merges with his mast, becoming a mobile assemblage able to float in the rough waters. "Hold[ing] acquaintance with the waves," he survives by shifting his relationship to the environment from a hostile to a friendly one, engaging in a conversational give-and-take not unlike the play of theatre itself. Here Taylor's moral space, composed of "webs of interlocution" (2016, 36), dovetails with Ingold's taskscape, composed of "the constitutive acts of dwelling" that mould land into landscape (2000, 158).

The Captain sketches what I call a virtue ecology, a scene of individual intelligence, prowess, and forward thinking ("courage and hope") beset by both good and bad fortune and extended into the environment through acts of attention and respect. In Aden's gloss, hope is a form of "spiritual perception that allows us to see beyond our current predicament and discern possibilities that might be sustaining." Hope and courage allow Sebastian to transform fragments from shipwreck into tools for survival: he experiences the mast as "living" upon the sea because he skilfully intuits its potential to save him. In the terms developed by Russell Bodi in his contribution to this cluster of essays, Sebastian's outlook transforms a zero-sum game in which the drowning man fights the waves to his death to a non-zero-sum game in which the skilled athlete participates in a shifting ecology of forces.

The image of Sebastian's efforts heartens Viola: "Mine own escape unfoldeth to my hope." As Aden put it, "The captain sees virtues in Sebastian, and she enacts those virtues in their conversation." Together, they begin to seek the outlines of a plan. What follows is a discussion of possible placements for our orphan/refugee/apprentice: should she serve Olivia or Orsino? Learning that Olivia has also lost a brother, Viola is attracted to the idea of seeking her patronage:

> O that I served that lady,
> And might not be delivered to the world
> Till I had made mine own occasion mellow,
> What my estate is. (1.2.37–40)

Viola identifies service to the "virtuous maid" who has "abjured the sight / And company of men" (1.2.32–7) with the opportunity for retreat and repair. This is Viola's first articulation of an attitude toward time that will later bear the name of Patience, countering Sebastian's more activist courage with stoical definitions of courage as fortitude and endurance. Her phrase "delivery to the world" merges her birth from the sea with the sense of a message or communiqué to be "delivered," in the manner of a letter, speech, or sermon, through her words and actions.

The Captain informs her, however, that Olivia is not accepting placements at the moment: "she will admit no kind of suit, / No, not the Duke's" (1.2.41–2). Viola decides to serve Orsino instead, conducting what career counsellors would call a skills-inventory: "I'll serve this duke. / Thou shalt present me as an eunuch to him. / It may be worth thy pains, for I can sing, / And speak to him in many sorts of music / That will allow me very worth his service" (51–5). She then restates her approach to time: "What else may hap, to time I will commit; / Only shape thou thy silence to my wit" (56–7). Here she alights on the plan to dress as a boy, but the term she uses is "eunuch." Drawing on the association between castrati and music, the image of the degendered persona, lacking the digit of connection, supports her yearning for quiescent repair, at once mournful and expectant. When Viola later compares her hidden state to "Patience on a monument," there is a whisper of Hermione in Viola's desire to withdraw from circulation, to lick her wounds. Dressing as a boy will in fact allow Viola more mobility, speech, and action than she would have enjoyed as a girl, but the assumed identity is designed to protect her from direct exposure to unwanted attention and attachment even as she builds connections between the two households and their principals.

In her work on capacity building in both ancient philosophy and contemporary international development work, philosopher Martha Nussbaum (1986) writes that repeated injuries to trust, desire, and expectation require extensive periods of hibernation and repair, especially when they harm people of good will, who are more likely to expose themselves to disappointment and betrayal than others who are more protective of their own interests.[12] That sense of damage may colour the declaration of trust that begins Viola's final speech to the Captain: "There is a fair behaviour in thee, captain, / And though that nature, with a beauteous wall / Doth oft close in pollution yet of thee / I will believe thou hast a mind that suits / With this thy fair and outward character" (1.2.43–7). The judgment indicates a certain caution on Viola's part; she is young, but not naive, somewhere between the "little tiny boy" and the "man's estate" shut "'Gainst knaves and thieves" in Feste's final song of innocence and experience (5.1.368–86). Her reference to pollution may point to some longer history of betrayal, abuse, or abandonment, the original sin that may have gotten the twins on that boat to nowhere in the first place. In any case, the word *eunuch* throws a faint sexual wash over Viola's "blank history" (2.4.107), while the figure of fraternal twins weaves the kind of gender complexity that Sebastian reveals when he tells Antonio that he is "yet so near the manners of his mother" (2.1.30). Whatever longer weather pattern has driven them to Illyria, Viola's devotion to her brother may have already been a survival strategy, a positive version of the two spent swimmers of *Macbeth* "that do cling together / And choke their art" (1.2.8–9).

Viola's need to correlate and evaluate the Captain's behaviour with his intentions, conducted as she herself plans to assume a disguise, reveals the precocious canniness of a damaged child but imputes some depth to the Captain as well. As Aden put it, "Viola practices vigilance when she evaluates the Captain's trustworthiness, and then gives him the gift of her trust: 'I *will* believe you.'" Aden hit on an insight developed by philosopher of management Sverre Raffnsøe

(2013), who argues that when we trust someone (by delegating a task, accepting their judgment, or acting on their recommendation), we allow them to extend their capacities while also building our own. Without trust, the world is harsh and lonely, and our skills are severely truncated. Although he is more lightly drawn than passionate Antonio, the Captain's knowledge of both shore and sea implies a worldly acquaintance with human failings and social disaster. According to Aden Michael, sometimes the best social workers are those that have themselves suffered the slings and arrows of outrageous fortune; in Aden's words, "As an immigrant from a war-torn country, I relate to my clients. I know what it means to be displaced, to be oppressed, to see the turmoil that war has caused."[13] If I were staging the play and wanted to recruit the Captain from a contemporary virtue ecology, I might look for inspiration to the work of Cedric Sturdevant, a project coordinator at My Brother's Keeper, a nonprofit in Jackson, Mississippi. Sturdevant serves a growing group of rural African-American men with HIV-AIDS.[14] Sturdevant embraces these impoverished, depressed, scared, and outcast men as his brothers because he has rehabilitated his own injured life from the same set of punishing circumstances. The virtue ecology tended by Sturdevant is shaped by poverty, racism, and homophobia; the life of a virus and its management in the institutions of public health; the uses and abuses of Christian teaching; and the human capacity for mutual care, trust, and connection.

Literature and theatre are laboratories and gymnasiums for inquiry into and exercise of human capacity in its communicative and skilled dimensions. Considering *Twelfth Night* as a work of capacity building invites us to consider the Captain as a caseworker with his own waterlogged baggage, Viola as a talented and charismatic but damaged young person, and their dialogue as an intake assessment. *Who are you, what brought you here, and why are you so alone? Who in this virtue-poor community can best employ, shelter, or foster you? What are your skills and talents, and what are your emotional needs and legal disabilities? What can we do together to create the conditions in which you can best build or rebuild your capacities? And why should you trust me?* This is an exercise in *placement*: orientation in an unfamiliar locale, followed by a taking stock of knowns and unknowns and an inventory of skills, conducted in partnership with a guide who himself embodies some history of moral luck, and culminating in a decision to take up residence and employment in a particular situation designed to shelter the protagonist and advance her fortunes.[15]

PLACEMENT IN SHAKESPEARE'S SOCIAL WORK

I became attuned to the word *placement* and its possible relevance to Shakespeare's social work in my focus group on adoption and foster care. One contributor to our conversation had herself been a teen mother forty years ago, was reunited with her daughter in their adulthood, and is now the grandmother of biracial children adopted by her birth son and his husband. When I referred to her as having "given her daughter up for adoption," she stopped for a moment and then quietly replied, "We say, 'I *placed* her.'" That gentle correction was momentous for me: the word communicated the complex calculus of forfeit and benefit assumed on all sides of the adoptive transaction and the dark opal of affects that issue from this difficult nativity.[16] My informant was articulating a "non-zero-sum game" framework for her multi-generational story of childhoods and motherhoods in transition.[17] From a dramaturgical standpoint, placement involves blocking, initiated in rehearsal by a director (captain/coach) working in concert with actors who are finding their ways into their roles. From the perspective of the taskscape, placement enlists the affordances of the setting, conceived as both the geographical locale and the institutional opportunities and inhibitions on growth experienced by different players on the scene. Thaisa and Marina in *Pericles*, Helena in *All's Well*, and Rosalind and Celia in *As You Like It* are among the characters of Shakespeare who undergo some version of this placement script. Other capacity-building patterns in Shakespeare might include abiding, incubating, and healing (the kind of sheltering in place that Viola desires from her employment); therapeutic conversations that clarify intentions, expose delusion, and disclose personhood (exemplified in the great scenes between Viola and Olivia, between Feste and Olivia, and between Viola and Feste); and role-playing and trust games (explored in both failed and successful forms in the gulling of Malvolio and the stage fighting between Sir Andrew and Sebastian/Viola).

And then there are the questions for the thought experiment itself. What capacities does reading for placement build for and with *Twelfth Night*? To be worth pursuing, the effort should deliver more than a new thematics. Instead, this approach aims to disclose recurrent patterns and techniques of social and psychic damage and repair that resonate across the ensemble of settings in which Shakespearean drama unfolds. The work of the theatre proceeds precisely by building the capacities of its many players. Forms of enskilment such as voice work, fight choreography, and expressive movement are always more than technical, since they engage the full person in linguistic, respiratory, affective, imaginative, and athletic exchanges. Each actor, moreover, has found their way to theatre through a range of social cuts and inclusions that combine the affirmative ("Hey kid, you can act!") with the demoralizing and the damaging ("Freak, geek, or queer?"). For every actor, theatre became a *place*, a home for creative work and a shared creative identity, what Hamlet calls "a fellowship in a cry of players" (3.2.28), by virtue of a *placement*, a process of seeking and finding, of losing and gaining, and of aiding and abetting.

Acclaimed actor-activist Lisa Wolpe shared with me that performing Viola at nineteen opened her up to the possibilities of what a person can be and do; she later found that acting Malvolio, Hamlet, Shylock, and Richard opened up even more. Wolpe worked with psychologist Carol Gilligan in an all-female multicultural theatre group called the Company of Women before founding the Los Angeles Women's Shakespeare Company; Gilligan's (1982) work on women's moral voices and comportments, issuing from the intersection of theatrical enskilment and psychology, resonates with many aspects of my project on Shakespeare's virtues. Wolpe now works on site with different groups of actors around the world, directing them in productions that leave them better trained and more able to make theatre on their own. Her career represents the potential of theatre to be a capacity-building enterprise for actors, ensembles, and communities.[18]

Thinking about placement in these multiple frames, from social services to dramaturgy to moral space, expands our sense of what kinds of circumstances, both historical and contemporary, *Twelfth Night* might articulate and transmit. Placement concerns the templates and scripts by which we seek orientation, meaningful employment, and new attachments. For teachers and administrators, placement describes how we help others connect to the worlds we share and how we can amplify our efforts at institution building through organizational intelligence and the gift of delegation. By turning to resources such as social work, long-form journalism, and design and organizational studies to explore how and with whom displaced persons conduct their searches for orientation, belonging, and meaningful employment, we can also build the capacities of Shakespeare studies in a changing higher education, public humanities, and vocational landscape.

NOTES

1 Aden Michael, interview with the author, 29 July 2017.

2 See, for example, Deborah Eade (1997). Capacities (or capabilities) are at the centre of Martha Nussbaum's (2011) moral philosophy and public policy work.

3 Sharon Roszia, interview with the author, 6 June 2017.

4 I was honoured to have as my reading partners Deborah N. Silverstein and Sharon Kaplan Roszia, authors of the 1982 article "Seven Core Issues in Adoption," which has been distributed on many adoption web sites as "Adoptees and the Seven Core Issues of Adoption" (Roszia and Silverstein 1999). See also Melina and Roszia (2010).

5 Sam Nasstrom, personal interview with the author, 7 December 2017. Our focus was on the willow-cabin passage.

6 Brynn Bodi, LMSW, has extensive experience working with families, children, and teens in home-based, boarding-school, and court settings around issues that include adoption, mental health, and homelessness. She currently works in a private-practice outpatient setting serving teens, adults, families, and couples.

7 See the *Los Angeles Times* story "Losing Gloria" (Presser 2017) for the survival strategies of young people whose families are split by deportation.

8 On homelessness, adaptation, and survival among LGBTQ youth, see Aviv (2012), a piece of literary journalism that resonates with many Shakespearean themes.

9 All subsequent quotations from the play refer to this edition.

10 See Tillich ([1952] 2000).

11 Brynn Bodi, personal communication, 30 December 2017.

12 Nussbaum (1986, 337) glosses Aristotle on the internal damage wrought by bad luck: "A sick person can be quickly healed … What does take time and repeated good fortune to heal is the corruption of desire, expectation, and thought that can be inflicted by crushing and

prolonged misfortune ... It takes a long time for the bereaved person to form new and fruitful attachments."

13 Social worker Brynn Bodi qualified Aden's claim: a social worker's own experience with trauma can lead to "lack of boundaries and over-identification (often seen with substance abuse clinicians or ones dealing with sexual trauma). However, if the social worker has done their own therapy and resolved their struggles individually, they have a great chance of demonstrating levels of empathy and understanding that many other providers could not provide for those specific issues." Personal communication, 30 December 2017.

14 For more on Cedric Sturdevant, see Villarosa (2017).

15 On placement, placement drift, and placement "pathways" ("the flow of children in and out of the child abuse and child welfare systems") see Usher, Randolph, and Gogan (1999). On employment placement and the maintenance of poverty, see Hasenfeld (1975).

16 Roszia and Silverstein (1999) identify "seven core issues in adoption" and argue that adoptee, birth parent, and adoptive parent all undergo variants of these crises in attachment: loss, rejection, guilt/shame, grief, identity, intimacy, and control.

17 As social worker Brynn Bodi pointed out to me, at stake here was more than a political correction of a received phrase: instead, my exchange with this birth mother points to the critical role of language in narrating a life story that allows for growth and repair: "The mom saying 'we say "placed"' is really saying 'I feel less guilt and shame by using this word.'" Brynn Bodi, personal communication, 30 December 2017.

18 Interview with Lisa Wolpe, 26 January 2018. See also Stein (2016).

REFERENCES

Aviv, Rachel. 2012. "Netherland." *New Yorker*, 10 December. http://www.newyorker.com/magazine/2012/12/10/netherland.

Eade, Deborah. 1997. *Capacity-Building: An Approach to People-Centred Development*. Oxford: Oxfam.

Gilligan, Carol. 1982. *In a Different Voice: Psychological Theory and Women's Development*. Cambridge, MA: Harvard University Press.

Hasenfeld, Yeheskel. 1975. "The Role of Employment Placement Services in Maintaining Poverty." *Social Service Review* 49 (4): 569–87.

Ingold, Timothy. 2000. *The Perception of the Environment: Essays on Livelihood, Dwelling and Skill*. New York: Psychology Press.

Melina, Lois Ruskai, and Sharon Kaplan Roszia. 2010. *The Open Adoption Experience*. New York: Harper Collins.
Nussbaum, Martha. 1986. *The Fragility of Goodness*. Cambridge: Cambridge University Press.
– 2011. *Creating Capabilities*. Cambridge, MA: Harvard University Press.
Presser, Lizzie. 2017. "Losing Gloria." *Los Angeles Times Magazine*, 1 June. https://story.californiasunday.com/losing-gloria.
Raffnsøe, Sverre. 2013. "Beyond Rule: Trust and Power as Capacities." *Journal of Political Power* 6 (2): 241–60.
Roszia, Sharon Kaplan, and Deborah N. Silverstein. 1999. "Adoptees and the Seven Core Issues of Adoption." *Adoptive Families* 32: 8–13.
Shakespeare, William. 2008. *Twelfth Night, or What You Will*, edited by Roger Warren and Stanley Wells. Oxford: Oxford University Press.
Smyth, John. 2011. *Critical Pedagogy for Social Justice*. New York: Continuum/Bloomsbury.
Stein, Navida. 2016. "Interview: Lisa Wolpe on Gender Parity in Theater and Playing Shakespeare's Famous Male Roles." *StageBuddy*, 26 July. https://stagebuddy.com/theater/theater-feature/interview-lisa-wolpe-gender-parity-theater-playing-shakespeares-famous-male-roles.
Taylor, Charles. 1989. *Sources of the Self: The Making of Modern Identity*. Cambridge, MA: Harvard University Press.
– 2106. *The Language Animal*. Cambridge, MA: Harvard University Press.
Tillich, Paul. (1952) 2000. *The Courage To Be*. 2nd ed. New Haven, CT: Yale University Press.
Usher, Charles L., Karen A. Randolph, and Harlene C. Gogan. 1999. "Placement Patterns in Foster Care." *Social Service Review* 73 (1): 22–9.
Villarosa, Linda. 2017. "America's Hidden H.I.V. Epidemic." *New York Times Magazine*, 6 June. https://www.nytimes.com/2017/06/06/magazine/americas-hidden-hiv-epidemic.html?_r=1.

8

LESSONS FROM A STREET FIGHTER

Reconsidering Romeo and Juliet

RUSSELL J. BODI

A few encounters with a sixty-eight-year-old former street fighter crystallized for me the real-life implications of what game theorists such as John Nash and many martial arts experts have spent a lifetime exploring. Bobby McMillan, a different kind of lifelong learner, possesses extraordinary insights that illuminate those aspects of Shakespeare's work that, like Bobby himself, are grounded in violence and conflict. I first encountered Bobby at a fitness centre, where he was passionately excoriating a mixed martial arts fighter for not practising "the real thing." I learned from my visits with McMillan that only a topic like fighting could disrupt his customarily non-confrontational demeanour. Usually, Bobby enters the gym wearing a hooded, impermeable garment reminiscent of a monk's cowl, which he wears throughout his stay, even into the sauna, where he sits meditatively in what serves as a kind of sweat lodge for him. I recognize him by the distinctive, two-inch dreadlock that adorns his chin and protrudes from beneath the cowl. I see no swagger, but a man who keeps his gaze downward or level, eschewing interaction, yet not reluctant to respond to my inquiries. Subsequent to his outburst, I was compelled to ask him a number of speculative questions. What Bobby the Street Fighter advocates is not the result of intense academic enterprise – Bobby can neither read nor write and has spent many years in prison – but stems from decades of equally intense fist-to-body combat. His world view coincides with and illustrates what game theorists call the "Nash equilibrium" and manifests a source of countercultural wisdom that echoes aspects of Shakespearean drama as a lived art reminiscent of fight choreography and staged conflict in theatre, film, and ballet. Most importantly for my study, Bobby the Street Fighter explains how there is cooperation within a fight, what the fighter's best weapon is, and what causes his greatest injuries – insights relevant to dramatic combat scenes in Shakespearean theatre.

Through Bobby's eyes, I can see how theoretical analyses of conflict and decision making, once limited to economic negotiations and games, fit into literary studies because they provide insights into volition, context, and will. Literary critics tend to dismiss game analyses on the grounds that they create reductive conclusions, but, when coupled with skill theory, these systems can provide a coherent view of interiority and commitment. Still, many of the practices and the terminology of theorists such as John Nash have proven valuable in assessing the most advantageous positions for what we can call "players" in literary and real-life conditions. Beginning with the assumption that all interactions are competitive, especially interactive games and martial arts bouts, the Nash equilibrium explains that cooperation and equal distribution of assets mutually affect *both* actors in a conflict situation, demonstrating systematically that the best advantage for one can also be the best for the opposing player. Thus, we understand the essence of the non-zero-sum equation. Game formulas apply to all Shakespearean situations where self-interest and community interest are at stake. So, public fight scenes in *Romeo and Juliet*, usually viewed as zero-sum equations, enable actors and scene producers to evaluate the balance and identities of not just the participants but the community at large. While scholars traditionally view Shakespeare archivally, through literary contexts and from established performances, there is much to be gained through interviews with and the observations of genuine street fighters and martial arts experts, thus accessing experiential knowledge and an enduring sense of art from practitioners in contemporary settings. Stage and film directors, choreographers, and scholars can capitalize on the theoretical outlook of an actual street fighter, whose view of combat scenes acquires greater authenticity, especially since he never read "Shakespeare" but has breathed the violent aspects of a Shakespearean reality.

COOPERATION

In *Romeo and Juliet*, those fights that begin with playful banter and escalate to fatal bloodshed demonstrate Shakespeare's typical agonistic circumstances. In these combative scenes, however, we see certain elements of cooperation, especially since there are no sudden ambushes, and the choice of weapons is understood by players on both sides from the start. Equally important, especially in staged combat, the verbal exchanges preceding all fighting underscore the ritualized, remarkably intimate, enduring aspect of combat. In Act 1, Scene 1, Abraham's question, "Do you bite your thumb at us, sir?" (37), begins the belligerent thrust and parry of words that leads in turn to swordplay, signifying the nature of gentle warfare (Shakespeare 2003).[1] Bobby the Street Fighter underscores this aspect of the play's combat scenes when he explains the simple nature of cooperation within street fighting. He readily asserted, "You give and you take."[2] His quick answer gave me the impression that he has given such matters much advance consideration. In his expert words, Bobby explained how he would go into a battle expecting to be hit – even injured. Such acceptance of the inevitable manifests gravitas and gentility, an indication that the fighter is willing to share blows. Sheer brawling would likely violate the deliberately restricted and ritualized nature of a fight, which possibly explains Samson's circumspection before engaging in their fight with Abraham. By questioning, "Is the law of our side if I say ay?" (38), Samson verifies that he does not initiate the ensuing combat alone.

Conflict becomes cooperative when players consider their expectations to be germane to the interchange, almost like a debate. One way to characterize cooperative interplay involves the concept of zero- versus non-zero-sum equations. Zero-sum games locate one player's winning in direct proportion to the other player's loss. Thus, a $+1-1=0$ situation creates the conception of a total winner and a total loser. The zero-sum point of view locates the victory of others as a threat to the person or community. Extended to the world view of Verona, this phenomenon can lead to a myopic sense of competition (e.g., an escalating arms race or cyclical revenge). However, the goal of a non-zero-sum society is exchange: according to anthropologist Robert Wright, "Human nature's laser-like focus on ultimate payoff is a prime mover of cultural evolution. Instinctively enlightened self-interest is the seed that has grown into modern society" (2000, 26). So, even fights can exist with an understanding of cooperation on both sides, more like an unwritten contractual agreement or peace treaty than a fight for status. In Nash's terminology, this kind of combat appears to be close to a non-zero-sum equation, because self-interest is gauged in terms of equal distribution for both opponents – equilibrium in practice. In Bobby's case, though he endeavours to "touch" or "kill" his opponent, he defends himself by keeping his zone of contact at a distance while working for a fall. Yes, he works to win, but his understanding of conflict and cooperation embraces the possibility of loss.

As an excellent illustration of tacit cooperation, Verona's primary families must cautiously measure every word and action in carefully choreographed, dance-like reciprocity, a dynamic unmistakably illustrated in Prokofiev's ballet based on the play. In the Royal Ballet's 1966 production, the initial fight scene plays against the strident screaming of the upper range instruments, mostly violins, pitted against a *basso continuo* and the clash of swords enhancing the rhythm. The combatants dance in a simulacrum of a real fight. In this production, both sides suffer equal casualties as each family heaps its deceased youth onto a single, symbolic pile in the middle of the stage, like a repentant offering before the "moved prince." Another display of mutuality occurs when Romeo and Tybalt carefully lay down their swords as another political offering to Escalus. The symbolism demonstrative of a true non-zero-sum situation shows dramatically what Bobby McMillan means by "you give and you take."

For the Montagues and Capulets, even though they are eager to engage in battle in Scene 1, the prospect of loss is especially devastating. When Capulet meets with Paris, he remarks, "The earth hath swallowed all my hopes but she; / She's the hopeful lady of my earth" (1.2.14–15). Like Montague, the loss of an heir means the total termination of his line. The mutuality of the progenitors' stakes creates a greater reason to cooperate than to contend, which may explain Capulet's tolerance of Romeo and his friends at the masque. Escalus forces a double-bind, zero-sum state, wherein the fathers must suffer either social indignity or the prince's wrath.

Tybalt, Mercutio, and, later, Romeo represent different motivations for engaging in combat. In Tybalt, we see an avid, impetuous sportsman, unable or unwilling to contain his lust for fighting. As the primary representative of a new generation of Capulets, an aggressive Tybalt seeks out a challenge: "What, art thou drawn among these heartless hinds? / Turn thee, Benvolio, Look upon thy death" (1.1.53–4). With the alacrity of one who lies in wait for this opportunity, Tybalt turns an effort to affect peace into the chance to prove himself. Family reputation is unmistakably more pressing than the injunctions against fighting. Thus, some productions of the play show that Tybalt fights with the bravado typical of an honour-fight, minus the verbal jousts. A man in need of action, he displays signs of chivalry that mesh with his determination, a zero-sum combatant depending on a worthy Montague to complete his identity. Of course, Romeo's intervention complicates Tybalt's quest for honour in Act 3.

Often, the goal of fighting is more about continuing the playful exchange than winning. If Bobby drops his opponent immediately, the game is over and the playful spell breaks. Victory and/or defeat essentially spoil the game, which explains why viewers of a boxing match are notoriously angry if they have paid to see a fight that ends with a first-round knockout. In Franco Zeffirelli's 1968 film version of *Romeo and Juliet*, the depiction of 3.1 shows a protracted view of fighting and humorously demonstrates an element of cooperation between Mercutio and Tybalt. When Romeo tries to intervene, they dismiss him in an extravagant display of collaboration. Once they sideline Romeo, they bow and resume their deadly fight. Similarly, in the Royal Ballet's version, Mercutio, unmistakably the superior fighter and more agile dancer, enjoys the dangerous game against a stolid though menacing Tybalt. When Tybalt loses his rapier, Mercutio makes an exaggerated move to retrieve it, then launches the weapon with his back to Tybalt as high as the proscenium arch, while laughing and dancing merrily. Tybalt's only demonstration of skill consists in successfully catching the weapon. Mercutio merely wants to continue playing, likely because he has the upper hand. Ironically, Romeo's non-zero peacemaking manoeuvre spoils the game for both players, which leads to Tybalt, mistakenly or not, ending the bout when he hits Mercutio.

So, is there interdependence in fights in Verona? On the surface, there appears to be nothing but zero-sumness. The problem for the youth of Verona is that unambiguous cooperation must exist as both tribal factions attempt to demonstrate domination and manhood within a common venue, since they primarily represent the current generation of feuding families. If Romeo is accused of being "womanish," then he depends on Tybalt to help him prove otherwise. Tybalt's statement, "Here comes my man" (3.1.45), marks a turn in his focus from Mercutio to that worthier object to prove himself a contender in Verona. Likewise, Mercutio's death subsumes Romeo's previous non-zero nature, and he must *be a man* about finding justice instead. Ironically, he depends upon Tybalt to establish his courage and manhood.

While Romeo and Tybalt may not understand the full range of their ancient and mutual opposition – since they have always lived with it – they know of Escalus's attempt to broker peace in Verona through his recent proscriptions against street fighting. Typical of young men, at least during their fighting, Romeo and Tybalt are more concerned about vanquishing the immediate enemy than about generational extermination. However, Mercutio's dying words, "A plague o' both your houses!" (3.1.93), mark another level of affinity between Capulets and Montagues, insofar as they are both to blame for his death. At this point, Romeo loses any sense of non-zero play. His rage blinds him to all notions of cooperation, as he can focus only on revenge, an ultimate measure of zero-sumness, particularly weighty given Romeo's status in Verona.

Seemingly independent of the feuding families, Mercutio does not emerge as a fighter until Act 3. As Romeo's friend, he does not represent the Montague family's honour. His greater allegiance could more easily lie with Prince Escalus, his kinsman. Nevertheless, Mercutio has caught the pervasive spirit of youthful combat in Verona, particularly its playful aspects. With friendship underpinning his motives for fighting, Mercutio's defiance of family and his embrace of friendship likely makes fighting more appealing, making him a more spirited and complicated combatant. To Benvolio he quips, "Why, thou wilt quarrel with a man that hath a hair more or a hair less in his beard than thou hast" (3.1.14–15), jokingly noting the supposed zero-sumness of Benvolio's nature. Later in the same scene, Mercutio makes light of Tybalt's use of the word "consort" as a musical term, which becomes undoubtedly threatening: "Here's my fiddlestick; here's that shall make you dance" (38–9). Tybalt, perhaps acknowledging Mercutio's superior wit, turns away from the verbal fray to a more immediate target, marked by Romeo's entrance. Tybalt's disengagement from Mercutio's verbal game and his new focus on Romeo enrages Mercutio, who may now view himself as the weaker opponent. Thus, when Romeo backs away from Tybalt, Mercutio takes that "submission" as a reason to fight. Romeo's "dishonourable" vileness provokes a fight for a friend's honour. Ironically, when Romeo intercedes on Mercutio's and Tybalt's behalf, the usual give and take of a sword fight turns tragic. Whether by accident or by deliberate action, play loses its non-zero-sum aspects at that moment, and the participation becomes decidedly more serious and emotional and less controlled. Bobby's theory of give and take holds true, but in this case that exchange turns vengeful. Mercutio never understands "why the devil" Romeo came between them – a misprision that Romeo cannot set right in Mercutio's mind.

By sharp contrast to the other fighters in the play, Romeo resists the impulse to engage in combat. Clearly, once he sees Tybalt as a newly acquired relative, he cannot violate the sanctity of family. "Tybalt, the reason that I have to love thee / Doth much excuse the appertaining rage" (3.1.53–4). By not disclosing the "reason," Romeo miscalculates both Tybalt and Mercutio. When he bids farewell and essentially walks away from the fight, Tybalt thinks he is jesting. No one in this scene understands the familial affinity that Romeo has with Tybalt, especially Mercutio, who chastises Romeo for what he mistakes as "dishonourable ... submission."

Still, the calmness of Romeo's disposition might point to another interpretation of Romeo's reluctance to compete. In the combative realm of Verona, the first impulse to "turn and draw," overtakes simply *turn*ing. When asked about entering a fight, every legitimate sensei and martial arts expert insists on employing all means to avoid combat. One sensei arrived at a potentially violent scene. Onlookers expected to see him exert his physical authority but were surprised when he dissuaded the combatant from using violence. Another sensei explains that practitioners must always meet confrontation with an open hand. A clenched fist is a sign of aggression, and combat is reserved for defensive measures. Though Mercutio and Tybalt view Romeo's "farewell" as a sign of weakness and submission, his reluctance may instead represent reserved and understated confidence. Overt displays of prowess, the kind we see in Tybalt and Mercutio, are anathema to the expert. Students in the martial arts are schooled from the time they begin sparring that they must not misuse their dangerous supremacy, which might explain Romeo's attempts to negotiate a peaceful resolution rather than enjoin the "appertaining rage" he faces. Romeo's recent marriage forces him to see advantages on both sides. The battle for family supremacy is meaningless to Romeo, whose vision now transcends tribal battles in a non-zero-sum reality.

Many productions of *Romeo and Juliet* show Romeo's unwillingness to engage in fighting as the result of a soft or naive nature, possibly brought on by his recently acquired effeminacy – his marriage to Juliet. In the Franco Zeffirelli and Baz Luhrmann (1996) versions, Romeo seems to be driven exclusively by blind rage and tearful aggression when he finally fights. While these performances may portray Romeo as a more sympathetic character, it is possible that his reluctance to engage in fighting stems from his superior skill and experience in fighting. After all, in ballet renditions, the most skilful dancer always plays Romeo. Thus, like a sensei, Romeo enters combat only when the mitigating violence has gone too far. In Verona, where negotiation and conciliation are countercultural, demonstrations of skill and the need for revenge create their own version of cooperation: When one side takes a life, the other side must take revenge.

BEST WEAPON

One way to enter a conflict is to know the available weaponry and its possible applications, so I asked Bobby what his best weapon was. He quietly responded, "*the other guy.*" In many ways, his explanation goes beyond what the best martial arts aficionados have said, and his wisdom explains conflicts in Shakespeare. Every karate sensei and martial arts expert I interviewed agreed that the mind is the best weapon. As Sun Tsu contends in *The Art of War* (2000), a warrior gauges the opponent's weakness and irritates it and can use feints for surprise. Sun Tsu, like Bobby, emphasizes the spiritual nature of martial arts as it pertains to his acquisition of skill. An extension of game theory, skill theory is more nuanced in its approach to conflict situations. Theorists such as Eric Leifer always maintain that true skill comes in knowing what the opponent will do, even before the opponent does. While game theory offers a finite number of alternative measures, skill theory accounts for what Leifer describes as players who are "embedded" in the game, making the encounters "metatheoretical" (1991, 6). In Verona, the decisive *ex ante* disposition in the two families to fight creates those equal prospects that Leifer describes. From birth, the progeny of the two feuding families are equally embedded in an "ancient grudge" (Prologue). Thus, the process that governs the play's primary engagements must involve something beyond the players' choices. The embodiment of knowledge, technique, and ability enter the equation, making skill in weaponry a complicating factor in any discussion of *Romeo and Juliet.*

When I spoke with two mixed martial arts experts, they explained that there can be great advantage in using the opponent's momentum and energy against him, thus exposing his weakness. Martial arts explanations may come close to approaching what Bobby told me from his more vernacular and street-trained knowledge. To use another player requires more than an appropriation of momentum, energy, and knowledge of what that player will do next. There is a certain guiding of the other player's will, soul, and desire. This phenomenon is easiest to see in *Othello*. Bobby's theory of weaponry surfaces in Iago's use of his primary opponent, Othello. Once Iago justifies his reason to destroy Othello, he exploits weaknesses that the onstage and offstage spectators are unaware existed but that readily and tragically surface in Othello's character: jealousy, isolation, insecurity, and the quest for honour and justice. In Verona, we see similar use of "the other guy" in the testosterone-induced contests among Verona's juveniles, wherein an equal possibility for annihilation makes play stimulating. Missing, however, is the *ex ante* introspection we see in Iago, because Tybalt's interiority barely surfaces, allowing for directorial latitude in his portrayal.

Anthropological manifestations of any player *using* any antagonist generate rich possibilities for interpretation and staging. A moral code exists among pure street fighters, which explains Bobby's highly informed but bitter chastisement of the mixed martial arts proponent. There are certain prohibitions inherent in fist fighting, which preclude weaponry. Susan Snyder explains that technology, in Verona's case, swords, basically removes the proximity of fighters, making valour a moot point. "This [technological advancement] was not man against man, but man against machine" (1980, 203). For this reason, fist fighting stands as an even more intimate engagement than sword fighting. The further we are from the opponent, the less chance for a personal connection, which becomes important, especially in staged combat, where some fight scenes potentially include the more intimate use of fists.

With these insights in mind, we can return to the two staged fights, beginning with Act 1, Scene 1, which demonstrates how players alter the zone of contact. Samson directs Gregory to quarrel, but Samson, remembering the law, decides to "Let them begin" (1.1.31), allowing Abraham to feel the discomfort of responding aggressively. At this point, Abraham seems perfectly willing to retreat: "Quarrel sir? No sir" (42). Depending on the production, both sides may want either to fight or to avoid fighting, but no one wants to take responsibility for starting something illegal. Finally, Samson retorts with, "I serve as good a man as you" (44). More than the previous escalating rhetoric, this challenge to Abraham's manhood provokes a heated response. Like Iago, Samson targets his opponent's weakness and exploits it. Abraham returns the challenge, detecting Samson's weakness with "You lie" (49), to which Samson can only respond with the ultimate deep play challenge, "Draw, if you be men" (50). Samson now accepts responsibility for losing his composure.

Act 3 begins with a more dramatic show of verbal and physical aggression. The Zeffirelli Tybalt, played by Michael York, is a bully, a superior fighter with a commanding presence whose swagger makes him an easy target for Mercutio's sharp wit. His facial reactions to Mercutio's humiliating remarks show his keen sense of a public persona. Only by Romeo's fortunately locating a dropped weapon can he thwart Tybalt's killing thrust. By contrast, in Alvin Rakoff's BBC *Romeo and Juliet*, Tybalt, played by a very young Alan Rickman, is diminutive and far from intimidating. Mercutio is the more skilful and confident fighter, whose physical dominance matches his verbal jousting. Here, Mercutio playfully brings Tybalt down to his knees and holds his rapier to his throat, confident – until Romeo's untimely intervention – that he will eventually prevail. Later, an enraged Romeo rapidly chases Tybalt through the streets, dispatching him with ease upon catching him. Under Rakoff's direction, the chase, not the fight, is the more compelling action. In all productions, one character exploits another, either his weakness or his strength, as a positive gain. Romeo, however, sees that he has been the plaything of *the other guy*, his best weapon surrendered to another power – Fortune. Once he declares that personal forfeiture, he lives out that ominous proclamation of folly.

Tybalt likely employs Mercutio to destabilize Romeo, insofar as a three-person conflict model exemplifies and complicates Bobby's "other guy" principle. Likewise, as Romeo quarrels with Mercutio and Tybalt to persuade them to stop the fighting, he says, "Tybalt, Mercutio, the Prince expressly hath / Forbid this bandying in Verona streets, / Hold, Tybalt! Good Mercutio!" (3.1.76–8). Tybalt takes advantage of the secondary quarrel that temporarily and fatally distracts Mercutio from play. Once Romeo enters the fight, directors usually show him losing self-possession, as if his anger will free him to fight more effectively. While the Baz Luhrmann Romeo's incontinent weeping while gunning down Tybalt and the Zeffirelli Romeo's unbridled rage make for great drama, such portrayals do not necessarily echo reality. However, in Nureyev's Romeo, we see that his superior dance moves match his greater fighting ability and composure, more in keeping with what combat experts claim. The player who loses control of his emotions usually loses the match.

Sensei Randy Kopke (a black-belt sensei at Sylvania Family Karate in Ohio) explains more precisely how a karate expert uses his opponent: "As soon as the opponent starts to retreat, this is an opportunity to use that [momentum] against him and create a flight or cover up type of reaction."[3] Thus, in karate, "the other guy" manoeuvre favours balance and technique over brute strength. Sensei Kopke explains that he also uses the opponent's leverage against him, especially if he is bigger, in an effort to throw the aggressor. "If the opponent is trying to push me around, I will drop into a seating type position, so I can drop backwards onto my back clutching the opponent's arms or shirt and then throw him by placing my heel into his waist and just falling backward in a kicking motion ... quite dangerous to the opponent." Besides the physical appropriation of another player's movement, there are compelling psychological methods: Kopke explains that one way to emotionally disarm an opponent involves laughing at him after he has just landed his most impressive hit. Summoning the fortitude and heightened performativity despite pressure and pain is exactly what Mercutio does before his ultimate fall, disguising his defeat: "No, 'tis not so deep as a well, nor so wide as a church door, but 'tis enough, 'twill serve. Ask for me tomorrow, and you shall find me a grave man. I am peppered, I warrant, for this world ... Zounds, a dog, a rat, a mouse, a cat, to scratch a man to death!" (3.1.85–8). Just as Romeo claims in Act 2 that Mercutio "jests at scars that never felt a wound" (2.2.1), Mercutio is jesting at wounds in hopes of belittling his enemy and negating Tybalt's potency. Now Tybalt must muster his proficiency on a Romeo whose need for revenge awakens his manhood and clears his focus.

The successful fighter knows that success comes through patience. Bobby explained that a calm fighter must be observant and wait for his chance. Kopke concurs: "The person who maintains his emotions the best will more than likely win." As most coaches and athletes know, an athlete who is out of control is easier to defeat. So, when Mercutio chastises Romeo for being "calm," combat experts would see his rationale as counterintuitive. While anger and loss of composure may indicate manliness in fictive Verona, a realistic portrayal of a successful combatant would not show a tear-stained, rage-filled fighter. Appropriately, Nureyev's Romeo couples grace with control, exhibiting pure athleticism and determination – anything but rage.

The focus on the larger game minimizes many of the stochastic or unpredictable elements of the fight circumstances. The good fighter practises the art of patience and observation, which Bobby calls "spiritual" and understandably transcendent. What Bobby calls "art" combines performance, technique, and imagination in a meaningful representation of what his life means. Stage representations of the play's fight scenes might effectively adapt lessons from real street fighters and practitioners of martial arts to create not just realistic techniques, but attitudes and comportments that pervade character representations.

INJURY

Finally, I asked Bobby what causes his greatest injury. I was thinking that a bare-knuckles fighter would likely sustain the most injuries to his hands or what Kopke calls a "full blow to the body," whether from a kick or a punch, especially if it is unexpected. However, in Bobby's view, what hurts the most is hitting the ground. The ground stereotypically "rushes up" to meet characters who trip or faint, or who are pushed down.

Hitting the ground epitomizes the zero-sum realization of a clear winner and a clear loser. Moreover, falling embodies the tragic realization that comes with collapse. There are three significant falls in *Romeo and Juliet*, each delineating a different aspect of the pain of loss. Mercutio, in realizing that he is losing his life, begins by quipping, "a scratch; marry, 'tis enough" (3.1.86), oscillating between cursing the entire culture that led to his bloody death and joking about being "a grave man" (87). In the Royal Ballet's production of Prokofiev's ballet, Mercutio jokingly pretends to be injured during his fight with Tybalt, which makes his actual death scene confusingly ironic to the bystanders. In the end, Mercutio feels the physical and emotional agony of witnessing the end of life and of the warring factions that caused it: "They have made worms meat of me" (94). His choice of "they" elevates his perspective on the futility of feuding families and points to the totality of his curse, "A plague o' both your houses" (93), which underscores the irony of Verona's zero-sum culture.

Mercutio's fall creates a turning point in the play: the playful but bitter banter that characterized the earlier encounters now turns deadly. Romeo, in blaming himself for being "effeminate," soon declares that he is now drawn in: "This but begins the woe others must end" (107). He abandons gentle conformity and allows determination to supplant it. Upon confronting Tybalt, Romeo's concern is more about Tybalt's "slander" of Mercutio than a friend's loss of life. Tybalt's subsequent challenge insults Romeo's manhood: "Thou, wretched boy" (117). Theatrical productions vary in how Tybalt responds – leaving in triumph, running away in guilty terror, or being dragged off by friends. Once Romeo accosts him, there are no textual clues to indicate his response. Tybalt, not inclined to provide philosophical underpinnings, simply fights and silently dies. However, in the ballet, Tybalt's death throes display an exaggerated and protracted, even ponderous, struggle into death, in contrast to his earlier arrogance.

Romeo's most noteworthy fall, usually associated with his death scene, is clearly not his most painful moment. Instead, if we examine Bobby McMillan's viewpoint on the pain of falling, Romeo's tragic realization that he is "fortune's fool" hurts more poignantly than the merciful cessation of his own life. After he kills Tybalt, all succeeding scenes – melancholic with Juliet, disconsolate in exile, persistent with the apothecary, argumentative with Paris, and finally resigned in death – take on a dreamlike quality that creates in Romeo a tacit acceptance of what Fortune offers. After the killing of Tybalt, he likely saw it all coming.

As both a literary scholar and former public school teacher and coach, I have melded many areas of experience to help me approach the common ground shared by sportsmanship and drama. Having taught literary theory to "non-literary" students, I have grown to appreciate how tacit knowledge enlivens my own perceptions of literary moments. In that context, I see significant value in people like street fighters and martial arts experts as players or "gamers" who use ethical training and experience to mould their approaches to conflict and to life. Theories of game and skill constitute assessments of opponents' manoeuvres and of attitudes inherent in combat, which apply to stage combat in such plays as *Romeo and Juliet*. Similarly, in comedies like *Much Ado about Nothing* and *Twelfth Night*, players assess and "use" other players, and cooperation often leads to comic miscalculation.

Bobby the Street Fighter is a cultural and intellectual anomaly, yet his insights are not limited by technology or time, because the interpersonal dynamics of fist fighting span millennia. Such fighting is elemental in its brutality but also in its inherent tendency toward cooperation. Bobby's education began when his sister first began beating him, continuing through his older brothers' consistent fighting with him, often two at a time, and led to long periods of solitary confinement in prison. (I did not ask why, but I can imagine.) His ruminative wisdom carries with it an edge that few will experience, but that can benefit our study and understanding of Shakespeare, if we have the courage and humility to listen.

NOTES

1 All subsequent quotations from the play refer to this edition.
2 Bobby the Street Fighter, interview with the author, March 2017.
3 Randy Kopke, email exchange with author, 10 August 2017.

REFERENCES

Leifer, Eric M. 1991. *Actors as Observers: A Theory of Skill in Social Relationships*. New York: Garland.

Shakespeare, William. 2003. *Romeo and Juliet: Texts and Contexts*. Edited by Dympna Callaghan. Boston: Bedford / St Martin's.

Snyder, Susan. 1980. "Ourselves Alone: The Challenge to Single Combat in Shakespeare." *Studies in English Literature, 1500–1900* 20 (2): 201–16.

Sun Tsu. 2000. *The Art of War*. Translated by Lionel Giles. Leicester, UK: Allandale Online Publishing.

Wright, Robert. 2000. *Nonzero: The Logic of Human Destiny*. New York: Pantheon Books.

9

ROOTING FOR SHAKESPEARE

Cooking through Timon of Athens

DAVID B. GOLDSTEIN

We sit down to dessert and the conversation turns to tubers. We are studying the passage in *Timon of Athens* in which Timon, half-starved and digging in the wild earth outside the city, finally unearths a root for sustenance. In the flow of his invective on the nature of human wickedness, he barely breaks his stride to announce his sought-for discovery:

> Yield him who all the human sons doth hate,
> From forth thy plenteous bosom, one poor root!
> Ensear thy fertile and conceptious womb;
> Let it no more bring out ingrateful man!
> Go great with tigers, dragons, wolves, and bears;
> Teem with new monsters whom thy upward face
> Hath to the marbled mansion all above
> Never presented! – O, a root! Dear thanks! –
> Dry up thy marrows, vines, and plow-torn leas,
> Whereof ingrateful man with liquorish drafts
> And morsels unctuous greases his pure mind,
> That from it all consideration slips –
> *Enter Apemantus.*
> More man? Plague, plague!
>
> (4.3.185–97)[1]

Most scholars and theatre artists take at face value that Timon's root is meant to be a poor, shrivelled thing. The root is apparently the most debased and heavily material form of food that either Timon or the play's authors, Shakespeare and Middleton, can imagine. The point, at this stage of the play, is that Timon is reduced to the bare necessities. Like Edgar in the hovel of *King Lear*'s heath, he is the "unaccommodated man" (3.4.107), stripped of all social interaction, reduced to none but a bodily relationship to the earth.

But this is not how one of my dinner guests sees the scene. When we hit the root speech, she points out that, in many belief systems, "root vegetables are a mystical bridge between worlds." She continues:

> As I was reading the play, I kept feeling that Timon is continually missing this blurry line between extremes. Is he involved in friendship? Hospitality? Ritual? Are people beautiful or horrible? But root vegetables form a bridge between the revealed world that you see, and the world below that you don't see. And for him to be gnawing on a root, as if trying to break it apart and internalize it, is like trying to bring together these worlds that seemed confusing and separate from one another. Perhaps for this moment he can begin to see the possibility of a bridge.

The speaker is Risa Alyson Cooper, executive director of Shoresh (Hebrew for "root"), a Toronto organization that connects members of the Jewish community with land-based education, charity, and food production. She knows something about roots, and so does everyone else at the table. The other participants respond quickly and thoughtfully. One calls it a "beet-centred vision" of the play. Another considers the class politics of root vegetables as food for the poor, and we wonder whether roots would ever have been found on Timon's table in the play's first half. A third considers the paradox that, although roots are often full of sugar and starch, they are viewed as if they are the opposite of a treat, a point that in turn resonates with the metaphors of sweetness and confectionary sprinkled throughout the play. All of these comments remind me of Peter Holland's insight that "Timon's spade is not the sign of the farmer or cultivator but of someone who differently and indifferently works the earth with no notion of a future, of planting, of creating a resource for food" (2009, 21). In the eyes of actual farmers such as Risa, or Gavin Dandy, a founder of Everdale, one of the first community-supported agriculture (CSA) farms in the Greater Toronto area, the scene looks a bit different. Our conversation implies that, while Timon may see his act as narrowly consumptive, the play may hold space for a more expansive approach. Anytime someone digs in the earth, deeper connections to farming, rootedness, and the nature of the human will necessarily emerge. The conversation leaves Timon and then returns to him, this time in the form of a meditation upon his status as an urbanite in a simultaneously primal and alienating environment. It is a fruitful and fast-moving conversation, and I do not want it to end.

The meal in which the discussion is taking place is a methodological experiment in Shakespeare criticism: to analyze a play through and from within its meals, in which a team of food professionals helps plan, cook, and eat a meal that develops themes and issues from the text, and then serves and consumes the meal while discussing key scenes from the play. Will the discussion generate new insights about the play, about the creation of knowledge, about the relationship between text, performance, and lived experience, about the relationship between scholarly and other kinds of professional expertise? My hope is that it will, and that the experience of bringing the group together over a meal that is materially and philosophically related to the play will open up new lines, not only of inquiry into the play, but of connection out of it, to other kinds of professionals besides those of us who make our living reading and analyzing literary texts. When we place a text on a dinner table, who speaks and what do they speak about? How does the text itself speak? And what sustenance does each participant, food, and text provide? What follows is a description of and progress report on the first of these experiments, which occurred at the Depanneur in Toronto, in November 2017. I will defer the full results of the experiment, including the new reading of the play that this event made possible, to a future publication.

THE PLAY

Scholars have primarily approached *Timon of Athens* as a play about money and misanthropy. But its most conspicuous feature, unanticipated in the play's classical sources, is its trio of meals, which both anchor and challenge the play's otherwise bipartite structure.[2] First there is the potlach-like banquet that opens the play and communicates the central tension between Timon and his sycophantic guests. This is followed by the broken banquet of Act 3, in which Timon serves lukewarm water and (possibly) stones to the same courtiers.[3] The formal meals are echoed in the final parodic meal of

Act 4, in which Timon digs in the earth for roots. These scenes place the play in a line of thinking about eating and performance that stretches through the work of both the play's co-authors, including – in Shakespeare's case – the cannibal banquet in *Titus Andronicus*, the awkward wedding meal of *Taming of the Shrew*, the al fresco meal in *As You Like It*, the violent banquets of *Macbeth*, and the harpy-guarded mirage of *The Tempest*.[4] In *Timon of Athens*, eating – specifically in its avatar of the banquet and its parodies – conveys fundamental aspects of the play's structure and meaning.

Scholars have long identified the play as particularly rife with metaphors of eating, especially as relating to flattery, hypocrisy, cannibalism, bestiality, and degeneracy (Spurgeon 1935, 198–9; Morse 1983; Fitzpatrick 2007, 113–19). Jody Greene (1994) has noted the relationship between metaphors of cannibalism and the play's undercurrent of homoeroticism, while more recently Simon Estok has connected that nexus of imagery to a burgeoning scholarly interest in the play's ecocritical subtexts, asking, "What does this play have to say about diet, power, and male relationships?" (2015, 91). Meanwhile the banquet scenes themselves have garnered attention among recent critics as sites for discussions of the relationship between hospitality and friendship, and as a performance of humanist collapse (Noschka 2016; Battell 2018; Lanier 2016). *Timon of Athens* stands as a play particularly concerned with eating – in speech, imagery, and action – in the canons of both Shakespeare and Middleton.

By reframing this concern with eating as central to the play, not primarily or exclusively as a metaphor for other issues but as fundamental to its central questions, we can develop a new reading of *Timon of Athens* that responds to urgent issues in current food politics. The thematics of misanthropy and finance can tell us something about the dynamics of eating as much as the other way around. Indeed, our contemporary context teaches us that food, finance, and fellow feeling are inextricable. We cannot separate the systems of production and consumption of food from the systems of capital that govern, shape, or threaten them; nor can we engage seriously in discourse about the culture of food without encountering questions about the status, rights, and responsibilities of other people, not to mention of the animals and plants that produce the food we consume. To imagine the play in this way is necessarily to open a dialogue with professional food-thinkers; they, in turn, can help literary critics attune readings of the play to larger concerns about cuisine and culture.

THE METHODOLOGY

It is one thing to think about the play from the perspective of its meals. It is another to think from within them. How does cooking and eating a meal constitute research? As Marjorie Garber reminds us, Claude Lévi-Strauss's famous formulation "good to think with" (*bon à penser*) first appeared in the context of food. Animals that are chosen as totems, he writes in *Totemism*, "are chosen not because they are 'good to eat' but because they are 'good to think'" (Garber 2012, 97). As Garber points out, Lévi-Strauss invokes the category of eating only in order to marry it to the category of thinking. Food is good to think with because thinking is good and can attach itself to any material pathway through consciousness. The question that Garber goes on to ask, "whether the humanities are 'good to eat' or 'good to think with'" (98), is precisely at issue here.

In considering how to think with food, I am first of all interested in how food*making* is itself a form of thinking. For the philosopher Lisa Heldke, who describes foodmaking as a "thoughtful practice" (1992, 203), and for the sociologist Luce Giard, who extends Michel de Certeau's theories of quotidian performance into the culinary realm of "doing-cooking" (Certeau, Giard, and Mayol 1998, 151), foodmaking is both an embodied act and an intellectual one, in which one gains knowledge about the world and oneself through the practices of culinary creation. In challenging the standard philosophical account that separates intellectual work from physical labour, placing the first hierarchically over the second, these thinkers join a growing consensus that the old Platonic-Cartesian stabilities no longer apply. Food and eating form a particularly charged instance of the challenge to mind-body dualism, since knowledge starts with taste (in the case of the breastfeeding baby), as the etymology of "sapience" (Latin *sapio*, taste) reminds us (Perullo 2016; Serres 2008; Van Esterik 2015). All these thinkers suggest to us that to plan, cook, serve, and, by extension, eat food is to learn something about the environment in which that food features. In the case of this experiment, to cook through a play scene is therefore to open ourselves to a kind of knowledge of that environment that might not be available to us solely via intellectual thought, or even through performance, were we to act it out.

At the same time, the question of performance does enter into the methodology, since all meals are performances that fall somewhere along the continuum from the most mundane (eating a hamburger alone in one's car) to the most elaborate (a royal wedding, a state dinner). Meals have themselves become an active terrain of performance art in recent years, as in the ground-breaking work of Gordon Matta-Clark, and more recently of Rirkrit Tiravanija, Jess Dobkin, and Jennifer Rubell, to name a few. In the case of the present experiment, the meal's performative elements are downplayed, or are activated only insofar as they encourage conviviality and conversation, since the free flow of ideas is the ultimate goal of the experiment. But echoes of the play's performative context remain, such as the theatrical flourish with which the first course, of "lukewarm water" (see below), was served to the participants. (The Depanneur, sadly, was not equipped with the silver covered dishes that appear in the play, but the effect was nevertheless dramatic.)

If the experience of doing-cooking produces knowledge, then the experiment represents a sort of doubling of the grounds of knowledge, or a circling back to them, whose goal is to engage people with professional knowledge of food in a culinary process that in turn produces intellectual knowledge. I teach courses on food and writing in which my students are required to cook, and I have learned that invariably the experience of cooking produces a deeper understanding of texts. But here I wondered if a group of participants already trained in culinary thinking would produce not just a deeper but a different tissue of sapience and, further, if discussing the play might cause the participants to think differently about the stakes of their own professional investments.

THE PARTICIPANTS

Over the past two decades, Toronto has become a city generously bestowed with culinary expertise and an important hub of the contemporary food movement. In drawing together a group of eight official participants for the *Timon* banquet, my only two criteria were that I would invite a) only people who have thought deeply about, and have some professional connection with, food, and b) no English professors. The final group consisted of the following:

Marianne Apostolides, writer, author of the memoir *Inner Hunger: A Young Woman's Struggle through Anorexia and Bulimia*, as well as a play then in workshop, *Feast*

Karen Campbell, founder and youth director, Everdale Farm

Risa Alyson Cooper, executive director, Shoresh
Gavin Dandy, founder and executive director, Everdale Farm
Ayal Dinner, founder, West End Food Co-op
Len Senater, chef-owner, the Depanneur
Ryan Whibbs, chef and professor of hospitality and culinary arts at George Brown College

I also invited Ren Bucholz, an intellectual property lawyer who is a deeply knowledgeable amateur chef, and who helped me develop the original project idea and the menu.

The group covered a range of expertise, including farmers, chefs, activists, non-profit directors, teachers, and writers, some of whom I knew well and some of whom I had never met. I made digital copies of the play's three scenes of eating: 1.2, 3.6, and 4.3, and sent them to the participants. I encouraged them to approach the text through the lens of their own interests, considering questions of food access, production, and security, as well as hospitality, commensality, and any other issues that their reading might elicit. I also requested menu advice from the amateur and professional chefs in the group, and together we developed a menu for the evening. Having already settled on inviting Len Senater, whose innovative restaurant experiment, the Depanneur, has become a centre of culinary thinking and teaching in Toronto, I contracted to rent the Depanneur for the banquet, and Senater took a lead role in the meal's planning and execution. On the night of the dinner, I cooked alongside Senater, Apostolides (whose expertise in Greek cuisine, as well as the depth of her writing on food and identity, made her a crucial participant in the cooking and conversation), and Whibbs. Once the other guests arrived, everyone pitched in with the cooking, serving, and cleaning to make the evening a communal and commensal endeavour that blurred the lines among participant, eater, and audience.

THE MEAL

As is usually the case with Shakespeare, we have little to go on if we choose to build a meal from the specific foodstuffs eaten in the play. While metaphors abound, of material comestibles we discover only a handful, and they are the most basic and iconic ones at that: water, wine, and roots. In the first banquet, the cynic Apemantus ostentatiously drinks water, presumably in contrast to the wine flowing in the cups of Timon and his guests (although the wine is inferred rather than mentioned). "Those healths," he announces, "will make thee and thy state look ill, Timon. / Here's that which is too weak to be a sinner: / Honest water, which ne'er left man i' th' mire" (1.2.54–7). The water returns as a physical object in the second banquet, where Timon describes his banquet as consisting of "smoke and lukewarm water," the latter of which he proceeds to sprinkle in their faces (1.2.89–92). The only other food to appear onstage is the aforementioned root, whose appearance is often, in performance, played for laughs. In the 2017 production of *Timon* at Stratford, Ontario, that inspired this study, Joseph Ziegler scrabbled in a hole in the stage before suddenly revealing something akin to a shrunken parsnip. It hardly looked edible.

To learn from food in the play thus requires a different approach from that of historical recreation, since there is nothing in the play to recreate.[5] Nor is it particularly useful to reconstruct an Elizabethan feast, since the play is set in Athens and is not concerned to reference specific historical eating practices. In fact, the stage direction that opens Act 1, Scene 2 in the original published version, the First Folio text, describes the meal as "a great Banquet" (Shakespeare 1623, 82), which is perhaps surprising since the term *banquet* was most often used to describe a course of sweetmeats served after the main meal (Wilson 1991). It is possible that such a post-prandial event is indicated here, since the central activities seem to consist of toasts and a masque, which would be consistent with an Elizabethan dessert banquet. Yet the meal of Act 3, which is clearly meant to comment on and revise this one, seems to trade on its recipients' expectation of a full meal. Thus even if we felt it important to enter the banquet through a proper recreation of it, we would have little clear textual guidance for its contours. And this seems to me precisely the point of Shakespeare and Middleton's choices here. The meals of *Timon of Athens* at times evoke particular historical culinary motifs, and of course directors will stage them in whatever ways will contribute most powerfully to the overall stage concept. But the text itself is curiously generic, as if exploring the theatrical phenomenon of public eating rather than a specific iteration of it.

Since Shakespeare and Middleton appear to approach the foodstuffs of the play more from a symbolic than a material perspective, "thinking with" as much as "performing through," I felt free to consider how food in the play might produce complex and overlapping expectations, for both Elizabethan and contemporary audiences. I decided therefore to develop a menu that would think through and with the play in three ways: Elizabethan cookery (the cuisine of the play's authors and original audience), Greek cuisine (the cuisine of the play's imagined present), and the play's culinary philosophy, or the ways that the play considers and performs food and drink in order to realize its aesthetics. I did not make consistency of approach a goal or virtue, but rather looked for serendipitous intersections among the three vectors.

The final menu consisted of four courses:

1 Hors d'oeuvre: "lukewarm water" (aïgo bouido)
2 First course: potato and walnut skordalia, winter salad with raisin and caper vinaigrette, roasted root vegetables
3 Second course: beef or white bean stifado, white rice
4 Dessert: pear-pumpkin spoon sweet with ice cream and shortbread[6]

Aïgo bouido is a southern French hors d'oeuvre that, as its name ("boiled garlic" in Provençal) suggests, is essentially water boiled with garlic, salt, and perhaps a few other herbs (I augmented the broth with more herbs and with dried mushrooms to further deepen its flavour.) Its purpose is to provide a subtle way of activating the palate at the start of the meal. As a metaphor for thinking through food in *Timon of Athens*, it is almost too perfect. A banquet that actually begins with lukewarm water! A soup that is one step away from a solitary root! A dish that is designed to point the diner inward, toward the subtleties of taste and knowledge! The resonances of the dish continue down through the play. The dish is a trompe l'oeil that works in the opposite direction from Timon's second banquet, in that it first appears to be nothing but ends up tasting like something. It also conjures Timon's third scene of eating, in reminding us that roots are not all that we think they are: they are profound, tasting of earth and substance (indeed the participants commented on just this aspect of the dish).

The first course paid homage to the Greek and Elizabethan contexts of the play, while once again pointing back to the importance of root vegetables. Skordalia is an elemental Greek dip, composed of a stout-hearted quantity of olive oil and raw garlic blended with either stale bread or, as in this case, potatoes. Accompanying it were roasted carrots and parsnips, with the result that participants dipped roots (or at least underground stems) into roots, becoming a kind of literal human link in a tuberous cycle. (Replacing bread with potatoes also had the bonus of allowing the gluten-free participants to partake of it.) Thinking of humans as a way station in the life cycle of roots brings to mind and challenges Timon's speech about the cycle of life in Act 4, in which all relationships are reduced to thievery:

> The sun's a thief, and with his great attraction
> Robs the vast sea; the moon's an arrant thief,
> And her pale fire she snatches from the sun;
> The sea's a thief, whose liquid surge resolves
> The moon into salt tears; the earth's a thief,
> That feeds and breeds by a composture stol'n
> From gen'ral excrement. (4.3.434–40)

Timon's interpretation of composture (manure) as a thing the earth steals from its inhabitants and unethically consumes in order to breed more life is undeniably wacky, giving earth a moral agency that it applies nonsensically to robbing creatures of that which those creatures least value. It is a radically different way of thinking about soil fertility from that of contemporary organic farmers, and the appetizer was designed to encourage how we might rethink the importance and problematics of Timon's speech from a contemporary ecological perspective.[7]

Alongside the roots and dip we served a salad from Francine Segan's *Shakespeare's Kitchen*, inspired by the Italian and Spanish imports that filled seventeenth-century English recipe books. The combination of dried fruit, lemons, and English vegetables (in this case, cabbage, cucumber, and beets) is a fairly common Elizabethan experiment in sallet making, but borrows from the same Mediterranean context as the other elements of the meal.

For the main course, I cooked meat and vegetarian versions of a classic country Greek dish, stifado, which likely dates back to the high Middle Ages (Wright 2002, 28) but which is relatively unknown outside of Greece today. It is a stewing technique using red wine and red wine vinegar, but what makes it unusual is its combination of spices, uncommon in Greek cuisine but instantly recognizable to an Elizabethan palate: wine, cumin, cinnamon, cloves, and allspice. The resulting dish – earthy, sweet, sour, and dense – conjures a distinctively late medieval pan-European sensibility, and in a single dish crosses early modern English, ancient and modern Greek, and modern North American boundaries.

To complete the emphasis in the play on undervalued edible plants, as well as the fusion between southern and western Europe, dessert consisted of a traditional Mediterranean concoction, found in various versions from Spain to Turkey, in which fruit is simmered in water and then sugar syrup until it reaches a consistency somewhere between pudding and jam. I adapted a recipe for balkabak tatlisi, a Turkish pumpkin spoon sweet. Pumpkins, native to North America, are as iconic on this side of the Atlantic now as they were alien to the other in the sixteenth century, and yet they or their seeds were popular foods at the Globe theatre (Bowsher and Miller 2009, 149–50). I added pear, since it is the closest easily obtainable relative to the medlar, a fruit that Apemantus produces for Timon to eat in Act 4 (4.3.303–10). I served it with local vanilla ice cream, for another cross-cultural touch (the vanilla was from Africa, the milk and cream from Ontario), accompanied by classic Scottish shortbread.

Given the importance in the play given to drinking and toasting, and the tension between Apemantus's cynical glass of water and Timon's insistence upon stronger stuff for his guests, it seemed necessary to serve wine with dinner. We poured a Jafellin aligote, a country white from Burgundy; and a local Niagara red, the Chateau des Charmes gamay noir. They were hearty wines, chosen to pair well with the meal rather than for any thematic connection, in keeping with the emphasis on conviviality and commensality. However, I also brought along a few bottles of Great Lakes Pompous Ass English Ale, which seemed an appropriate beer for the occasion.

Although, as the principal investigator, I took the lead in developing the meal, I solicited advice from those with time to offer it. Ren Bucholz helped brainstorm ideas about the methodology and coherence of the meal as a whole. Len Senater contributed the suggestion of the winter salad, and took command of its preparation, as well as acting as a wise and steady consultant as we cooked in his restaurant kitchen that afternoon. Marianne Apostolides took the lead on the skordalia, while Ryan Whibbs addressed himself to the root vegetables and was involved in much of the final cooking. Anyone who did not arrive in time to cook lent a hand with serving and cleanup. It was unquestionably a group effort, in which we all became researchers, creators, servers, and consumers of the meal.

The meal was served family style, to encourage both informality and conviviality, and because it would not seem odd either to ancient or modern Greeks or Elizabethans, all of whom would have helped themselves from nearby platters rather than having their dishes plated individually in the kitchen. I used the four courses of the meal to structure the discussion. The hors d'oeuvre was devoted to setting the parameters for the evening and talking about the play and its context, including its authorship, critical ministrations, and importance to my own research. Each of the following courses was devoted to one of the scenes I had distributed to the participants (though some members of the group had gone on to read the whole play). I was struck by how different the experience must have been from reading a better-known play, such as *Hamlet* or *King Lear*, which many of the participants would already have encountered and considered. *Timon* was a new adventure for everyone, and created opportunities for unanticipated lines of thought.

PRELIMINARY CONCLUSIONS

While the conversation ranged broadly, it kept returning to three major issues in the play: the dynamics of hospitality, the play's competing philosophies of eating, and the question of food access and security. Of these, only the first has been given much attention by critics, and I anticipate that it is along these three lines that the play will open itself to a more complete analysis. Under the pressure of professional culinary expertise, the play's food-related aspects began to take on the shape of a master trope, in which virtually all the critical issues that circulate in the play return in some way to the basic questions of eating: what we eat, how we eat it, with whom, where, and why. The movements of the play's characters, plot, and ideas – from relationships around eating and drinking; to lending, buying, and selling; to war and sex; to, finally, questioning the purpose and boundary of humanity itself – come back to the core question of what it means to eat, and to know the self and the other through eating, or, as is mostly the case in this play, to fail in that endeavour.

The question arose, implicitly and explicitly, how our reading of the play might be affected by experiencing it through the material performativity of a meal, as opposed to a seminar room, a library chair, or a theatre seat. Strikingly, questions and comments about the food we were all eating kept weaving in and out of the experience of analyzing the play, and no one, least of all me, seemed concerned to separate them. This was the case for the discussion that followed the comment with which this chapter began, Risa Alyson Cooper's "beet-centred" reframing of the play.

As we were concluding a meal constructed largely of root vegetables, the question of their status both in our cuisine and in our very bodies was much on our minds. The farmers and food activists at the table pointed out that, although we might think that the status of roots has changed considerably over the centuries, they are still considered humble, cheap culinary resources. They are still derided as filler, or as fattening or empty carbohydrates, no match for the noble meat of the paleo diet or the pure wholesomeness of kale. As Risa noted, roots – and the edible underground stems, such as the skordalia's potatoes, that are biologically but not ideologically different from true roots – sit in the middle, neither quite in the earth nor out of it. They are exalted in no way, neither sentient nor sunlit. They do their work in the dark, painstakingly converting soil to starch. The reasons for belittling roots have shifted, but human discomfort with rootlife persists. We do not like to be reminded that we are ultimately earthen, that we too are neither in the earth nor out of it – at least until we are returned to it in the permanence of death. Roots remind us of our inherent organicism. This is the last thing on Timon's mind in the first half of the play, when he believes that he is not subject to the fundamental laws of either finance or mortality. In the second half, all he can see is dirt and death. When he announces his own ending, saying egotistically, "Sun, hide thy beams; Timon hath done his reign" (5.2.222), it is as if he cannot imagine the sun shining once he is under the ground. But the antidote to his narcissism is root-thinking. The sun hides its beams from roots, yet still nourishes them, and roots in turn nourish higher organic life. The organic system is neither one of "reigning" nor of "thievery." There is only reciprocity.

Putting the pressure of culinary expertise on the play exposes the centrality of its culinary preoccupations. At the same time, it activates the play's ability to speak to contemporary concerns about our own relationship to food, and what that relationship means with respect to our relationship to other humans and to the wider world. Scholars have a particular and unique ability to open texts and examine their innards for what they can tell us about our cultural moment and about the cultures that came before us. We are like ancient Greek seers, poring over the entrails of our sacrifices. But we also have the ability to hold those textual bodies open for others to view and interpret. This opening, which is essentially the act of opening another's mind for analysis, carries great risks and responsibilities, but it also carries rewards – of increased connection, understanding, and growth. Finding inventive ways to perform that openness and connectivity will form a crucial aspect of the next generation of humanities scholarship.

NOTES

I am grateful to the Social Sciences and Humanities Research Council of Canada for its generous support of this project.

1 All references to Shakespeare's plays are to Shakespeare (2002). The version of *Lear* cited is *King Lear: A Conflated Text*.

2 Bulman (1974) argues convincingly that the idea of the banquets comes from the anonymous academic play *Timon*. On the importance of the banquets in the dramatic structure and on their wider humanist context, see Lanier (2016).

3 While most critics take for granted that stones are served, and while stones painted to look like artichokes figure in the anonymous *Timon*, there is no definitive textual evidence for their presence. The only reference to stones comes at the end of the scene, which closes with a rhyme on bones and stones that leaves room for interpretation, as the reference could be specific or generic (3.6.118–19).

4 As for Middleton, as Meads (2001) notes, "he accounts for, or intersects with, a good number of plays containing banquets." A fuller investigation of Middleton's approach to food and eating, and how *Timon* fits into this context, awaits a future project.

5 On the interpretive possibilities of culinary recreation, see Albala (2010).

6 The recipes were adapted, sometimes extensively, from the following sources: aïgo bouido: Waters (1996, 160); potato and walnut skordalia: Kochilas (1996, 43); winter salad with raisin and caper vinaigrette: Segan (2003, 73); beef or bean stifado: Jenkins (1994, 334–5); pumpkin and pear spoon sweet: Goldstein (2000, 191–2).

7 Timon's topsy-turvy ideas about compost were not generally shared by his contemporaries (Eklund 2017).

REFERENCES

Albala, Ken. 2010. "Cooking as Research Methodology: Experiments in Renaissance Cuisine." In *Renaissance Food from Rabelais to Shakespeare*, edited by Joan Fitzpatrick, 73–88. Aldershot, UK: Ashgate.

Battell, Sophie. 2018. "'Thou Weep'st to Make Them Drink': Hospitality and Mourning in *Timon of Athens*." In *The Routledge Companion to Shakespeare and Philosophy*, edited by Craig Bourne and Emily Caddick Bourne, 220–33. New York: Routledge.

Bowsher, J.M.C., and P. Miller. 2009. *The Rose and the Globe – Playhouses of Shakespeare's Bankside: Excavations, 1989–1991*. London: Museum of London Archaeology Monographs.

Bulman, James. 1974. "The Date and Production of *Timon* Reconsidered." *Shakespeare Survey* 27: 111–27.

Certeau, Michel de, Luce Giard, and Pierre Mayol. 1998. *Practice of Everyday Life*. Vol. 2. *Living and Cooking*. Translated by Timothy J. Tomasik. Minneapolis: University of Minnesota Press.

Eklund, Hillary, ed. 2017. *Ground-Work: English Renaissance Literature and Soil Science*. Pittsburgh, PA: Duquesne University Press.

Estok, Simon. 2015. "Queerly Green: From Meaty to Meatless Days and Nights in *Timon of Athens*." In *Ecological Approaches to Early Modern English Texts*, edited by Jennifer Munroe, Edward J. Geisweidt, and Lynne Bruckner, 91–8. Aldershot, UK: Ashgate.

Fitzpatrick, Joan. 2007. *Food in Shakespeare*. Aldershot, UK: Ashgate.

Garber, Marjorie. 2012. *Loaded Words*. New York: Fordham University Press.

Goldstein, Joyce. 2000. *Sephardic Flavors*. New York: Chronicle Books.

Greene, Jody. 1994. "'You Must Eat Men': The Sodomitic Economy of Renaissance Patronage." *GLQ: A Journal of Lesbian and Gay Studies* 1 (2): 163–97.

Heldke, Lisa M. 1992. "Foodmaking as Thoughtful Practice." In *Cooking, Eating, Thinking: Transformative Philosophies of Food*, edited by Deane W. Curtin and Lisa M. Heldke, 203–29. Bloomington: Indiana University Press.

Holland, Peter. 2009. "Feasting and Starving: Staging Food in Shakespeare." *Shakespeare Jahrbuch* 145: 11–28.

Jenkins, Nancy Harmon. 1994. *The Mediterranean Diet Cookbook*. New York: Bantam.

Kochilas, Diane. 1996. *The Greek Vegetarian*. New York: St Martin's.

Lanier, Douglas. 2016. "Cynical Dining in *Timon of Athens*." In *Culinary Shakespeare*, edited by David B. Goldstein and Amy L. Tigner, 135–56. Pittsburgh, PA: Duquesne University Press.

Meads, Chris. 2001. *Banquets Set Forth: Banqueting in English Renaissance Drama*. Manchester: Manchester University Press.

Morse, Ruth. 1983. "Unfit for Human Consumption: Shakespeare's Unnatural Food." *Jahrbuch der Deutschen Shakespeare-Gesellschaft West* 119: 144–7.

Noschka, Michael. 2016. "Thinking Hospitably with *Timon of Athens*: Toward an Ethics of Stewardship." In *Shakespeare and Hospitality*, edited by David B. Goldstein and Julia Reinhard Lupton, 242–64. New York: Routledge.

Perullo, Nicola. 2016. *Taste as Experience: The Philosophy and Aesthetics of Food*. New York: Columbia University Press.

Segan, Francine. 2003. *Shakespeare's Kitchen*. New York: Random House.

Serres, Michel. 2008. *The Five Senses: A Philosophy of Mingled Bodies*. London: Continuum.

Shakespeare, William. 1623. *Mr. William Shakespeares comedies, histories, & tragedies: published according to the true originall copies*. London.

– 2002. *The Complete Works*. Edited by Stephen Orgel and A.R. Braunmuller. New York: Penguin.

Spurgeon, Caroline. 1935. *Shakespeare's Imagery and What It Tells Us*. Cambridge: Cambridge University Press.

Van Esterik, Penny. 2015. "Commensal Circles and the Common Pot." In *Commensality: From Everyday Food to Feast*, edited by Susanne Kerner, Cynthia Chou, and Morten Warmind, 31–42. London: Bloomsbury.

Waters, Alice. 1996. *Chez Panisse Vegetables*. New York: Harper Collins.

Wilson, C. Anne, ed. 1991. *"Banquetting Stuffe": The Fare and Social Background of the Tudor and Stuart Banquet*. Edinburgh: Edinburgh University Press.

Wright, Clifford A. 2002. *Real Stew*. Boston, MA: Harvard Common Press.

10

"REDEEMING TIME"

The Dramatization of Desistance in 1 Henry IV

JEFFREY R. WILSON

In William Shakespeare's *1 Henry IV*, at the end of our introduction to Prince Hal, a drunkard and juvenile delinquent who is nevertheless poised to inherit the English crown, he steps aside to justify his criminal lifestyle (it is his drinking buddies that he refers to in the opening line of this soliloquy):

I know you all, and will awhile uphold
The unyoked humor of your idleness.
Yet herein will I imitate the sun,
Who doth permit the base contagious clouds
To smother up his beauty from the world,
That, when he please again to be himself,
Being wanted he may be more wondered at
By breaking through the foul and ugly mists
Of vapors that did seem to strangle him.
If all the year were playing holidays,
To sport would be as tedious as to work;
But when they seldom come, they wished-for come,
And nothing pleaseth but rare accidents.
So when this loose behavior I throw off
And pay the debt I never promisèd,
By how much better than my word I am,
By so much shall I falsify men's hopes;
And, like bright metal on a sullen ground,
My reformation, glittering o'er my fault,

> Shall show more goodly and attract more eyes
> Than that which hath no foil to set it off.
> I'll so offend to make offense a skill,
> Redeeming time when men think least I will. (Shakespeare 2016, 1.2.170–92)[1]

The first time I read this soliloquy – with its imagery of the sun breaking through the clouds, of metal shining brighter when set against mud – it made immediate sense to me because it made sense *of* me. It clarified a central aspect of my own juvenile delinquency. I can clearly remember consciously thinking in the days of my criminal youth exactly what Prince Hal is thinking in this soliloquy: *I am, to be sure, destined for greatness. I shall, in my life, achieve glory and fame; I'm sure of it. People will someday tell my story and hold me up as the exemplar of a human being, and, when they do, the central part of that story will be the adversity I overcame. My current criminal lifestyle – along with all the pain and suffering it causes myself, my family, and my friends – will be the conflict that is resolved in the plot of my life. My life will be like a good story in which, against all odds, our hero's true nature is revealed through his struggle with and conquest of some seemingly insurmountable difficulty.* What's most fascinating about this line of thought is that the imagined narrative of desistance from crime in the future is actually a justification for the persistence of a criminal lifestyle in the present.

Working up from Hal's "redeeming time" soliloquy to some modern examples, this chapter addresses the problem of planned desistance from crime, especially insofar as planned desistance can actually contribute to the present persistence of criminal behaviour. What I call the *dramatization of desistance* in Hal's soliloquy encourages us to bring Shakespeare into dialogue with the emerging field of "narrative criminology." Theorists in this field attend to narratives of crime not as retrospective recitations of past criminal behaviour but as constitutive events that can contribute to crime. As Lois Presser and Sveinung Sandberg wrote in the collection that certified the establishment of the field, *Narrative Criminology: Understanding Stories of Crime*, "Narrative criminology is any inquiry based on the view of stories as instigating, sustaining, or effecting desistance from harmful action" (2015, 1).

Both the stories we tell ourselves (e.g., Hal's stories) and the stories our cultures tell (e.g., Shakespeare's stories) influence our orientation toward law and society. But if narratives can contribute to crime, they can also contribute to criminology. Shakespeare's narratives can help us build criminological theories. Thus, this chapter works from Shakespeare to a testable social scientific hypothesis for the dramatization of desistance: *in both the private stories we tell ourselves and the public stories our cultures create, narratives imagining desistance from crime can become a juvenile delinquent's justification for the persistence of criminal behaviour.*

This effort to activate Shakespeare for the social sciences may seem unconventional in light of traditional literary studies – the formalism focused on the structure and operation of a text, the historicism placing a work in its proper context – but using Shakespeare to develop social scientific theory flows from the fairly obvious fact that literature helps us understand life. Yet the challenge of multiple disciplinary methodologies operating at once – the close reading and qualitative analysis associated with the humanities, the theoretical formulation and quantitative analysis associated with the sciences – can be daunting for any analyst aiming beyond amateurism. Thus, as I built and evaluated the notion of the dramatization of desistance, I sought to bridge the gap between humanistic and scientific thinking by arranging a series of conversations with scholars from the field of narrative criminology. Shadd Maruna, professor of criminology at the University of Manchester, and Lois Presser, professor of sociology at the University of Tennessee, were kind enough to share their expertise.[2] Maruna is a specialist on desistance whose award-winning book *Making Good: How Ex-Convicts Reform and Rebuild Their Lives* (2001) emphasized the role of narrative in rehabilitation (he also wrote the foreword to Presser and Sandberg's *Narrative Criminology*). At the time of my interview with Presser, she had just completed *Inside Story: How Narratives Drive Mass Harm* (2018), a book examining the "narrative sway" of "storied realities" that are both "strategic and impactful, something we manipulate and something that manipulates us."[3] Our conversations are incorporated in my attempt to theorize the dramatization of desistance in the second half of this chapter, but first comes the foundation for this theory in an account of Hal's "redeeming time" soliloquy from the perspective of traditional literary studies.

APPLIED SHAKESPEARE: FROM LITERARY CRITICISM TO CRIMINOLOGICAL THEORY

Hal's soliloquy comes early in *1 Henry IV*, the second play in Shakespeare's second tetralogy. At the start of *1 Henry IV*, the noble and warlike King Henry IV – having recently deposed Richard II and taken the English throne for himself – is disappointed in his dissolute son and heir to the crown, Prince Hal, who spends all his time drinking in the pubs in Eastcheap. After claiming in his "redeeming time" soliloquy that his delinquency is actually part of his master plan to make his future kingship all the more impressive, Hal warns his favourite drinking buddy – the jolly knight Sir John Falstaff – that once he becomes king he will reject Falstaff and the other friends of his youth. Soon, civil war erupts in England, waged by a rival faction trying to claim Henry IV's crown for itself. The young Hal and his Eastcheap friends fight for King Henry in the war. At the battle of Shrewsbury, Hal (now seventeen years old) fights heroically, saves his father's life, and helps win the war against the rebels. Henry IV later dies and, at the age of twenty-seven, Prince Hal becomes King Henry V. At his coronation, Henry V does indeed reject his former friend, Falstaff. Only two years later, at age twenty-nine, Henry V wins victory in the famous Battle of Agincourt, England reclaiming lands previously lost to France, after which he marries Catherine of Valois and settles down to rule over a time of peace and prosperity in an expanded English nation. Thus, when he dies at the young age of thirty-six, Henry V is celebrated in England as a national hero.

Clearly, time is tangled up in knots in Hal's soliloquy. He seems to know how his story will end before it even begins. Hal sees the same thing looking forward into his life that Shakespeare saw looking backward upon it. In other words, the mythologized legend of Henry V that developed after the fact in histories looking backward was repurposed by Shakespeare as a psychological transaction the character experiences in the moment.

Historicist critics have shown the story of a profligate Hal reforming his behaviour later in life was already well established in Shakespeare's sources (Bullough 1973, vol. 4). Even before Shakespeare, the story of Henry V invoked the biblical parable of the prodigal son from the Book of Luke: a wastrel son who squandered his inheritance returns to apologize to his father, who lavishly celebrates the boy because he "was dead, and is alive again: and he was lost, but he is found" (15.31).[4] But Shakespeare's version, built around the phrase "redeeming time," also quotes from the Epistle to the Ephesians: "Take heed therefore that ye walk circumspectly, not as fools, but as wise, Redeeming the time: for the days are evil" (5.15–16). Teaching good Christians to make the most of the time allotted to them here on earth by living virtuously and working to secure their salvation, these biblical passages helped form the foundation of the Tudor morality plays staging a protagonist beset by the temptations of the world, the flesh, and the devil, another tradition informing Hal's soliloquy. As John Dover Wilson wrote in his influential book, *The Fortunes of Falstaff*, which saw Hal as an Everyman pulled between the vices at Eastcheap and the virtues at court, "Before its final secularization in the first half of the sixteenth century, our drama was concerned with one topic, and one only: human salvation" (1943, 17).

Formalist criticism of Hal's soliloquy has noted it is "the play's only verse soliloquy, and one that sets the tone of all performances" (Kastan 2002, 162n). Immediately after Hal's soliloquy ends the second scene of the play, King Henry IV starts the next scene saying, "I will from henceforth rather be myself" (1.3.5): the question of stable selfhood runs throughout *1 Henry IV*. Prince Hal's "reformation" is the thematic core of the play, with King Henry IV (an illegitimate ruler) and Sir John Falstaff (a dishonourable nobleman) also implicated in an overarching effort "to redeem the time by securing the throne against the forces of disorder in the land" (Dickinson 1961, 45–6). That mission is achieved only at the end of *2 Henry IV*: "I know thee not, old man," Hal says to Falstaff (5.5.45), a callback to the "I know you all" in the opening of Hal's soliloquy at the start of *1 Henry IV*. Hal then spurns Falstaff by invoking his multiple selves – "Presume not that I am the thing I was, / ... I have turned away my former self" (54–6) – and commands his former friends to do as he has done: "reform yourselves" (66).

Reformed man and national hero, or Machiavellian prince and manipulative master of political theatre: that is the central question dominating discussion of Prince Hal. Dover Wilson's notion of a sincere, straightforward reformation – Hal's soliloquy a choral voice controlling the audience's understanding of character and plot – has largely lost out to the Machiavellian reading. "Hal only *acts* the role of the prodigal," Alan Young argued in 1979, meaning "dissipation and reformation, as made clear by Hal's soliloquy, are matters of contrived surface appearances" (1979, 200–1). Here Hal "performs the performance of a parable" (Montrose 1996, 97). Because we in the audience are the unwitting target of this political theatre, however, "Hal's justification of himself threatens to fall away at every moment into its antithesis" (Greenblatt 1985, 30).

Greenblatt's word "justification" points to a third, less common approach to Hal's soliloquy – the one pursued in this chapter. Despite their differences, both the National Hero reading and the Machiavellian Prince reading are politically oriented interpretations overlooking the psychological valences of Hal's soliloquy. With his characteristic psychological insight, Samuel Johnson inaugurated this reading in 1765: "This speech is very artfully introduced to keep the prince from appearing vile in the opinion of the audience; it prepares them for his future reformation; and, what is yet more valuable, exhibits a natural picture of a great mind offering excuses to itself, and palliating those follies which it can neither justify nor forsake" (1765, 123). The modern inheritor of this line of thought has been Harry Berger Jr, who, with equally characteristic psychological insight, noted Hal in his soliloquy "sounds like he is making a speech, rehearsing a preformulated scenario, before an audience," and Johnson's comment on Hal's soliloquy "becomes more interesting if we redirect it toward the only opinion and audience of which the soliloquist can be aware" – that is, Hal himself (1997, 306). Read not as a political manoeuvre designed to manage the opinions of the theatrical audience, but as a glimpse into the protagonist's mind, Hal's soliloquy is, according to Berger, "a contentious, meanminded, and cynical speech even as it solicits moral self-justification" (Newstok and Berger 2011, 148). Here Hal is not a master Machiavellian schemer who has sought out a bad reputation to make his future reputation even more impressive; instead, he is a distraught boy, Hamlet-like in his self-delusion, grasping at excuses to justify the situation he has found himself in through no conscious design of his own.

In traditional literary criticism of Hal's "redeeming time" soliloquy – historicism, formalism, and even the psychological approach – thought generally travels backwards from us to Shakespeare to his sources, and an understanding of Shakespeare is the goal of the scholarly examination. That's how literary studies usually work, but that pursuit avoids something the general public – lovers of literature – grasps more fully than scholars: even as the meanings of

Shakespeare are the immediate concern of academic Shakespeare studies, the meanings of lived experience are the ultimate concern of our engagement with literary texts. The psychological approach viewing Hal's soliloquy as an approximation of a human thought process acknowledges its generalizability: while the particulars may change, Hal's soliloquy and subsequent story are phenomena actual human beings can go through and relate to, allowing for an interpretive reciprocity between the fictional and the real, the particular and the general. Abstract theories can elucidate concrete examples – criminology can help us interpret Shakespeare – but Shakespearean examples can also build criminological theories (Wilson 2014). It is only a short step from literary criticism to criminological theory when, as Lois Presser said to me, "a story or concept in literature reflects a collective narrative that sustains some criminal or otherwise harmful pattern."

HAL'S REFORMATION AND LIFE-COURSE CRIMINOLOGY

Our current criminological theories of desistance illuminate how a seemingly irretrievable juvenile delinquent like Prince Hal could stop his life of crime and become the virtuous and prosperous King Henry V (and, likewise, they can elucidate other prodigal son stories). In 1964, David Matza's *Delinquency and Drift* noted that between 60 and 85 percent of juvenile delinquents do not become adult offenders: "Moreover, this reform seems to occur irrespective of intervention of correctional agencies and irrespective of the quality of correctional service. Most theories of delinquency take no account of maturational reform" (1964, 22). Picking up on this point, Sheldon and Eleanor Glueck's *Of Delinquency and Crime* argued "the physical and mental changes which enter into the natural process of *maturation* offer a chief explanation of improvement of conduct with the passing of years" (1974, 149; emphasis in original). In 2001, John Laub and Robert Sampson identified the notion of "life-course criminology" as "the most compelling framework for understanding the processes underlying desistance and the role of social context in shaping the dynamics of desistance" (2001, 3). Laub and Sampson emphasized the moderating role of "key institutions of social control in the transition to adulthood (e.g., employment, military service, and marriage)" (19). From a "life-course" perspective, Hal's "reformation" from rogue to hero came about due to his strong social and institutional bonds: his connection to his noble father, his place in the royal line of succession, his military service in the Battle of Shrewsbury, his marriage to Catherine, and his job as king of England all came together to serve as institutional corrections on the individual vagrancies of Hal's youth, creating a reformation born not out of personal reflection, enlightenment, and self-determination but instead out of a responsiveness to the most powerful pulls on one's actions at different stages of life, whether the pull of delinquency in youth or of responsibility in adulthood. Hal's purportedly heroic "reformation" was really just everyday maturation facilitated by ordinary social bonds to ordinary institutions.

THE DRAMATIZATION OF DESISTANCE AS A TECHNIQUE OF NEUTRALIZATION

Our current criminological theories of desistance are not able to explain, however, Hal's "redeeming time" soliloquy and its imagined or projected desistance in the future that is really no desistance at all in the present. "I think that the character of Prince Hal perfectly captures a real type and a real sociological process," Maruna told me. "However, he would not be familiar in today's mainstream criminology." This gap in our current criminology is especially regrettable because the rationalization and justification of crime, what Gresham Sykes and David Matza called "techniques of neutralization," is a central part of juvenile delinquency. Sykes and Matza positioned their idea against the dominant theory at the time, which saw juvenile delinquency stemming from a youth's attachment to a subculture holding values contrary to those of mainstream, adult culture. That older theory held that what mainstream culture defines as *wrong* holds no sway over the delinquent because the subculture defines delinquency as *right*. From this perspective, Hal's connection to the Eastcheap subculture leads him to express its values instead of those of the royal English court, from which Hal is detached. Not so, Sykes and Matza argued, for the theory of subcultural values is belied by the fact that juvenile delinquents still feel guilt, like Prince Hal: the motive for his "redeeming time" soliloquy is his recognition that he is doing something wrong in Eastcheap. He feels a need to rationalize his actions. Hal remains connected enough to the royal court to hear its nagging voice in his conscience: his values still come from the court, yet his mind has found a way to justify to himself the violation of those values. "Unquestionably, young people involved in crime seek to neutralize their behaviours to assuage their consciences," Maruna told me. "This is one of the best established truths in criminology." These justifications occur not only after the fact, but also before criminal action. They allow juveniles to commit crime in the first place because they "neutralize" the mainstream values they hold. Sykes and Matza identified five "techniques of neutralization":

> *Denial of responsibility*: "I didn't mean it."
> *Denial of injury*: "I didn't really hurt anybody."
> *Denial of the victim*: "They had it coming to them."
> *Condemnation of the condemners*: "Everybody's picking on me."
> *Appeal to higher loyalties*: "I didn't do it for myself." (667–9)

Sykes and Matza never said there could only be five techniques, and what I have called "dramatizing desistance" can be a "technique of neutralization," one with applications far beyond Shakespearean drama.

To Maruna, "Our most famous example of a modern Prince Hal is surely George W. Bush, who famously said something along the lines of 'When I was young and irresponsible, I was young and irresponsible,' and somehow (miraculously) his indiscretions from his past were swept under the rug." The "October surprise" in the 2000 US presidential campaign was that Bush had been arrested for drunk driving (Kellman 2000); he subsequently faced (and dodged) questions about past cocaine use (Seery 2007). Shortly after winning the election, Bush – whose political persona hovered between bumbling idiot and corporate stooge – found himself responsible for crafting the nation's response to the terror attacks of September 11th, 2001. The prodigal son was forced to become a national leader, as Mackubin Thomas Owens argued in 2004 with reference to Shakespeare: "As a youth [Prince Hal] is dissolute to say the least … Upon his father's death, he becomes a war leader of the first rank. President Bush's youth was never as dissolute as Hal's, but like the future Henry V, he became an effective war leader after 9/11." The viability of this analogy has been challenged by Shakespeare scholars Newstok and Berger (2011), but what interests me here is the potential effect of the analogy being made in the public discourse. It seems likely to me that young playboys of privilege, seeing Bush's story of youthful vagrancy left behind, could very well use that narrative to neutralize any pressures they might feel – from themselves or others – to conform their behaviour to cultural norms and laws. Here the dramatized desistance is a historical account of someone else's reformation, not an imagined account of one's own in the future, but the effect of witnessing that dramatization could be the same: persistence in juvenile delinquency and crime.

The examples of Prince Hal and President Bush suggest precisely what Maruna insisted to me: the dramatization of desistance is a specifically white-collar phenomenon (overlooked in prior criminological research because criminology tends, Maruna said, "to focus almost exclusively on the highly disadvantaged who typically fill our prisons, police stations, and probation offices"). When I think about my own youthful rebellion, it was bound up with feelings of undeservedly being born into privilege: my family was upper middle class by small-town America standards, and I felt I hadn't really done anything to earn that advantage in life. I wanted to succeed on my own merits, so I degraded my starting point to create a level playing field. Even as I turned to juvenile delinquency and crime, however, I remained connected enough to mainstream American values to feel guilt and shame, which were neutralized by self-narrativizing this affair into a future prodigal son story.

At the same time, examples exist that suggest the dramatization of desistance is not restricted to the upper class. We see it at work in a lower-class setting in the Notorious B.I.G.'s song "Juicy," considered one of the greatest hip-hop songs of all time by *Rolling Stone* magazine. Dealing drugs by the age of twelve and arrested for selling crack cocaine at seventeen, B.I.G. spent nine months in prison in the early 1990s (Lang 2007, 9). The lead single off his 1994 debut album, "Juicy" tells a rags-to-riches story of B.I.G. moving from childhood poverty to juvenile delinquency to maturation and success as a rapper in adulthood. In his signature tone – deep yet nasal, almost out-of-breath – B.I.G. raps:

> I made the change from a common thief
> To up close and personal with Robin Leach ...
> I never thought it could happen, this rappin' stuff
> I was too used to packin' gats and stuff ...
> We used to fuss when the landlord dissed us.
> No heat, wonder why Christmas missed us.

Birthdays was the worst days.
Now we sip champagne when we thirsty.
Damn right I like the life I live,
'Cause I went from negative to positive.

The music video for "Juicy" frames the song as B.I.G. telling a news reporter his life story of overcoming adversity to achieve the American Dream. The video skips from scenes of hard times, getting arrested on the street corner, to time in prison paying his debt to society, to signing record deals with music industry executives in his new mansion, to hosting lavish parties in the luxury pool in his backyard.

There are two central points to make about the dramatization of desistance in "Juicy." First, the song may have contributed to criminal persistence in some of B.I.G.'s audience. Largely young, black, working-class men and women who were scraping by, his listeners were no doubt inspired by "Juicy" to aspire to work hard, achieve success, and secure a more comfortable life. At the same time, it seems likely that some in B.I.G's audience who were living the lifestyle of his youth could have used his story of overcoming adversity to imagine a similar story for their future selves. They could then justify to themselves the persistence of a criminal lifestyle as what had to be done to get by, something that was only temporary, something other successful people such as B.I.G. had to do themselves, and thus something the juvenile delinquent wouldn't strive too hard to avoid. Like Prince Hal, some in B.I.G.'s audiences could use their imagined future reformation as justification for their continued criminality.

Second, B.I.G.'s dramatization of his own desistance may have been – like Prince Hal's – a technique of neutralization allowing him to persist in delinquency. After "Juicy," he continued his lifestyle as a glorified Tony Montana mafioso type. In the mid-1990s, he had additional arrests for harassment, assault, drugs, and weapons charges, and he was accused of being involved in the murder of fellow rapper Tupac Shakur. That murder was part of an East Coast / West Coast gang rivalry that ultimately resulted in B.I.G.'s murder by West Coast rivals in 1997. It's plausible that the dramatization of desistance in "Juicy" and B.I.G.'s other songs alleviated the drive to maintain a reformed life free of criminality – in B.I.G. himself and his audience alike.

THEORIZING THE DRAMATIZATION OF DESISTANCE

The examples considered thus far – Hal, Bush, Biggie – provide enough of a pattern for us to theorize the structure and logic of the dramatization of desistance. It begins when mainstream culture promoting mainstream values is disrupted by the juvenile delinquent, whose criminal behaviour both stems from and promotes subcultural values. Because he is still firmly attached to mainstream culture, however, the delinquent employs any number of techniques of neutralization to minimize his guilt and shame. One of those techniques is the dramatization of desistance. Desistance is not just a mainstream value; it is a mainstream *narrative*. In the formal terms of literary studies, the story of desistance draws upon the genre of heroic romance, which relates tales of good conquering evil. More specifically, the romance genre tends to involve narratives of overcoming adversity through an individual's admirable exercise of strength, talent, and will power. Historically, as the romantic fairy tales of knights defeating dragons were modernized, there was an internalization of adversity in this kind of story: antagonists transformed from the external enemies of the protagonist to his or her inner demons. The narrative of overcoming adversity thus shifted from a story of good conquering evil out in the world to one of good conquering evil in the mind of the protagonist. In these modern romances, overcoming adversity is often presented specifically as desistance from crime. These public stories of desistance – whether presented as historical or fictional – thus become available as models for the private stories of future desistance that juvenile delinquents tell themselves. The delinquent's dramatization of his or her desistance is an expression of guilt and shame about the present represented through the imagination of virtuous action in the future. An appeal to one's planned character in the future is then used to neutralize guilt over one's character and actions in the present.

Clearly, it's not just cultural and subcultural *values* that come into conflict with juvenile delinquency; cultural and subcultural *narratives* also clash. Specifically, the mainstream narrative of desistance from crime – heroic romance as the story of good conquering evil in the life and mind of a protagonist – comes into conflict with the subcultural narrative of juvenile delinquency, a story grounded not in fictional romance but in gritty reality. Fantasy and history collide, generating tension in the mind of the young criminal. The dramatization of desistance is one way of neutralizing this unrest: one imagines a future in which one follows the typical "life course" of a human being, maturing from juvenile delinquent to law-abiding adult. That imagined narrative of desistance in the future eases the guilt and shame one feels about being a criminal in the present. The heroism implied in this overcoming narrative makes it all the more appealing to adopt. And this neutralization of one's nagging conscience then clears the way for the continued criminal behaviour that one knows is wrong.

Thus, while a criminological theory like "life-course criminology" can be used to help us understand the events in one of Shakespeare's plays, the trajectory of thought is not always from theory to Shakespeare, as if the understanding of Shakespeare's plays were the end-all, be-all of life. Shakespeare's plays can help us build criminological theories like the dramatization of desistance: here Shakespeare is the means rather than the end of interpretation. His works are not the final object of analysis. An understanding of life is the end-game, and Shakespeare is the avenue through which we come to understand life. Traditionally, theory building in the social sciences is done on the foundation of empirical evidence, usually quantitative data but sometimes case studies. Shakespeare's plays offer a special kind of case that, because it is artistic, has a conceptual density already at work. Theories built from these narratives have the potential to catch hidden aspects of crime that traditional criminology working with "real world" data has missed. Shakespeare can thus be a valuable resource for the social sciences because his works prompt observations that (1) help us understand ongoing experiences in life, (2) we might not recognize without the Shakespearean intervention, (3) are not true simply because they are in Shakespeare's texts, and so (4) need to be rigorously (i.e., scientifically) tested.

When I asked my criminologists how they would test the dramatization of desistance empirically, Presser proposed "research should involve interviews and seek to compare eventual offending rates (in time 1) of persons vowing desistance to a greater versus lesser extent (in time 2)." Admittedly, that would be a difficult study to conduct. Maruna's suggestions would produce less reliable results but could be collected more feasibly:

> I suppose one could use a natural experiment, identifying states with robust protections against the stigmatization of adolescents

> versus those that routinely treat teenagers as adults, and compare whether young people in the former group offend at a greater rate ... Alternatively, one could do exploratory interviews with very privileged young people who use and deal drugs, engage in computer hacking, cyber-bullying, etc. (precisely the types of samples we lack in criminology) about their offending and how this impacts their sense of identity. It might be nice to do interviews with young people in more disadvantaged circumstances manifesting similar behaviours as a comparator. This would not be a proper "test" of the theory, but it would be a useful first step to look at the viability of the theory in the way young people think about and account for their activities.

SHAKESPEARE FOR THEORY

When we think of "Shakespeare and theory," it's usually the literary theory that blossomed in the second half of the twentieth century. Abstract ideas about how art is created and interpreted can help us understand Shakespeare's works: here thought flows from theory to Shakespeare, but we can also reverse this trajectory, as I have sought to do in this chapter: Shakespeare can be used to build theory.

In Maruna's words, humanistic texts, traditions, and scholarship are, for criminology, "absolutely needed and critical to the development of theory." He added, in what I see as the most poignant comment from his interview, that this method of using literature to develop theory is "simply making explicit what all of us do when we develop our theories in criminology (or any social science)":

> Yes, empirical evidence is necessary in the testing and development of theory, but theory is fundamentally a story, and we get these stories from the culture around us (literature, mythology, religion, folklore, film, and common wisdom). Yes, ideally, theories emerge from our own real-life case studies, but even though these are cases of "real people," the theory is based on our storied interpretation of these lives (not, somehow, on the lives themselves), and these are always filtered through the lens of the meta-narratives of a given culture.

All criminological theory is already fundamentally narrative. That's what a theory is: a story. That's also largely what literature is. And often criminological theory and literary narrative succeed or fail based on the same criteria: how well does the story told help us understand our lived experience by revealing hidden aspects of events that are identifiable as common human experiences yet are still troublesome and difficult to interpret? In other words, literature and criminology often serve similar functions in providing readers with highly formalized plots that can be used to identify, understand, and explain patterns of human behaviour, including the origins and outcomes of our stories of crime and justice, hidden aspects usually imperceptible when we are desperately grasping for a foothold of interpretation while *in medias res*.

Shakespeare holds a special place in this prospect. On the one hand, as Manura pointed out, "Shakespeare has had an enormous impact on western culture (indeed probably global culture), and his ideas have impacted the justice system in tangible ways, frequently cited by jurists and legal scholars, so it makes sense that we continue to go back to his writings to understand just how that justice system works." There are substantive affinities between Shakespeare's representations of law and order and modern critical legal studies, for instance, because both emphasize the human in the system: the human fallibility that Shakespeare expertly captured – think Portia in *The Merchant of Venice* or Angelo in *Measure for Measure* – ensures the justice system will never run as systematically as it claims.[5] On the other hand, Shakespeare has something to offer criminology that other literary representations do not, at least not to the same extent. I am referring to the massive, centuries-long discourse of Shakespearean criticism (represented in this chapter by the competing critical opinions on Hal's "redeeming time" soliloquy). If it is true that Shakespearean representations of crime can reflect generalizable criminal patterns, and criminology's job is to identify, explain, and prevent those same patterns, then Shakespearean criticism is a huge, untapped resource for criminology: every interpretation of Shakespearean crime is a criminological hypothesis waiting to be theorized and tested.

NOTES

I would like to thank Lois Presser, Shadd Maruna, Julia Reinhard Lupton, and Russell Bodi for comments and conversations about the ideas presented in this chapter.

1 All subsequent quotations from the play refer to this edition.

2 Unless otherwise cited, quotations come from my interviews with Maruna on 15 November 2017, and with Presser on 3 December 2017.

3 I am grateful for the opportunity to see a pre-publication copy of Presser's book.

4 All biblical references are to *The Bible and Holy Scriptures* (1560), i.e. the Geneva Bible. I have modernized the spelling.

5 I owe this point to an unpublished student paper (Paladino 2016).

REFERENCES

Berger, Harry, Jr. 1997. "Making Trifles of Terrors: Redistributing Complicities in the Ethical Discourses." In *Making Trifles of Terrors: Redistributing Complicities in Shakespeare,* edited by Peter Erickson, 288–334. Stanford, CA: Stanford University Press.

The Bible and Holy Scriptures. 1560. Translated by William Whittingham, Anthony Gilby, and Thomas Sampson. Geneva: Rouland Hall.

Bullough, Geoffrey, ed. 1973. "Henry IV." *Narrative and Dramatic Sources of Shakespeare*. Vol. 4. London: Routledge.

Dickinson, Hugh. 1961. "The Reformation of Prince Hal." *Shakespeare Quarterly* 12 (1): 33–46.

Dover Wilson, John. 1943. *The Fortunes of Falstaff*. Cambridge: Cambridge University Press.

Glueck, Sheldon, and Eleanor Glueck. 1974. *Of Delinquency and Crime: A Panorama of Years of Research*. Springfield, IL: C.C. Thomas.

Greenblatt, Stephen. 1985. "Invisible Bullets: Renaissance Authority and Its Subversion." In *Political Shakespeare: New Essays in Cultural Materialism*, edited by Jonathan Dollimore and Alan Sinfield, 18–47. Ithaca, NY: Cornell University Press.

Johnson, Samuel, ed. 1765. *The First Part of King Henry the Fourth*. In *The Plays of William Shakespeare*. Vol. 4. London: J. and R. Tonson.

Kastan, David Scott, ed. 2002. *King Henry IV Part 1*. London: Arden Shakespeare.

Kellman, Laurie. 2000. "Bush Once Pleaded Guilty to DUI." *Washington Post*, 3 November. http://www.washingtonpost.com/wp-srv/aponline/20001103/aponline095357_000.htm.

Lang, Holly. 2007. *The Notorious B.I.G.: A Biography*. Westport, CT: Greenwood Biographies.

Laub, John, and Robert Sampson. 2001. "Understanding Desistance from Crime." *Crime and Justice* 28: 1–69.

Maruna, Shadd. 2001. *Making Good: How Ex-Convicts Reform and Rebuild Their Lives*. Washington, DC: American Psychological Association.

Matza, David. 1964. *Delinquency and Drift*. New York: John Wiley and Sons.

Montrose, Louis. 1996. *The Purpose of Playing: Shakespeare and the Cultural Politics of the Elizabethan Theatre*. Chicago: University of Chicago Press.

Newstok, Scott L., and Harry Berger, Jr. 2011. "Harrying after VV." In *Shakespeare after 9/11: How a Social Trauma Reshapes Interpretation*, edited by Matthew Biberman and Julia Reinhard Lupton, 41–52. Lewiston, NY: Edwin Mellen.

Notorious B.I.G. 1994. "Juicy." On *Ready to Die*. CD. Bad Boy.

Owens, Mackubin Thomas. 2004. "George W. Bush as Henry V." *National Review*, 12 February. http://www.nationalreview.com/article/209492/george-w-bush-henry-v.

Paladino, Niko. 2016. "Shakespeare in Law: The Bard as a Critical Legal Scholar." Unpublished undergraduate paper, Harvard University.

Presser, Lois. 2018. *Inside Story: How Narratives Drive Mass Harm*. Berkeley: University of California Press.

Presser, Lois, and Sveinung Sandberg. 2015. "What Is the Story?" In *Narrative Criminology: Understanding Stories of Crime*, edited by Presser and Sandberg, 1–20. New York: New York University Press.

Seery, John. 2007. "The Bush Cocaine Chronicles: Complicity and Cover-Up." *Huffington Post*, 4 January. https://www.huffingtonpost.com/john-seery/the-bush-cocaine-chronicl_b_37786.html.

Shakespeare, William. 2016. *The Norton Shakespeare*. 3rd ed. Edited by Stephen Greenblatt. New York: W.W. Norton.

Sykes, Gresham M., and David Matza. 1957. "Techniques of Neutralization: A Theory of Delinquency." *American Sociological Review* 22 (6): 664–70.

Wilson, Jeffrey R. 2014. "Shakespeare and Criminology." *Crime Media Culture* 10 (2): 97–114.

Young, Alan R. 1979. *The English Prodigal Son Plays: A Theatrical Fashion of the 16th and 17th Centuries*. Salzburg: Universität Salzburg.

PART THREE

LIVING WITH SHAKESPEARE

11

NUTSHELLS AND OPEN TRIALS

Editing and Cinematography in Live Broadcast Shakespeare

R.W. JONES

A funny thing happened when I attended the Royal Shakespeare Company's recorded live performance of *Much Ado About Nothing*, billed as *Love's Labour's Won*, at a hip movie house in Austin, Texas, thousands of miles from Stratford-upon-Avon. In Act 2, Scene 3, Benedick "overhears" Leonato, Don Pedro, and Claudio stage their discussion of Beatrice's love for him. The scene invariably invites a multitude of sight gags, and this production proved no exception, with Benedick popping through curtains, accidentally appearing in plain sight, and ultimately ensconcing himself within a large, fully trimmed Christmas tree. The increasing absurdity of each appearance kept the laughs rolling in the RSC's theatre, with the bit culminating in Benedick's face replacing the centre of the Christmas tree star, electrocuting the credulous bachelor in the process. This climax provoked the largest laugh of all and lent revelatory force to the line "He does show some *sparks* that are like wit" (Shakespeare 2006, 2.3.181–2). Yet when the same sequence screened for the film audience within the packed Alamo Drafthouse in Austin, that uproarious sequence was no longer that uproarious and merited only some light chuckles. Even granting the received notion that live performances generate more laughter than taped ones, the disparity was startling. We were still a community of laughers after all, and other moments had gotten laughter from both crowds – why not this one?

The answer, I believe, resides in cinematography and editing, and their relationship to space, time, and audience expectation. I will return to this specific moment later. For now, I will examine the camera work of two of the most popular and publicized live theatre broadcasts in recent years – National Theatre (NT) Live's *Hamlet* and the Branagh Theatre Company's *The Winter's Tale*.

The Lyndsey Turner–directed *Hamlet* owes much of its visibility and market power (the show sold out a year in advance) to its lead, Benedict Cumberbatch, who earned a passionate and wide following for his titular role in TV's *Sherlock*. As he has gone on to star in both Hollywood blockbusters and prestige films alike, viewers have had little chance to miss him on-screen, and it seems that even casual admirers flocked to their local movie theatre to witness his stage rendering of the Prince of Denmark. According to the National Theatre, 800,000 people had seen the broadcast as of early 2017 (a record for NT Live), and further encore screenings occurred in fall 2017 and spring 2018, with another round slated for spring 2019. The production itself received mostly positive reviews, with general approval for Cumberbatch's "rational" Hamlet, but critics diverged on Turner's spectacular visual and sound effects and Es Devlin's elaborate set, which bordered on the baroque. Some found this grand design exhilarating and politically trenchant; others saw clutter and obtrusiveness. And though Cumberbatch exhorted his fans to refrain from snapping photos or recording his performance with their phones, the production unmistakably laid its focus on its magnetic star, both courting this impassioned obsession and trying to manage its impolitic expression.

Reviewers consistently returned to the word "cinematic" to describe Turner's most innovative effects, such as the blast of sound and debris that smashed through the upstage hall doors at the conclusion of the first half, creating an ashen wasteland as the play space for the second half. No less subtle was the handling of Hamlet's famed soliloquies: in these moments, a spotlight caught Cumberbatch, as the rest of the stage and cast receded into darkness and slow motion, so that "Hamlet's consciousness seemed to crash into the foreground," as James Loehlin put it (2016, 2). Blurring the lines of media, Turner constructed a theatrical effect to perform a cinematic function – the voice-over or interior monologue. The director of the broadcast, Robin Lough, followed suit in his editing or "mixing," reinforcing the audience's privileged access to Hamlet through cutaway reaction shots and close-ups.

Lough's stated approach accords with the espoused objectives of many of the companies producing live broadcasts. "The cinema audience," Lough told *Screen Daily*, "should always feel totally engaged with the stage production without ever noticing how the transformation to screen is taking place" (Sandwell 2012). However, as budgets have increased and technology has advanced (the NT Live *Hamlet* used eight cameras in its filming), directors have felt licensed and liberated to use more pans, tracking shots, and reaction shots. The broadcast event has consequently come to resemble the filmic more than the televisual. The audience's experience of the play then becomes mediated through the comfortable grammar of film and its established signs. As Janice Wardle (2014) puts it, "the dispersed audiences are located in a *cinematic* space, where they have been conditioned to become adept, whether consciously or unconsciously, at interpreting complex, cinematic, codes and conventions." Therefore, even sophisticated filmic techniques, employed by Lough and others, feel "natural" and mask the distinct choices that construct and shape theatrical meaning and interpretation precisely because of their cinematic familiarity and legibility.

In Lough's *Hamlet* broadcast, one of the moments that exemplifies technique subtly moulding viewer perspective occurs after Hamlet requests "a passionate speech" from the First Player (Shakespeare 1982, 2.2.428). The First Player's recitation of the chaotic fall of Troy and Pyrrhus's murderous rage provides occasion for the auditors onstage to react in separate, often telling, ways. Hamlet may be rapt by the performance or, like Claudius later, touched inwardly by its parallels to his own circumstances; Polonius may be uncomfortable, perhaps due to his own dramatic sensibilities that find the tale too graphic or too psychologically harmful to the speaker, or out of concern for its effect on Hamlet; and the players may have a whole host of reactions, individually or collectively, toward their company-mate, or Hamlet, or Polonius. Essentially, the scene exhibits watching of performance and exploring its effects on those very watchers, and thus it anticipates in several ways the staged *Murder of Gonzago* a few scenes later.

In the midst of the initial section of the speech before Polonius's interruption, the First Player speaks these lines: "So, as a painted tyrant, Pyrrhus stood, / And like a neutral to his will and matter, / Did nothing" (2.2.476–8). Scholars have long noted Pyrrhus's parallel to Hamlet through the echoes of this speech, and these lines in particular, as they reflect Hamlet's own reluctance to take decisive, violent action in revenge for his father's death. From a theatrical standpoint,

"Did nothing" stands as a short line in the Second Quarto, and the presumed pause this may indicate marks Pyrrhus's hesitation but also gives performative space for productions to mark Hamlet's reflexive application of the line to himself. During the filmed Turner *Hamlet*, Lough chooses this exact moment, in the pause after "Did nothing," to cut away to a close-up of Cumberbatch. Because of their familiarity with film conventions, an audience needs little guidance to realize that this line has special meaning for Hamlet, and, as he recognizes its acute relevance to his own circumstance, so do we. Again, this cutaway appears as a natural choice, but it is by no means obligatory. For instance, a longer or wider shot could have allowed us to take in both the Player and Hamlet at once, as we watch Hamlet's recognition dawn rather than being told that it has already awakened. Or a cutaway could have included any of the other characters onstage – Polonius, or the other players, or even the First Player himself. Do they notice Hamlet's reaction? Is anyone concerned or curious about the effect this speech is having on the erratic heir to the throne who recently lost a father? In Lough's editing, these questions become incidental and unnecessary. What the cut does offer, though, as many of both Lough's and Turner's choices do, is a special, exclusive entree into Hamlet's mind.

Lough's technique here is a savvy one. Not only are the viewers gaining privileged access to Cumberbatch, even when he is not speaking (perhaps a consolation for not seeing him in the flesh?), but the cut also keeps with Turner's thematic concerns. Since the cutaway isolates Hamlet in close-up, with little background, he is all foreground and the rest of the space is cut out, as if it were essentially ceasing to exist for the viewer. Although conventional, the device complements Turner's soliloquy effect, freezing time for those in the surrounding space, while we are, for the length of the shot, alone with Hamlet/Cumberbatch. We are not asked to critically observe Hamlet in context, but to join in his mind space. What happens in the scene around Hamlet as he takes in this charged accusation ("Did nothing") becomes insignificant. We are, with Hamlet, trapped in the box of the camera frame, alone with his thoughts, with full access to him, but not to the world he inhabits. In a moment, we return to a wide shot, and "time" continues, although the production itself has never stopped. The preponderance of moments like this further extends Turner's project of a Hamlet enclosed in a prison, or a nutshell if you will – trapped within his adolescence, boxed in by his own play castle, shut off from others by his own mind, and contained by spotlights, the camera frame, and even Cumberbatch's own celebrity.[1]

In film terminology, a series of individual shots cut together is *montage* (of which our conventional use of the word is only a minor variant). The term refers not to the content of the shots but to their succession, which produces a new meaning that they could not possess in isolation. A close-up of Cumberbatch would mean little if we did not recognize its relation to the previous shot of the player delivering the line "Did nothing." In the words of film critic and theorist André Bazin, "The creation of a sense or meaning [is] not objectively contained in the images themselves but derived exclusively from their juxtaposition" (1967, 25). In this way, viewers still put the meaning together but are guided by the director, who determines what they see and when. Bazin contrasts this to the technique of the *shot-in-depth*, where the image, or the *mise en scène* (what is contained in the frame of the camera), encompasses multiple elements, often in deep focus, which may come in and out of the frame as the camera moves without cutting. Essentially a longer "take," with more emphasis on composition, depth, and/or camera mobility than on cutting or editing, this technique preserves "continuity of dramatic space … and its duration" (34). As such, elements of the *mise en scène* exist in a dialectical relationship, commenting on one another, altering the meaning of the individual elements because of their placement and existence within the frame – or out of it. The viewer thus becomes aware of what the camera has chosen *not* to look at, as well as what to pursue, what to investigate, and so on. Films are of course made of an abundance of both techniques, but, for Bazin, shots-in-depth require more participation from the viewer, who "is called upon to exercise at least a minimum of personal choice. It is from his attention and his will that the meaning of the image in part derives" (36). Here Bazin appears to approach what theatre advocates tout as a prime virtue of that art – the freedom of the viewer to examine multiple elements of the stage picture at once – what, in film, we might call "simultaneity." So, while the succession of shots orders meaning in montage, when confronted with "simultaneity," the viewer must construct the meaning from the interaction of elements within the same shot.

If Lough's direction of *Hamlet* skews toward montage, then the contrasting technique was on display in the broadcast of *The Winter's Tale*, the standard-bearer for Kenneth Branagh's year-long repertory company at the Garrick Theatre. Like the Cumberbatch *Hamlet*, *The Winter's Tale* (co-directed by Branagh and Rob Ashford) featured plenty of cinematic star power, with Branagh as Leontes, performing Shakespeare onstage for the first time in twenty-five years, and Judi Dench as Paulina. On the film's "opening day," when it was broadcast live to theatres in the United Kingdom, it grossed $1.66 million, earning the top spot for the day, and improbably beating out franchise blockbuster *The Hunger Games: Mockingjay, Part 2*.

Benjamin Caron, Branagh's collaborator on the BBC's *Wallander*, directed the broadcast, emphasizing, along with the production, the communal over the individual. Especially during the scene of Hermione's trial, Caron's cinematography often captured reactions in the same shot, rather than using cuts, limiting the audience's connection to a single character and offering critical perspectives from which to view Leontes' fatal jealousy.

At first glance, Caron's direction appears less sophisticated than Lough's, seemingly lacking the number of cameras and some of the more cinematic techniques Lough employs. For instance, Caron's shots are wider: an establishing shot of the entire stage opens every scene, lending to the feel of older filmed productions with one camera. Caron uses fewer close-ups – a surprise, given the titanic statures of Branagh and Dench. He films the principal characters with long and medium-long shots, and these more expansive shots end up capturing ancillary characters in the background. The effect reminds the cinematic audience of the public nature of Leontes' breakdown and Hermione's humiliation. In fact, the play is full of anonymous witnesses, from the opening discussion of Leontes' and Polixenes' affection for one another, to the women surrounding Hermione in her late pregnancy, to the trial scene. Unlike a private, domestic drama like *Othello*, *The Winter's Tale* often proceeds in full view of the court, and Caron captures this by angling shots to encompass multiple characters at once. For instance, in the trial scene, Hermione is centred upstage, with the trial's witnesses spread out in two lines that flay out along diagonals toward the downstage corners. Caron shoots Hermione at an angle, rather than a full close-up, so that the closest witness to her upstage remains in the frame.

Additionally, Caron adeptly captures principal characters in "two-shots," which contain both speaking characters in the same shot, rather than the more familiar cinematic device of shot–reverse shot, which follows a cause-and-effect linearity. A particularly strong

Figure 11.1 | Paulina (Judi Dench) faces Leontes (Kenneth Branagh), who looks away.

example of this method occurs when Paulina demands that Leontes recognize his irrationality and claim his newborn daughter as his own. In the middle of the scene ("On mine own accord, I'll off," Shakespeare 2008, 2.3.64), Branagh appears closer to the camera facing out, with Dench over his right shoulder (figure 11.1). The shot mirrors a later moment in the trial scene, with Hermione (Miranda Raison) pleading with Leontes, again with Branagh facing out, and Raison in the frame behind him (figure 11.2).

In these moments, the viewer sees the reactions of both characters simultaneously, emphasizing Leontes's impenetrability and wilful delusions. Additionally, each shot contains onstage witnesses to the interactions. By the second half, the wide angles of Caron become necessary, with the crowded activity on the stage for the sheep shearing, an approach that accords with the communal nature of the play, which culminates in a final public event. The animation of Hermione's statue occurs amid an onstage audience who serve as witnesses who must, along with Leontes and even the offstage audience, "awake [their] faith" (5.3.195). Caron's style emphasizes the social aspect of the play, and although he rarely includes shots of the theatre audience, the figures onstage watching the story unfold remind us of our role as witnesses and, eventually, participants.

The choices that Caron and Lough make in their direction and editing each serve the thematic purposes of their respective productions. Far from arbitrary decisions or simply following a generic

Figure 11.2 | Leontes faces the camera, not Hermione (Miranda Raison).

style, the cinematography of each shapes an audience's experience of the play and responds actively to the prevailing ideas of each production – that is, featuring Cumberbatch and the audience's connection to the individual in *Hamlet*, and augmenting Branagh's emphasis on the social and, in turn, the ensemble in *The Winter's Tale*.

Returning to *Much Ado* at the RSC, then: upon re-viewing the Christmas-tree scene, I noticed that the director, who again happened to be Robin Lough, had divided those moments of comic surprise into a series of cuts. As the scene begins, Benedick (Edward Bennett) appears in long shot, where the audience can see his full body and the majority of the stage – this perspective replicates most accurately the live audience's viewpoint. When the others enter, Benedick dips behind a large curtain (the "arras") that hangs just behind a piano that sits upstage on the left, and the majority of the shots for the next sequence alternate between long and medium (from the waist up). Balthasar sings at the piano, and, at one point, Benedick pops his head just above Balthasar's and then, as if disembodied, rises upwards between the curtains (figure 11.3). During this sequence, the camera cuts to a close-up, capturing the two heads in line and catching Benedick's expressions as he mugs through the ending of the song.

The next few cuts go back to medium or long, but when Benedick has an aside, the camera again cuts to a close-up of just his face peeping through the break in the curtain. When he emerges in plain sight, the frame returns to a long shot, and then Benedick hides behind the

Figure 11.3 | Benedick (Edward Bennett) appears above Balthazar (Harry Waller).

trimmed Christmas tree. Several similar moments of facial reveal ensue, where Benedick's head pops out of the centre of the tree on lines such as "In everything but in loving Benedick" (Shakespeare 2006, 2.3.160). On the line "Hero says surely she will die" (170), Benedick's face appears inside the star at the top of the tree (figure 11.4), just before the electric lights are re-lit by the tricksters and he is electrocuted, cueing the line, "He doth show some *sparks* that are like wit" (181–2; emphasis added).

Bennett is a fantastically expressive actor, and the close-ups afford the cinema audience what the theatre audience might not see – the detail and range of his expressions of boredom, amusement, shock, embarrassment, and so on, as the scene progresses. But in the cuts to a close-up, something seems lost as well, and that might be what Bazin calls "the comedy of space" (1967, 52). For us, the cinema audience, Benedick's reveals are not surprises at all, for we register a cut in the split second in which it occurs, and, given the progress and pattern of the scene, we know the camera is cutting away to Benedick. Like in the cut-away to Hamlet discussed above, Lough eliminates the rest of the space with a close-up, and yet the comedy in the *Much Ado* scene seems predicated and contingent upon that

Figure 11.4 | Benedick hides in the star atop a Christmas tree.

very space. Although we know in general where Benedick might be (behind the arras, behind the tree), we don't know *exactly* where he is, or where he will appear next. The theatre audience enjoys the surprise of his sudden appearance, and "finding him" as it were, and it shows in their laughter. But for the cinema audience, there is no reward for locating Benedick, because the camera has already done our work for us. To take another genre, compare, for instance, a horror film where the shock comes from something appearing *in* the frame, not the camera cutting away to it. Lough's direction here has advantages and disadvantages, and it makes narrative sense to show a close-up of the speaker, but the disparity in the laughter in the two theatres should clue us in that we are witnessing essentially two different productions – the play and the film – and that the meaning of each is constructed independently.

The success of both of these broadcasts and the technological ability to distribute them internationally ensures that the live broadcasting of Shakespeare, and other "canonical" playwrights, will undoubtedly continue, offering access to major productions without the cost of travel and theatre tickets. Recently the National Theatre broadcast both parts of its nearly eight-hour *Angels in*

America production, potentially appealing to a younger demographic through the popularity of its young star, Andrew Garfield. With the production's eventual transfer to Broadway, one wonders if these broadcasts won't begin to operate in the inverse, publicizing a show that fans can then pay to see onstage. However, what exactly are audiences watching in the movie theatre when they attend a live broadcast? Neither the play itself, nor a feature film, these broadcasts lie closer to documentary or even to televised sports, which also employs multiple cameras to stage a "narrative" that can narrow, enhance, or stand at odds with what eyewitnesses experience. And, unlike at a play, the total audience – local and dispersed – sees the same director's vision beamed into their community, a vision that then stands in record as "the production." Additionally, these broadcasts increasingly tend to move away from the televisual and toward the filmic, with more close-ups, reaction shots, and mobile cameras, and fewer shots of the audience intruding into the fiction. While theorists of the live event and "communities of perception" will have much to say about this growing phenomenon, we must also be attuned to *how* these productions are working to produce a distinct vision of the play for a film-conscious audience.

NOTE

1 Because this broadcast has not been released on DVD, I am unable to reproduce any images from it here. The theatrical trailer may be viewed at https://www.youtube.com/watch?v=P5JZbeFvTZA.

REFERENCES

Bazin, André. 1967. *What Is Cinema?* Translated by Hugh Gray. Vol. 1. Berkeley: University of California Press.

Loehlin, James. 2016. "Looking Before and After: The Cumberbatch *Hamlet*." Paper for "The Shakespearean Text and Contemporary Performance" seminar, Shakespeare Association of America Conference, New Orleans, LA.

Sandwell, Ian. 2012, "NT Live: 'It's about Getting Back to What the Core of the Theatrical Experience Is About.'" *Screen Daily*, 18 October. https://www.screendaily.com/blogs/nt-live-its-about-getting-back-to-the-core-of-what-the-theatrical-experience-is-about/5047936.article.

Shakespeare, William. 1982. *Hamlet*. Edited by Harold Jenkins. London: Methuen.

– 2006. *Much Ado About Nothing*. Edited by Claire McEachern. London: Bloomsbury.

– 2008. *The Winter's Tale*. Edited by Mario DiGangi. Boston: Bedford / St Martin's.

Wardle, Janice. 2014. "'Outside Broadcast': Looking Backwards and Forwards, Live Theatre in the Cinema – NT Live and RSCLive." *Adaptation* 7 (2). https://dx.doi.org/10.1093/adaptation/apu017.

12

FILMING THEATRE

A Tale of Two Merchants

PETER HOLLAND

> Antonioni once told me that he had directed a few plays, and I asked him whether he wanted to do more theater work. "No," he said. "Always the same shot."
>
> Stanley Kauffmann, "Notes on Theater-and-Film"

I

In 1637 the artist Gian Lorenzo Bernini staged a remarkable performance in Rome. "When the curtain had fallen, one saw on the stage a flock of people partly real and partly only feigned, who ... seemed almost to represent those on the other side, who had come in great number to see the comedy." This second audience on the stage was seated in a second auditorium so that there were, it seemed, "two theaters." Two actors on stage "proclaimed the reality of the two rival theaters" and pretended to draw the two audiences. After a while, they "came to realize that the group each beheld was deemed illusory by the other."

> Then, the time having come for making the best of this theatrical paradox, the two braggarts decided "that they would pull a curtain across the scene and that each would arrange a performance for his audience alone," of which one ... was in fact submitted to the real spectators. But ... "it was interrupted at times by the laughter of those on the other side, as if something very pleasant had been seen and heard." (Bernheimer 1956, 243)[1]

II

On a number of occasions in the past few years, I have experienced the same strange event, but one whose rival realities I interpret very differently. I settle down in my seat in the Browning Cinema on campus at the University of Notre Dame and find myself watching another audience on screen, also settling into their seats. My view of them is interrupted every now and again by information about forthcoming events in the same series, something I see but they do not. My view of this second audience is tinged with the sharing of emotions with them, anticipating what we are both about to see, and my eagerness is enhanced by the digital clock in the corner that times the countdown to the start. But there is also a second tinge colouring the moment, increased by affectionate memories of the space in which they are (the National Theatre, the Royal Shakespeare Theatre, Shakespeare's Globe, the Donmar Warehouse) and hence an envy that they are there and that this time I am not, that my experience of the event will necessarily, at least in my response in the moment to its imminence, always be lesser than theirs, that the separation and remediation from theatre to screen diminishes the object, that the actors will be performing for them and not quite for me. I know that the memory of being in those theatres strongly affects these feelings, for they are not present when I watch operas from the Met, a space I have never visited.

But, as I look at the audience settling around me in the cinema and see friends and colleagues, I know that they know I have been to these theatres more often than they have and that my envy of the audience on screen is matched by my friends' kind envy of me. And then, as I look at the audience settling on screen, I find myself wondering if I will see someone I know, not an uncommon event when I go to those theatres, but now knowing that, even if I did see a friend (and I never have on one of these occasions), they are not in fact there now. For, though I have the sensation of simultaneity, I know that it is not really the case, that, apart from broadcasts from the Metropolitan Opera, all of which are simulcasts, broadcasts in real time simultaneity with the live performance they are showing (for my cinema does not show "encore presentations" of opera any more, the audience numbers not justifying them), the audience I am seeing are not "live" any more, that, though once there, there earlier, there before, they have now left for homes or hotels. The simulacrum of the simulcast reveals its falsity, its faking of an event as a now which is really a then, a fiction in which I am a willing participant, sharing Dr Johnson's view of the audience's sense of the fictive locations of a drama: "The truth is, that the spectators are always in their senses, and know, from the first act to the last, that the stage is only a stage, and that the players are only players" (1916, 27).

It is not, of course, that I am intellectually fetishizing the real, the temporal connection of watching what that on-screen audience watches exactly as they watch it. It is a desire, a yearning, that is not quite like the imagining of place as real, be it Alexandria or Rome, that Dr Johnson was pooh-poohing, precisely because this entire event of watching as the onscreen audience once watched is an action that plays off the fact of its having been real elsewhere, earlier. Time slips, but the reality of that which is seen calls out for connection.

III

Has it started yet? Well, when does the play begin? As Tiffany Stern (2015) has reminded us, we have made assumptions about when a play began and when it ended that are far too bound up with the apparent limits of the printed book. In cinemacasts, as Michael Friedman prefers to call them, precisely in order to avoid limiting himself "to a consideration of 'live' or simultaneously shown versions of these performances" (2016, 457n1), it is clear when the transmission ends but less clear when the production begins.[2] With the house lights still up, NT Live broadcasts frequently move to an introduction by Emma Freud, whose management, COBJ, describes her as "the public face of the National Theatre."[3] As Erin Sullivan notes, "this sometimes heavy-handed framing is rather like being forced to read the program before the performance begins" (2017, 635). Others have been more irritated: as Ryan Gilbey (2014), a columnist in the *Guardian*, fulminated, "The next shock was finding that I had come to see Coriolanus starring Emma Freud .... The appearance of Ms Freud on screen, whipping us into a frenzy about what we were about to see, was at best superfluous ... and at worst obstructive." Freud's introductions and interval conversations show that NT Live has, in this and other respects, copied the Met Opera livecasts, often fronted by Renée Fleming. But it is also a part of a distinctively US cultural emphasis, with a venerable tradition on American television of signalling a high-cultural event by finding someone to offer an introduction to it, reassuring us (in Freud's case by her relentlessly excited delivery) that this may be good for us but is also likely to be enjoyable.

In case the introduction is insufficient, often with contextualizing from the director and cast members, Freud is likely to reappear during the interval, and the digital clock on screen during the interval counts down the time not to the second half of the production but to the interval feature. It seems essential in such conversation to bring up what the audience in the theatre or cinema may be thinking but might be inhibited from voicing precisely because of the heavy cultural burden carried by Shakespeare. So, in her interval discussion of the Donmar Warehouse *Coriolanus*, Freud was at pains to remind the director, Josie Rourke, that Tom Hiddleston, playing Coriolanus, had been named "the sexiest actor on the planet" by MTV. Checking with friends in the audience at the end, I find that many had indeed found him to be aptly named so. Though Gilbey (2014) thought these "hardly the words you want ringing in your ears as Act Two begins," they were clearly present in the unspoken responses of many.

What has usually gone unmarked is the sense of privileged access that the interviews in particular, sometimes in the auditorium, sometimes backstage, constitute. Although filmed during the interval, they are not accessible to the theatre audience, which cannot see backstage. Here is something for us in the cinema that those people cannot hear. Audience members caught on camera when the interview and/or introductory remarks are conducted in the auditorium, even right next to them, seem neither perturbed by nor interested in the introductions and such "special features" (which seem to be aching for a DVD release that never comes). But we in the cinema are intrigued. I do race back to my seat to catch the interval event, in part curious to see whether, for once, something intriguing will be said, but also because this is part of the show I am watching, whereas the theatrical audience's interval goings-and-comings are not. Missing it would not quite be like missing a scene of the play, but it seems to urge my presence.

IV

Whether annoyed by the length of the introduction or intrigued by its featuring an account of the play's stage history or a virtual tour of the theatre (Sullivan notes both, 2017, 635), I am ready for the play to start and the show to move from what my audience can "enjoy" and *that* audience cannot to that which both audiences have paid for. The framing is always only a bonus extra, hence my analogy with a DVD special feature. The play is what I have bought, at an unusual price – unusual in both directions: much higher than I would pay for a film, much lower than I would pay for a seat in the theatre (not choosing any longer to watch from "restricted view" or in the gods, that Olympian space the French think of as paradise).

The pricing and transmission dates of these broadcasts have not had much attention yet. Although film distributors always have significant degrees of control over screening dates and frequency (usually setting a minimum requirement for screenings but also permitting or refusing second-run screenings depending on proximity to other cinemas), event cinema is far more tightly controlled. When in 1964 *Hamlet*, directed by Sir John Gielgud and starring Richard Burton, was filmed by the technology called Electronovision as Theatrofilm, the screening times were exceptionally sharply defined. Released to nearly a thousand movie theatres, the film could be shown only four times, twice a day on 23 and 24 September 1964, after which the reels had to be returned to Warner Brothers, which destroyed them. NT Live broadcasts are similarly defined. Nicholas Hytner's production of *Julius Caesar* for the Bridge Theatre was screened in the United Kingdom for the first time on 22 March 2018 and in the United States on 15 April 2018. Each encore screening has to be cleared with the distributors. I finally saw an encore screening on 8 November 2018.

And, significantly, ticket prices are set by the distributors too, with a standard pricing structure for all venues. Regular ticket prices at my campus cinema are $7, but operas "Live from the Met" cost $23. Of course a decent ticket at the Met is much, much more than that, but the price differential between live theatre and these transmissions is much less extreme. There are some good seats at the Royal Shakespeare Theatre (RSC) for under £20, and the Travelex sponsorship at the National Theatre (NT), the most extended and remarkable arts sponsorship in the United Kingdom, means hundreds of seats at £15 each night. Except that I'm in the wrong country.

That the pricing is a statement matters, a reminder that culture is expensive; that the Met operates at a loss; that UK government subsidies are crucial for the RSC and NT; that the Globe, operating without such subsidies, is an exception in UK theatre; that $23 is affordable by academics and many in our local community; that Shakespeare may be our icon of culture but that the productions are not therefore cheap to mount; and, not least, that finding a major and ongoing income stream through these broadcasts is a sign of innovation in financial modelling. As Sullivan shows, between October and December 2015, the *Hamlet* starring Benedict Cumberbatch, discussed in the previous chapter, brought in £2.82m in ticket sales, considerably more than Jed Kurzel's film of *Macbeth*, starring Michael Fassbender and Marion Cotillard, released in the same month (2017, 628). Production costs for the *Hamlet* are not easily available but are unlikely to be anywhere approaching the $20 million the film cost to make.

V

Has the show started yet?

Yes, but the problem of analysis and the determinants of the pleasures of performance pose their own scholarly paradox. Much as I would like to write about an NT Live broadcast, my note-taking in the dark is not as good as it used to be, my memory not as retentive, and my reluctance to spoil the immediacy of reception by scribbling ever-increasing. As I have argued elsewhere, there is a paradox in film studies: the more the advances in the technology of film availability make possible close analysis of the object, the less willing film studies has been to undertake such work (Holland 2018). Yet, in Shakespeare studies, our approach to these broadcasts has been dominated, to an extent unprecedented in the study of Shakespeare on film, by a concern over camera work, shot-choice, camera location, editing, and the other aspects of the work of the screen producer, so often the apparently indefatigable Robin Lough.[4] In part this may be, I suspect, the consequence of our growing up with the discipline of close reading as an essential part of our intellectual and scholarly formation. But, to a larger extent, it seems to me to be the consequence of an awareness that the theatre performances, the director's approach, the set design, the materials of concept and production that are so dominant in our analysis of Shakespeare in theatre performance, are all no longer significant. Others, who see the theatre performances, will review and analyze those things; those writing about the broadcasts are not concerned to say anything that would be part of that reviewing/analytic practice. Instead, therefore, we have a self-conscious concentration on the filming processes, of what is seen and heard and how that manifests the transitions from one form of liveness to its remediation, to a degree that we have never previously concerned ourselves with.

There has been, as a result, an exhilaration in the writing about the filming, the excitement of a new kind of writing about Shakespeare performance that, at the very least, has never been so pronounced before. In work by Stone (2016), Sullivan (2017), Friedman (2016), the reviewers in a *Shakespeare Bulletin* gathering (Greenhalgh et al. 2014), and numerous other pieces, including Jones's chapter in this volume, what the screen director makes the cameras do and how the output is edited is excitingly and immediately present. A few years ago, none of us had the slightest interest in the potential of the TowerCam or the Moviebird 44. Now we have become experts. So, when I move now to analyze two versions of *The Merchant of Venice*, I need to attend closely to such details. I have therefore chosen to concentrate on two performances that have been released on DVD. I did not choose a play with productions that include NT Live whose distribution never moves from cinema to DVD and hence directly into my study.

Polly Findlay's *Merchant* opened in the Royal Shakespeare Theatre in May 2015 and was recorded for the "Live from Stratford-upon-Avon" series on 22 July 2015. Jonathan Munby's *Merchant* opened at Shakespeare's Globe in April 2015 and was recorded for "Globe on Screen" on 26 and 29 May 2015. The former is a single night's work, the latter a splicing together of two separate takes. Is it just the risk of such intrusions as low-flying helicopters at the Globe that has led to this normative practice for them of creating an edited version of two performances for transmission to cinemas as the "Globe on Screen"? Certainly I am unable to separate out which sequences come from which performance, though I have yet to try minutely examining the spectators standing in the yard, the group of playgoers most often visible in the DVD, to see whether I can detect individuals present in one and not the other, thereby giving me a chance of unsplicing at least parts of the performances.

It was not only that the two productions are easily accessible (as NT Live cinemacasts are not) that led to my choice, nor that they represent two different spaces whose effects on the work of filming are decisively different, nor that both were directed for the screen by the same person, the ubiquitous Robin Lough. It was also that neither production is especially good. The performance of Jonathan Pryce as Shylock apart, there is no particularly strong performance in the Globe's cast, and the directing is rather lacklustre. It is clear to me, for instance, that Munby has little idea what to make of the Antonio-Bassanio relationship, hinting rather coyly at homoerotic desire but unwilling to decide how much that might mean to either man. This is unquestionably a Shylock-centred version, likely to be best remembered for the elaborate staging at the performance's end of Shylock's baptism, an unscripted moment that here, with music and processions and Shylock's cries, leaves the insecure world of Belmont and therefore Shakespeare's ending far behind.

The RSC version fell under the shadow of Rupert Goold's glitzy 2011 RSC production, set in Las Vegas with the casket scenes as a game show, Launcelot Gobbo played by an Elvis impersonator and Patrick Stewart returning to Shylock, a role he had played for John Barton at the RSC in 1978. Goold had remounted the show in 2014 when he took over as artistic director of the Almeida Theatre. Like it or loathe it, Goold's *Merchant* had a verve that Findlay's did not.

DVD packaging is always chosen to reflect a marketing view – though not necessarily the director's view – of the production. No surprise, then, that Pryce is the cover image for the Globe's version, looking serious but not villainous, and with a quotation from the *Time Out* review ("Jonathan Pryce is electrifyingly good") just beside his head. Pryce's renaissance costume contrasts with the RSC's Shylock, dressed in modern dark suit and open-necked white shirt, with a yarmulke on his head as he grins at the knife he is holding (plainly from the Trial Scene). If the celebrity casting of Pryce is foregrounded on the one, the casting of a Palestinian-Israeli actor, Makram J. Khoury, was a key choice at the RSC. Little known in the United Kingdom, Khoury was significant, not least in press coverage (for example, Singh 2015), for his racial identity: an Arab playing the Jew. This Shylock is on the back cover of the DVD. The front of the RSC's DVD has Portia in red dress, leaning in shadows against the gold reflective wall that would prove to be the back wall of the set.

These two images of the production contrast sharply with the RSC production's own view of its emphases, for it was centred on Antonio, seen alone on stage at the play's and film's start, standing as close to the centre-point of the stage as can be, turning his opening lines, spoken through barely-held-back tears, as direct address to the audience. The camera work at the opening moves from a five-second wide shot of the whole stage, showing the audience around it, locating swiftly and efficiently the theatre space within which the performance will happen, before cutting sharply to a tight close-up on Antonio's face, then slowly pulling back to show the actors on a bench beside the theatre's old proscenium at audience left, from which Salerio will stand and move rapidly to join Antonio as the scene moves, here, from soliloquy to dialogue. This opening sequence is then echoed in brief at the start of 3.3, the first scene after the intermission: the same shot of the whole stage and much of the audience space, with Antonio alone on stage down-stage audience left, held for a moment before the scene fills and animates.

One of the characteristics of the RSC's DVD series is that, unlike the livecasts, they choose to erase the intermission as much as possible. There is, in effect, no intermission, neither in extent nor by, say, inserting an intertitle reading "Intermission" of the kind used in long feature films. The screen goes to black for a few seconds, and that might help note that this is the performance's divide. But I can only identify where the interval occurred for sure because the director's commentary mentions it, as is also true on, for example, the DVD of Gregory Doran's RSC *King Lear*. In *Merchant*, the shot sequence indicates the echo and hence the rhythm.

At the performance's end, again Antonio is alone on stage. As Gratiano leaves through what has been identified as the entrance to the house, Antonio starts to follow, veers away and slumps onto one of the side benches, outside the playing-area, now clearly having no place to be, no place to go to. The three moments – at beginning, middle, and end – serve to use Antonio's pain, isolation, and (self-)exclusion as the strongest temporal structuring device. The film, at the end, goes straight into the curtain call, the cast running back onto the stage and arranging themselves in fairly random order so that the second call puts Nerissa rather than the Duke in the row at the front edge of the thrust. But both calls put Jamie Ballard (Antonio) at the centre of this front row alongside Patsy Ferran (Portia), with Khoury (Shylock) more modestly placing himself in the second row. The camera work gives different views of the company calls – and there are no solo calls here – but it offers only three close-ups of an individual cast-member, one brief one of Portia as the cast assembles on stage and two much more substantial ones of Shylock, one in each of the two calls. For Lough and his team, this is Shylock's play and the company call has to be edited to show who matters most in the cast in a way that the play's director and cast effectively refute.

The curtain call also serves to reveal something else that the filming has, until then, kept oddly hidden: the source of the performance's music. Music at the RSC has long been live, partly because the negotiations with the Musicians' Union meant that live music was the same cost as pre-recorded, although it also meant that the Shakespeare Memorial Theatre (the theatre's name before the creation of the RSC) for a while in the 1950s experimented with electronic music, often composed by Roberto Gerhard, when "radiophonic music" was a distinctly avant-garde phenomenon. For a long time, especially before the remodelling of the Royal Shakespeare Theatre, the musicians were backstage and invisible. Now they are usually in side-galleries to the stage. In Doran's *King Lear*, there is a shot of the brass players, wearing their headphones, in their performing space as a cutaway during a scene change that created onstage the long table for Lear and his knights in 1.4. Quite why it is better to see the musicians than the scene change is beyond me, but at least it gives us a chance to see those we have been hearing – and, in his director's commentary, Doran notes how welcome that is. What it does not do is fully locate the musicians in relation to the stage space, with the result that, although now known to be live, they are also delocalized.

In Findlay's *Merchant*, transitions between scenes are occasionally punctuated by five choristers, deliberately girls as well as boys, placed right at the top of the vast golden and reflective wall that forms the back wall of the set and that creates an image of the strength of the Venetian state. The choristers, as Findlay (2015) comments, create "the sense of religious structure, of religious institution" so that "those children [are] singing songs that carry the weight of religious authority" that controls the play's world. There is other music as well, but it is not until the curtain call that we are allowed to see what the theatre audience has always found it perfectly easy to see: the four adult singers in the side gallery on audience left and the four instrumentalists on audience right. The end credits roll over a shot of the auditorium as the audience is leaving, accompanied with some diegetic sound (that is, sound in the film that derives from something shown on screen, unlike, say, film music underscoring) of their chattering and seats tipping but overlaid with a music track that, since the musicians are not there any longer, becomes the one and only recorded music track in the production, a sound that is not of the performance but only an underscore for the film's credits. The liveness of the music throughout the performance time in this "live from" broadcast is, then, confused by the reluctance of the camera to find the singers and band members.

It is easy, of course, to dwell on what fails, what is rewritten, what is missed. It seems odd, for instance – given the choice to have Shylock step off the main playing area down to the audience level after he says he'll "stay no longer question" (Shakespeare 2005, 4.1.343) and for him to play everything thereafter down there – that we cannot see his final exit, leaving the frame still facing toward the stage and beginning to turn as he passes out of sight. Audiences are, it seems to me, fixated on Shylock's departure, and we are refused the view. But such strange decisions are part and parcel of a deliberate eschewal of what Sullivan has dubbed "bravura moments," the crane shots and high-angle shots, the self-regarding editing and movement that had been so memorable and effective in the earliest RSC explorations of the genre, like the very first overhead shot that begins *Richard II* (Sullivan 2017, 648–55; Holland 2016). Indeed, so unremarkable is the editing (as well as the shot choices), so carefully concerned not to draw attention to itself, that it seems hardly surprising that the entire director's commentary never once mentions the filmic particularities of what Findlay and her assistant director, Oscar Toeman, are presumably watching on a monitor as they record the commentary conversation.

Part of the reason for refusing to show Shylock's back as he exits is that the Duke has already begun speaking, deliberately cutting across the exit, and the rule under which almost all the editing is done in this filming is that s/he who speaks must be in shot. The result is an almost unremitting focus on the speaking actor shot from the waist up. Inevitably, the cinema audience wants to see the speaker in Shakespeare; it would not be satisfied with a reaction shot that left the character speaking as an off-screen presence. This problematizes the filming of long speeches, but almost any speech longer than a couple of lines here necessitates a continuous focus on the speaker that can be numbingly boring. Theatre audiences can choose to look away; cinema audiences are assumed to prefer that the camera does not look away. Theatre does not make conventional shot-and-reverse filming of dialogue possible or desirable, but what the livecasts' technique tends to replace it with, as here, is not an engaging alternative.

Filming in Shakespeare's Globe presents different problems. The openness of the space has produced a method of filming using cameras in the first gallery, just above the heads of those standing in the yard. The film of Munby's *Merchant* opens on the pre-show music, with a packed stage of masked dancers and musicians already in action. It is some minutes before the first line of dialogue, and, till then, the emphasis on energy, fun, a song in Italian, raucous music, much whooping and hollering, by-play among the cast, and then a playlet of Cupid and his arrows, all suggesting Venetian carnival, encourages us to become familiar with the space, especially when (at 2:35 but not motivated by anything we are seeing) we are switched to a camera in the second gallery, giving us a wide-shot of the full theatre so that we can see the hundreds of standers and the sky above. Just in case we have not got the message about the nature of the society in which the play will take place, two elderly Jews are kicked and spat on by the revellers. Only after four minutes does the stage clear and Antonio and the "Salads" begin 1.1. If we have been watching closely enough, we will recognize Antonio as the man picked up by the camera earlier as he removes his mask, sighs, and makes his sad, non-revelling way over the stage. None of this is exactly subtle, either as theatre direction or as filmmaking.

As Erin Sullivan comments on the Globe filming of the *Henry IV*s, the team had adopted "a filming style that's not dissimilar to the theatre's typical approach to playing: clear, measured, technically spare, simple but hopefully not simplistic" (2017, 641). Yet, two further characteristics are also dominant. The first is the heavy emphasis on a range of wide shots of the full width of the stage structure, making the nature of that performing space repeatedly and emphatically visible in ways that are never as true of RSC or NT Live filming. That also involves shots across the yard, showing and sharing the crowd of spectators, the visible presence of the community of audience that, while occasionally present in the other filming spaces, is never as central to playgoing as it is in the Globe. The result is that, from time to time, we are able to see the camera and camera operator placed on the other side of the yard, making process visible in a way rigorously avoided elsewhere. But the nature of the shot also produces a flexibility that the RSC *Merchant* does not have. A wider range of shots is available, since the wide shot is so frequently used, allowing reactions to be seen, because the speaker does not have to be the sole focus of the camera's attention. The sense of watching with the audience is also markedly stronger, given the frequency with which those in the yard are in shot and the number of entrances and exits through the yard that the cast use. Community and place combine effectively to make the show one shared, not simply observed, supported by the loud laughter that is so strong a feature of Globe audiences' response – by contrast, the Stratford-upon-Avon audience is noticeably quiet.

The second is the problem of voice. Of course actors at the Royal Shakespeare Theatre are projecting into a large auditorium, but that never involves the volume that is necessary at the Globe (hence the experiment with the actors wearing microphones to amplify their voices during the 2016 and 2017 seasons).[5] The result can make the viewer of the filmed event hear the actors as shouting, creating a disjunction between voices and their spatial relationship to the other characters to whom they are speaking. The nature of the combination of voice and space marks out the there of the performance, not the here of the film's streaming. It points to my absence, my distance, my separation.

VI

The phenomenon of livecasts leaves the film's spectators unsure how to respond. As we watch the audiences applauding – and, at the Globe, cheering – we want to join them, to do something that our spectatorial acts for film usually inhibit us from doing. We don't applaud the movie but we want to applaud the theatre performance. When I watch the Metropolitan Opera broadcasts, I and my co-viewers applaud at the end of an aria, as we would were we there, as we hear/see those spectators doing. We would like to be part of that sound reaching the performers, to join the immediacy of liveness, and yet we cannot. We know, even when the now of the performance and the now of the watching coincide, that our sound cannot travel, that the applause is a sign not of connection but of separation. And in that awareness we leave the cinema frustrated, incomplete, aware that the experience is partial, that it is always marked by the different directions of departure. As, at the end of F1's text of *Love's Labour's Lost*, Armado might be telling us (or perhaps only others in the play's fiction), "You that way, we this way" (Shakespeare 2005, 5.2.914). I might have liked to have persuaded myself I was at the Globe or the Royal Shakespeare Theatre or the National, but I leave back into South Bend, Indiana.

NOTES

1 The quotation stitches together Bernheimer's quotations from an eyewitness and a later commentator as well as his own summary.

2 It is probably the case that the influence of the excellent collection of essays on the phenomenon edited by Aebischer, Greenhalgh, and Osborne (2018) will result in our settling on the term "'live' theatre broadcast" for these screenings. I am not yet quite prepared to abandon the options of playing with the terms that have constituted other possibilities, such as livecast, live froms, simulcast, alternative content, cinecast, cinemacast, streamed transmission, outside broadcast, digital broadcast cinema, captured live broadcast, event cinema, theatrofilm. My campus cinema is wedded to calling them "captured live broadcasts" and is not going to change simply because academic discourse has settled on a different term.

3 See http://cobj.co.uk/client/emma-freud.

4 Rachael Nicholas (2018) records Lough's having directed thirty screen productions of Shakespeare between 2009 and 2017.

5 Actors in broadcasts from the National Theatre also wear microphones, often awkwardly visible when the costume or wig will not adequately conceal them, but these are for sound recording for the broadcast, not a permanent feature of the production.

REFERENCES

Aebischer, Pascale, Susanne Greenhalgh, and Laurie E. Osborne, eds. 2018. *Shakespeare and the "Live" Theatre Broadcast Experience*. London: Arden Shakespeare.

Bernheimer, Richard. 1956. "Theatrum Mundi." *Art Bulletin* 38 (4): 225–47.

Doran, Gregory. 2017. "Director's Commentary." *King Lear*. RSCLive. DVD.

Findlay, Polly. 2015. "Director's Commentary." *The Merchant of Venice*. RSCLive. DVD.

Friedman, Michael D. 2016. "The Shakespeare Cinemacast: *Coriolanus*." *Shakespeare Quarterly* 67 (4): 457–80.

Gilbey, Ryan. 2014. "Coriolanus at National Theatre Live: Cut the Chat and Get On with the Show." Review of *Coriolanus*, NTLive. *Guardian Online*, 31 January. https://www.theguardian.com/stage/2014/jan/31/coriolanus-national-theatre-live.

Greenhalgh, Susanne et al. 2014. "Live Cinema Relays of Shakespearean Performance." *Shakespeare Bulletin* 32 (2): 255–78.

Holland, Peter. 2016. "*Richard II* on Screens." In *The Text, the Play, and the Globe*, edited by Joseph A. Candido, 155–72. Lanham, MD: Fairleigh Dickinson University Press.

– 2018. "Shakespeare on Screens: Close Watching, Close Listening." *Shakespeare Survey* 71: 186–93.

Johnson, Samuel. 1916. *Johnson on Shakespeare*. Edited by Walter Raleigh. Oxford: Oxford University Press.

Kauffmann, Stanley. 1972. "Notes on Theater-and-Film." *Performance* 1 (4): 104–9.

Nicholas, Rachael. 2018. "Appendix: Digital Theatre Broadcasts of Shakespeare, 2003–2017." In Aebischer, Greenhalgh, and Osborne, 227–42.

Shakespeare, William. 2005. *The Complete Works*. 2nd ed. Edited by John Jowett, William Montgomery, Gary Taylor, and Stanley Wells. Oxford Shakespeare. Oxford: Clarendon Press.

Singh, Anita. 2015. "RSC Casts Palestinian Actor as Shylock in The Merchant of Venice." *Telegraph*, 26 February. http://www.telegraph.co.uk/culture/theatre/theatre-news/11437574/RSC-casts-Palestinian-actor-as-Shylock-in-The-Merchant-of-Venice.html.

Stern, Tiffany. 2015. "Before the Beginning, After the End: When Did Plays Start and Stop?" In *Shakespeare and Textual Studies*, edited by Margaret Jane Kidnie and Sonia Massai, 358–74. Cambridge: Cambridge University Press.

Stone, Alison. 2016. "Not Making a Movie: The Livecasting of Shakespeare Stage Productions by the Royal National Theatre and the Royal Shakespeare Company." *Shakespeare Bulletin* 34 (3): 627–43.

Sullivan, Erin. 2017. "'The Forms of Things Unknown': Shakespeare and the Rise of the Live Broadcast." *Shakespeare Bulletin* 35 (4): 627–62.

13

SHAKESPEARE ADAPTATION IN THE AGE OF THE CAMERA PHONE

Spectacle and Experimental Seeing in Ralph Fiennes's Coriolanus

HAYLEY O'MALLEY

In our hyper-mediated and increasingly networked twenty-first century, new visual technologies – especially the ubiquitous camera phone – capture and circulate images with unprecedented ease and speed. This moment of media change has inaugurated new forms of state power, but it has also opened up new opportunities for art-making and socio-political critique. Perhaps surprisingly, since it adapts a Renaissance play about Republican Rome, Ralph Fiennes's 2011 film *Coriolanus* offers a particularly compelling case study for the ways today's media technologies shape the aesthetic and political ambitions of twenty-first-century film and art-making more broadly.[1] In this chapter, I focus on *Coriolanus* to ask, what effects do visual images have in our ever-shifting and over-saturated mediascape? And how can a play-text penned over four hundred years ago help us develop and practise forms of media literacy appropriate for the twenty-first century?

Fiennes's *Coriolanus* anachronistically weaves today's media technologies into its plot and, in doing so, reveals how visual technologies shape contemporary Shakespeare film adaptation. Media technologies within the *mise en scène* of *Coriolanus* mark the modernity of the setting – "a place calling itself Rome," in a nod to John Osborne's 1973 version – updating it to look like our world.[2] But they also signal Fiennes's own reliance on such technologies as he adapts the aesthetics of early modern drama for digital film. I argue that Fiennes experiments with a handheld-camera aesthetic and digitally curates found documentary footage in a way that ultimately produces an intimate engagement with current political crises and opens up the possibility for a feminist counter-narrative actualized in images, rather than in Shakespeare's words. Fiennes's film also, I argue, showcases how Shakespeare's plays, particularly in their metatheatrical energies and complex representations of politics, offer an ideal resource for generating audience self-reflection about the ways we read and respond to media images in the twenty-first century.

I focus my close readings on one particularly rich site of convergence between aesthetic experimentalism and timely political critique: the film's sustained attention to boyhood. By mapping this thematic interest, one that intensifies a set of allusions already present in the play-text, I suggest that, as presented in Fiennes's film, the spectacle of children and speculation about their points of view can inspire audiences to embrace more self-conscious modes of seeing the world – the always already mediated world – of the twenty-first century.[3]

One of Shakespeare's less-read plays, *Coriolanus* tells the story of the Roman general Caius Martius, later dubbed Coriolanus, whose relish for combat makes him fearless and fearsome on the battlefield but ill-suited to play the public relations game required for success in government. Ostensibly set during the early Roman Republic, the play raises difficult questions about political options and ethics in times of crisis (the play begins during a famine). Those questions would have resonated with Globe groundlings – who likely remembered the grain shortage that led to the 1607 Midland Revolt – just as they did for theater-goers in the 1930s who watched the play and thought of fascism. Yet Shakespeare raises such questions through a play seemingly uninterested in deep interiority – Coriolanus rarely soliloquizes, and then only briefly – and with a protagonist who is flatly unlikeable, without any of Richard III's Machiavellian charisma or Macbeth's tragic oscillation between maniac and man. Having directed and acted in the play, Fiennes was well positioned to claim, "*Coriolanus* is a terrifying play," but he would quickly add, "though I've always found the part of Coriolanus himself to be curiously addictive" (Carson 2013, 220).

Fiennes's *Coriolanus* is the first film adaption of the play, and it seems to have been a labour of love: Fiennes not only made his directorial debut, but he also played the title role, co-wrote the screenplay, helped edit, and was one of the producers.[4] That amount of involvement – especially in a film with a budget under $8 million – also gave him a degree of auteurist control and the licence to experiment aesthetically, something he perhaps craved after playing Lord Voldemort in the big-budget *Harry Potter* movies. Forced to fundraise like any independent filmmaker, but freed from at least some of the creative constraints imposed by studio conglomerates, Fiennes could rely on advances in digital technologies to produce high-quality war footage – without breaking the bank – that he could then splice with found footage of conflict available in the public domain. And while the war scenes are grittily realistic – cinematographer Barry Ackroyd also worked on *The Hurt Locker* – Fiennes finds space, even within a taut two-hour running time, to offer a series of non-combat, "silent" vignettes that similarly rely on images, rather than Shakespearean dialogue, to tell a story. These vignettes allow Fiennes not to stray from Shakespeare's original language, even if he sometimes rearranges it to new effect, as in a prisoner interrogation scene, which ends with the prisoner's death.[5] At the same time, the vignettes also enable Fiennes to rely on the power of his camera to produce complex characterizations for characters relegated to very minor speaking roles – especially Martius's wife, Virgilia, and his son, Young Martius.

But turning to independent film did not, apparently, free Fiennes from his association with the *Harry Potter* films.[6] A week before filming for *Coriolanus* began in Belgrade, Fiennes told reporters that he had difficulty casting children: apparently, some were skittish around the man they knew as Lord Voldemort. Perhaps this explains the surprising lack of youths in the film's opening scenes of protest. The initial absence of children's bodies, however, highlights the affective potency of childhood when it does appear in the film.

While recent Shakespeare films like Richard Loncraine's *Richard III* and especially Julie Taymor's *Titus* have foregrounded children before the opening credits even conclude, Fiennes opens with a man sharpening a knife in a dark room, followed by a montage of social unrest. Shakespearean dialogue then begins when a group of plebeians, crammed into an apartment, resolve to protest the Roman government "in hunger for bread, not in thirst for revenge."

Figure 13.1 | Caius Martius (Ralph Fiennes) confronts the angry crowd.

According to the shooting script, they "are not wild-eyed radicals. They are normal people, from all walks of life. You and me" (Logan and Fiennes 2012, 3). They are also conspicuously adult.

From the apartment, the film cuts to an overhead shot of plebeian protesters marching. A few wear backpacks; they could be university students. But when the film switches to a hand-held aesthetic, and the camera shoots from within the crowd, frontal shots tend to frame middle-aged participants as a graying leader begins to chant, "Bread, bread, bread." Inspired, the crowd soon breaks through the gate of a Roman grain-storage compound, but police in riot gear are waiting, and we watch them brutalize the protestors' unprotected bodies. The camera work matches the scene's chaos: with footage chillingly reminiscent of numerous contemporary confrontations, the docudrama aesthetic intensifies the scene's emotional power.[7]

Into this fray strides Martius, and the horror at all-too-familiar police brutality metamorphoses with unsettling rapidity into enthrallment with his ability to dominate the plebeians. There is something exhilarating in the way Fiennes faces the crowd – alone, wearing only fatigues – exuding Terminator-like confidence (figure 13.1). He treats the adult crowd like a group of too-needy children, contemptuously calls them "fragments," and within moments, drains the group's energy. But I wonder whether I would be so captivated by Martius's power if bloodied youths lay on the pavement.

Social movement protest is often embodied by youths, if not necessarily children. Not only does Fiennes's adult-heavy casting not comport with that received image, but this lack of youth protestors also allows us, I think, to sympathize – perhaps counter-intuitively – with state power. And yet, such identification seems paradoxically to be part of a broader ethical project, for again and again, the film leads audiences to reflect on what types of mediated violence move us emotionally.

The film's childless protest scenes remind us that, in modern visual culture, over-saturated with violent images, a child in pain still registers as the suffering of an innocent and produces an affective shock that is difficult to dismiss. Remember Nick Ut's Vietnam War photograph of the "Napalm Girl" or the iconic images of the Soweto schoolchildren protest in South Africa. Think of Kevin Carter's more recent photograph of a vulture stalking a starving South Sudanese girl. These photographs produced "real world" effects – galvanizing anti-war protests, alerting the world to the abuses of apartheid. Performing what Judith Butler terms "ethical solicitation," such photographs suggest how hard it is for spectators to remain comfortably agnostic facing images of children.

The absence of children's bodies from *Coriolanus*'s protest scenes means that this point about children is always implicit at best. Yet, the *mise-en-abîme* intensity of camera phones held by protestors dotting the *mise en scène* foregrounds the self-referentiality of Fiennes's film and, in so doing, pushes audiences to consider how we react to similar phone-captured footage from contemporary "real life." I would venture that, for spectators of all ages, the images that come to mind will include youthful faces.

Let me now turn to two boys in Fiennes's *Coriolanus*. One is dead and the other is nameless. Neither appears in Shakespeare's play, and their combined screen time amounts to about thirty seconds. But their brief appearances urge audiences to consider the ethical effects of children in visual culture.

If Martius is "chief enemy of the people," as the plebeians claim (Shakespeare 1999, 1.1.7–8), he is also chief defender of the state, squaring off in the city of Corioles with the Volscian militia led by Gerard Butler's Aufidius.[8] In Corioles, Aufidius encounters the dead body of a small boy. The aesthetics of this scene and Butler's performance present the child as the quintessential icon of innocence, while also inviting us to interrogate such framing of children.

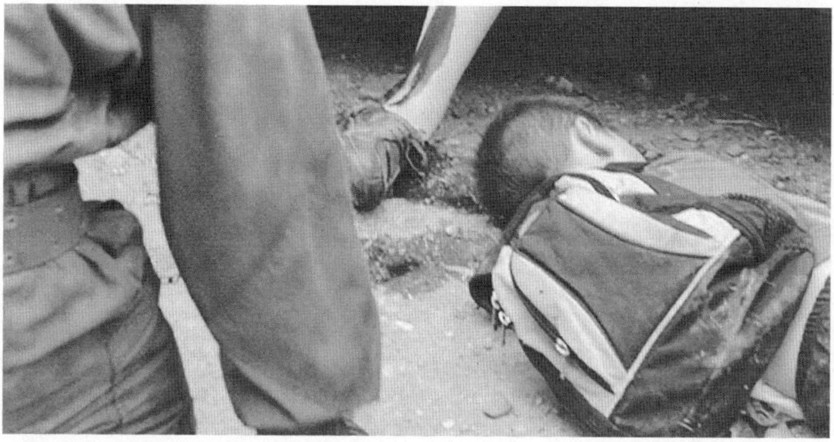

Figure 13.2 | The dead boy.

On one hand, the scene's aesthetics emotionally bind us to Butler's Aufidius. The camera follows closely behind him as he half jogs, half stumbles down the street: we spot the dead boy at almost the same time as he does. The boy lies face-down – his backpack still on – sprawled in the dirt just outside a mini-van (figure 13.2). The camera mimics Aufidius's glance as he surveys this gruesome tableau of civilian death: a woman grotesquely slumped in the backseat footspace; a man uncannily upright in the driver's seat. Aufidius sinks to his knees beside the boy, and, face anguished, rakes the dirt with his hand. For a few moments, his ragged breathing is the only commentary, leaving us to ask: was the boy gunned down as he raced toward his parents? Did he die having first witnessed their murder? What could possibly be the point of such killing? When Aufidius begins to speak, we are primed to share his emotion, his outrage.

But not long into Butler's scripted speech, the vignette starts to feel staged. He does not eulogize the boy. How could he? A dead boy is not in Shakespeare's play. Instead, Aufidius talks of Martius. The dead boy's body thereby becomes – merely? – justification for a continued fight against the Romans. We might wonder: how many times is the slaughter of innocents, especially children, used as justification for revenge? How many times would that revenge have been taken anyway? And how many films employ this trope of anguished father – or paterfamilias, as is the case here – goaded into violence by a child's death? Rather than continue to imagine the world of this particular Corioles child, we perhaps remember Russell Crowe in *Gladiator* or Mel Gibson in *The Patriot*.

Oscillating between total immersion in the filmic world and metacinematic alienation might, however, amount to an ethics of looking. The scene proper begins with a frontal view of Aufidius, who gazes straight ahead with glazed eyes. An overturned car, still smoking, and the body of a dead man lying nearby fail to garner his attention. Although we learn later that the Romans won this battle, Aufidius's demeanour does not code harried retreat but rather purposeful movement. The film cuts, the camera adopts its position just behind Aufidius, and, as a van comes into view, Aufidius slows to a walk. Is this his final destination? What does it hold that is so important? Butler, of course, has plenty of motivation to stop. But Aufidius? He, perhaps, has less. It is tempting to conclude that Gerard Butler is simply out of his depth with Shakespeare. But I actually think he is – intentionally or not – brilliant, and rather Brechtian, for his performance allows us to recognize the virtues of both surrendering to the affective impact of innocence and being sceptical of its potentially staged nature. Moreover, by completely ignoring the dead man's body, Butler showcases children's affective power: the boy's body stops him in his tracks – suggesting an affective hierarchy of war dead. Just as Gerard Butler ignores the man's body for the boy's, so too, according to Judith Butler, the mainstream news media tends to frame some lives as meaningful and grievable, while positioning others as dispensable.

The second boy appears in a later scene. Martius's victory in Corioles leads to his appointment as consul and the honorific title "Coriolanus," but his continued clashes with the plebeians ultimately result in his banishment from Rome. During a scene of his exile – with a full beard and long hair making him look more like Jesus than Voldemort – Martius appears profoundly affected by a nameless boy on horseback. I am not going to give a full reading of this scene, but I want to offer two reasons why it matters.

The intensity of Martius's gaze at the boy combines with shot framing and editing to endow Martius with an interiority that is rare in his characterization. Shakespeare's *Coriolanus*, as noted earlier, contains no significant soliloquies, and Fiennes builds on that in much of the film by presenting Martius as more machine than man. This particular sequence, however, raises numerous questions about Martius's psychology, hinting at a character complexity that we associate with Shakespeare's high tragedies and perhaps making us yearn for a more intimate glimpse into his consciousness via a Hamletian soliloquy.

But maybe Fiennes has already given us such access. The silent interaction between Martius and this boy joins a number of other interpolated non-speaking scenes to argue – despite Fiennes having cut the famed "allegory of the belly speech" – for the body's ability to speak.[9] The message of these silent scenes is not always clear, but such ambiguity is often the logic of soliloquies. Conspicuously cinematic, these scenes also constitute, for me, the most emotionally affecting moments of the adaptation – including the opening scene of Aufidius slowly sharpening a knife in the darkened room, illuminated only by the glow of a television screen; the violent eroticism of head-shaving ceremonies; and Jessica Chastain's Virgilia tiptoeing through her own home. By foregrounding body language along with filmic grammar, these non-dialogue scenes expand the agential possibilities of characters and bodies typically marginalized by their exclusion from verbal speech.

The sequence with the boy on horseback reveals Martius's human complexity, but when it comes to warfare, his desires are unambiguous. In Corioles, he ends a pump-up speech to his troops by roaring, "Make you a sword of me." As he charges back into combat, he is an Achilles of the digital age – a bellowing war machine out of the *Call of Duty* videogames, if not a CIA-programmed cyborg warrior. His son's relationship to violence is much more complicated, so I want to turn to this third boy, Young Martius, not only to continue thinking about silence and interiority, but also to consider how his ambivalence about violence speaks to twenty-first-century audiences confronted with a seemingly never-ending war on terror.

Poised on the threshold of adulthood, Young Martius, played by Harry Fenn, bridges the violence of distant wars and the so-called civility of the Roman home. He enters the film when Fiennes interrupts a scene of gritty combat in Corioles – a bus explosion has just slammed a squad of soldiers to the ground – by cutting to a shot of Young Martius aiming a gun at tin cans in his family's garden (figure 13.3). Lush and verdant, the garden is nevertheless precisely manicured, so, especially as captured in a symmetrically framed shot,

Figure 13.3 | Young Martius in the garden.

the effect is one of intense precision and control. In the background stands the family's Palladian villa, and on the balcony – like a ship's figurehead – Virgilia watches over her son. Young Martius is caught in-between: he stands within the sphere of feminine space even as he performs and invokes masculinized violence.

In this garden, the film begins to query whether innocence and violence can co-exist within the liminal space of boyhood. Young Martius is sheltered: supervised by his mother and enclosed by implicit villa walls, he is the image of upper-class childhood. But the deliberateness with which he takes each shot – a pacing that the camera mimics with longer takes and tripod-based stillness – is not only a world apart from Corioles but also seems the antithesis of the exuberant, fall-down-and-scrape-your-knee freedom of idealized childhood. If this is play, it does not look very fun. And yet, the seriousness with which young Martius approaches his task does not code serial-killer-in-training: there is nothing malicious in his demeanour. In fact, we might see him as something of a pacifist, confining his efforts to tin cans, rather than shooting squirrels. In that vein, his slowness could code reticence: a boy forced to complete a chore. When compared to the rigid conceptions of war held by adult characters, the range of possibilities for Young Martius's relationship to violence is refreshing in its realistic relationship to our present moment. In the post-9/11 world, pacifism that categorically opposes all war seems especially and naively utopian. At the same time, even the more hawkish must recognize the need for limits on violence in an era of chemical warfare and ever-proliferating drones. In this context, the complexity of Young Martius's response to violence helps index contemporary ambivalence about war.

The ambiguity of Young Martius's emotions also combines with the allure of childhood to foreground both the limits on our ability to know one another and how surprising and affecting that interpersonal ignorance continues to be. Young Martius's opacity is arguably more affecting than an adult version would be because of expectations audiences typically bring to bear on images of children. For while Tim Morris rightly frames childhood as "a form of Otherness, possibly its archetypal form" (2000, 9), adult spectators, having all been children once, are more likely to treat childhood as an Otherness penetrable by personal, lived experience. Images of childhood can thus garner our attention in their tantalizing comprehensibility, but, as we see more of Young Martius, we come to realize that our knowledge of him – like that of the "minor" and "major" characters in our own lives – is necessarily incomplete.

In the garden mini-scene, film aesthetics suture or bind us to Virgilia's perspective, but she too seems able only to guess at her son's state of mind. At the scene's end, we glimpse Young Martius as he looks back at his mother, and his brief expression raises a host of questions. Did he know that she was watching? Was he trying to impress her? Does he realize the intensity of her aversion to violence? From Virgilia's own enigmatic smile, it is impossible to tell whether she is congratulating or criticizing her son before she turns and retreats into the home. Later, in arguably the most affecting scene of the film, we see Virgilia's love for her son in explicit tension with the militaristic ambitions of Martius and his mother, Volumnia, the family she has married into. Virgilia silently enters her son's bedroom, cleans up war toys scattered on the floor, and then ever so lightly kisses his sleeping form. She dares not wake him, and she seems – dressed all in white – a ghostly mother. Only partially accessible even upon a mother's touch, Young Martius helps mark the powerlessness of Virgilia in a home alternately dominated by Martius and Volumnia, but the affecting power of this distance between mother and child also hints at the possibility of an everyday ethics: a recognition of the impossibility – even, and maybe especially, in surveillance societies – of assuming complete knowledge of each other.

By increasing the visibility of characters such as Young Martius and the only slightly more vocal Virgilia, but not providing them with additional dialogue, Fiennes does risk intensifying their marginalization by heightening their silences. Especially in Virgilia's case, spectators may grow impatient with her muteness: she has ample opportunity to speak; why doesn't she? Her silence can seem to result from individual choice, rather than a systemic problem, for Vanessa Redgrave's Volumnia has no qualms about asserting her opinions, and indeed her loquacity at the film's end saves the Roman state even if it also dooms her son. And yet the film's validation of silence through its numerous non-dialogue scenes gives both Virgilia and Young Martius the opportunity to express themselves – not by singing, which Volumnia at one point suggests Virgilia take up – but through a variety of non-verbal actions.

Silence has, of course, long been present in Shakespeare's plays – often courtesy of dumb shows like in *Hamlet* – as well as in cinematic adaptations: we might remember the plethora of Shakespeare adaptations during the silent film era or the way in which Akira Kurosawa's *Throne of Blood* (1961) and Grigory Kozintsev's *Korol Lir* (1971) let the camera soak up the landscape and argue visually for the absolute appropriateness of transposing Shakespearean drama into a new cultural setting. If Fiennes's turn to silence invokes a long film history, such a backward look is consistent with other recent Shakespeare film adaptations, namely Julie Taymor's reanimation of eighties camp in *Titus* (2000) and Joss Whedon's nostalgia for 1930s screwball comedy and Hollywood noir in *Much Ado About Nothing* (2013). All three of these films use silence as a tool for carving out space for contemporary concerns. In an admittedly risk-filled move, they rely on silence to propose an alternative for some of the most horrifically silenced Shakespearean women – Lavinia, Hero, Virgilia – as they pause the dialogue and create space for something like female agency. Over a century after early cinema's silent Shakespeare adaptations, these three films demonstrate how contemporary film can allow the bodies of children and women in particular to speak and be heard, and in doing so envision a genre of twenty-first-century Shakespeare film adaptation that uses the past to animate the present for the purpose of political critique and so to imagine a better future.

NOTES

1 For this line of inquiry and much else in this essay, I am indebted to and grateful for the scholarship, teaching, and mentorship of Katherine Rowe, Kimberly Benston, Robert Watson, Lars Engle, Sara Blair, and Jonathan Freedman. I also wish to thank Andrew Lanham. For particularly incisive readings of Shakespeare and modern media, see Cartelli and Rowe (2007); Burt (2002); and Starks and Lehmann (2002).

2 Žižek, for instance, lauds Fiennes for transforming Coriolanus into a figure of the radical Left, and argues, "Fiennes's *Coriolanus* is effectively like the saint's eye in an Orthodox icon: it looks specifically at us, at our predicament today, outlining the unique figure of a radical freedom fighter" (2012, xxix). Pittman, however, reveals the ethical problems of Fiennes's reliance on the Yugoslav Wars as updated context, showing how the film "accesses a fleet of Balkan stereotypes" and "unleashes unintended interpretive implications – that only in the Balkans can a suitable contemporary parallel be found to the self-destructive ethos of Coriolanus's martial masculinity. Thus the ailing post-imperialists of Great Britain or the United States need not apply the drama's searing, deconstructive lessons to themselves" (2015, 232).

3 For additional reading on Shakespeare and childhood, see Rutter (2007); Chedgzoy, Greenhalgh, and Shaughnessy (2007). Fiennes himself has compared Coriolanus to "a boy lost in a tunnel" and noted how, at the film's end, audiences should see that "he's a boy inside" (Carson 2013, 221).

4 Fiennes's post-production work importantly shaped the film: "When I began working on the film, I didn't want Coriolanus to be so hard, aloof, and arrogant that there's no way in. But when I was editing the film, I found that you can't make him someone easy to empathize with. It actually weakens him as a character. He is what he is" (Carson 2013, 225).

5 Friedman (2015) also discusses how Fiennes uses interpolated "silent" vignettes to expand the roles of secondary characters, although he ascribes less ambiguity to the characterizations of Virgilia and Young Martius than I do.

6 See Pittman (2015) for an extended discussion of how the "ghosting" of past roles played by the film's celebrity cast increases the ideological complexity of the film, especially around questions of masculine identity.

7 Comparing the telecast version of the Donmar Warehouse *Coriolanus* production and Fiennes's film, Friedman (2016) also emphasizes the emotional power of Fiennes's handheld aesthetic. But for Friedman, that aesthetic produces an uncomplicated allegiance between audiences and the plebeians.

8 The homoerotic relationship between Coriolanus and Aufidius has been the focus of several critical accounts of the film. See Garrison (2014) and Friedman (2015), in particular.

9 Fiennes viewed film as allowing different access to Coriolanus's character, claiming, "you can get closer to Coriolanus on film than you can on the stage" (Carson 2013, 221).

REFERENCES

Burt, Richard, ed. 2002. *Shakespeare after Mass Media*. New York: Palgrave.

Butler, Judith. 2009. *Frames of War: When Is Life Grievable?* London: Verso.

Carson, Susannah, ed. 2013. *Living with Shakespeare: Essays by Writers, Actors, and Directors*. New York: Vintage.

Cartelli, Thomas, and Katherine Rowe. 2007. *New Wave Shakespeare on Screen*. Cambridge: Polity.

Chedgzoy, Kate, Susanne Greenhalgh, and Robert Shaughnessy, eds. 2007. *Shakespeare and Childhood*. Cambridge: Cambridge University Press.

Friedman, Michael D. 2015. "The Hurt Roman: Homoeroticism, Intimacy, and Fratriarchy in Ralph Fiennes's *Coriolanus*." *Literature/Film Quarterly* 43 (2): 86–102.

– 2016. "The Shakespeare Cinemacast: *Coriolanus*." *Shakespeare Quarterly* 67 (4): 457–80.

Garrison, John. 2014. "Queer Desire and Self-Erasure in *Coriolanus* (2011)." Literature/Film Quarterly 42 (2): 427–37.

Logan, John, and Ralph Fiennes. 2012. *Coriolanus: The Shooting Script*. New York: New Market.

Morris, Timothy. 2000. *You're Only Young Twice: Children's Literature and Film*. Urbana: University of Illinois Press.

Pittman, Monique L. 2015. "Heroes, Villains, and Balkans: Intertextual Masculinities in Ralph Fiennes's *Coriolanus*." *Shakespeare Bulletin* 33 (2): 215–44.

Rutter, Carol Chillington. 2007. *Shakespeare and Child's Play: Performing Lost Boys on Stage and Screen*. London: Routledge.

Shakespeare, William. 1999. *Coriolanus*. Edited by Jonathan Crewe. New York: Penguin.

Starks, Lisa S., and Courtney Lehmann, eds. 2002. *The Reel Shakespeare: Alternative Cinema and Theory*. Madison, NJ: Fairleigh Dickinson University Press.

Žižek, Slavoj. 2012. Foreword to Sophie Wahnich, *In Defence of the Terror: Liberty or Death in the French Revolution*. London: Verso.

14

THE INDIAN SHAKESPEARE TRILOGY

Maqbool, Omkara, and Haider

AMRITA SEN

The rather well-worn cliché that William Shakespeare is a worldwide phenomenon is borne out not only by the sheer range of textual and stage adaptations of his plays – covering over 100 different languages – but also by his persistent presence in world cinema. As early as 1899, the London studio of British Mutoscope and Biograph Company recorded a scene from Sir Herbert Beerbohm's production of *King John* on 68 mm film. This first entry of Shakespeare into the newly developed world of motion pictures was followed by similar short productions by filmmakers in France, Germany, and the United States. Even outside the Western world, Shakespearean cinematic adaptations had an early start. It was in the silent era itself that some of the earliest movies inspired by the bard appeared in India (*Champraj Hado*, 1923) and China (*The Woman Lawyer*, 1927), the first based on *Cymbeline* and the second on *The Merchant of Venice*. From the very outset, therefore, celluloid Shakespeare was a global phenomenon. The recently popular term *global Shakespeares* is thus more an acknowledgment by film and literature critics of these plural cinematic (and performance) traditions than a sudden manifestation of Shakespeare in world cinema. For instance, what Sonia Massai's *World-Wide Shakespeares: Local Appropriations in Film and Performance* (2005) or the MIT Global Shakespeares online project aim at highlighting are the complex socio-cultural influences that go into the making of regional, particularly non-anglophone, Shakespeares. Such attention to multicultural adaptations of the Bard helps us not only to estimate his relevance worldwide, but also to recognize the complicated histories of Shakespearean transmission through empire and colonialism. This, then, is a new era in Shakespeare studies.

One of the most commonly discussed of these global Shakespeare traditions is Bollywood Shakespeare, so named after the cinema studios in Bombay (present-day Mumbai). The power of Bollywood itself, as Kenneth Rothwell argues, lies in it being part of "the vast Indian film industry, which in North Africa, the Middle and Far East has rivaled Hollywood in productivity and influence" (2004, 160). Moreover, given the colonial education system in the Indian subcontinent and the tastes of its middle class, the Indian film industry has long engaged with Shakespeare. Within the sphere of Bollywood Shakespeares, however, Vishal Bhardwaj's adaptations stand apart as exceptions. In part this is owing to the fact that, unlike other directors of Indian Shakespeares, Bhardwaj returns to the Bard's plays again and again. Bhardwaj started his first Shakespeare adaptation with *Maqbool* (*Macbeth*) in 2003 and followed up with *Omkara* (*Othello*) in 2006 and *Haider* (*Hamlet*) in 2014. While Indian cinema has from its earliest years included Shakespearean adaptations, never before has there been a Bollywood Shakespeare trilogy.[1] It is worth remembering here that, although Bollywood is among the wealthiest and best-known parts of the Indian film industry, it is not the only one. Regional Indian films have their own rich linguistic and cultural traditions and, not surprisingly, have also adapted Shakespeare's plays. For instance, the Bengali movie *Bhranti Bilas* (1963), based on *The Comedy of Errors*, was drawn from the nineteenth-century translation of Shakespeare's text by the noted social reformer Ishwar Chandra Vidyasagar. More recent Bengali appropriations such as *Hrid Majhare* (*Othello*, 2014) and *Arshinagar* (*Romeo and Juliet*, 2015), or even the Malayalam films *Veeram* (*Macbeth*, 2016) and *Kannaki* (*Antony and Cleopatra*, 2001), are suggestive of the continuing appeal of Shakespeare among local filmmakers and audiences. Bhardwaj's films therefore do not stand in isolation, but belong to a larger network of Indian Shakespeares, both regional and Bollywood. Nevertheless, despite involving noted directors and actors, most of these Indian Shakespeares (Bollywood or otherwise) have been solitary productions, with the filmmakers refraining from returning to the Bard. Bhardwaj thus gives us not only the first Bollywood Shakespeare trilogy but also the first Indian Shakespeare trilogy.

Within the larger context of world cinema, it is not unusual to find directors who have engaged with multiple Shakespearean play-texts.

Perhaps the most renowned international filmmaker to have left behind a body of Shakespearean adaptations is Akira Kurosawa. Sometimes criticized in Japan for having "too much Western influence," Kurosawa directed *Throne of Blood* (*Macbeth*, 1957), *The Bad Sleep Well* (*Hamlet*, 1960), and *Ran* (*King Lear*, 1985), helping to establish his reputation globally as "an iconic Japanese filmmaker" (Huang 2009a, 308n). Kurosawa's work represented a "kind of Shakespeare à *la japonaise*," wherein he transposed the plays onto a uniquely Japanese setting (Senda 1998, 22). Likewise, Bhardwaj's films have a distinctly Indian setting – an attribute owing in part to the origins of Bollywood Shakespeare in the Parsi theatre that flourished in Bombay in the late nineteenth and early twentieth centuries.[2] Unlike the older Parsi theatre, however, Bhardwaj's films remain rooted in contemporary India and explore specifically the fraught criminal and terror-ridden undercurrents of the subcontinent. Each film explores a distinct region in India and its unique socio-political context. This multiplicity leaves us with a family of texts that speak to one another, and to Shakespeare, in unique ways.

Not surprisingly, Bhardwaj's trilogy has received a considerable amount of scholarly attention. As the filmmaker has himself commented, "My films on his [Shakespeare's] tragedies have received acclaim; they are part of the curriculum in many universities. Recently, a girl from Lucknow completed her doctorate with my trilogy of tragedies as the subject" (Sundaram 2018). This critical interest has extended to Bhardwaj's individual films as well as to the trilogy as a whole. For instance, Poonam Trivedi (2007) and Douglas Lanier (2007), some of the earliest critics to comment on *Maqbool*, were quick to highlight how the film marked a new phase in Indian adaptations of Shakespeare in terms of its setting and characterization. Alexa Huang's special section, "Asian Shakespeares on Screen: Two Films in Perspective," in *Borrowers and Lenders* (2009b) brought together essays that examined the local as well as the global aspects of *Maqbool*'s significance and reception, juxtaposing it with Feng Xiaogang's *The Banquet* (*Hamlet*, 2006). Similarly, Mike Heidenberg (2014), Brinda Charry and Gitanjali Shahani (2014), and Jyotsna G. Singh and Abdulhamit Arvas (2015) dwell upon *Omkara*'s indebtedness to Shakespeare as well as to Indian and global cinema, bringing out the radical gender politics that mark Bhardwaj's films. *Haider*, the concluding film in Bhardwaj's tragic trilogy, has drawn the most mixed reviews. While

Trivedi (2014) sees it as a "a befitting new step in this long tradition" of indigenous *Hamlet*s on stage and screen, others, such as Paromita Chakravarti (2016) and Mridu Rai (2014), have criticized the film for its handling of the famed interiority of the character of Hamlet on the one hand, and its depiction of Kashmir on the other. Most recently, Amy Rodgers (2016) and Trivedi (2018) have engaged with the trilogy as a whole. Trivedi especially explores the "cultures of violence: urban, rural, and of the state" (23) that run through the trilogy, and the question of justice that the characters, particularly the women, have to face.

This chapter is interested in exploring how the political and the domestic worlds intersect in Bhardwaj's trilogy. Although they are set in different regions, one of the common themes that emerges in Bhardwaj's films is the quest for a home, a quest that is repeatedly threatened by the dystopic political realities of post-independence India. This domestic theme and its disruption become important precisely because Bhardwaj in his trilogy opts for contemporary settings instead of ones in mythical or historical India. Shakespearean tragic heroes are thus recast as ordinary, even at times middle-class, characters. Their primary concern, therefore, is no longer the acquisition or the future of an actual kingdom, although *Haider* comes closest in articulating a desire for political autonomy. Rather, the central characters, especially the women in Bhardwaj's films, all want to build their own homes, a domestic space that they imagine as their own and filled with their loved ones. In each instance, the domestic drama drives the plot forward, and the personal needs of the characters – their hopes, fears, and dreams –become most important. Through this domestic framework, Bhardwaj offers a stringent criticism of the political realities of modern India – its corrupt administrators, a thriving criminal underworld, and the plight of ordinary Indian women caught between the two. As we shall see, in the Indian Shakespeare trilogy, the domestic and the political come together to chronicle the fraught and often tragic realities of contemporary India.

THE BHARDWAJ TRILOGY

Speaking shortly after the release of *Maqbool*, Bhardwaj (2015) claimed that the film "happened by accident. I had no plans to take up Shakespeare. I had not read Macbeth; I didn't know what it was." Bhardwaj, nonetheless, returns to Shakespeare twice more, each time to take up a well-known tragedy, while avoiding the comedies altogether. The three tragedies that Bhardwaj choses – *Macbeth*, *Othello*, and *Hamlet* – are noted, among other things, for being political plays. If *Macbeth* examines questions of kingship and tyranny, then *Othello* and *Hamlet* both trace how the actions of individuals impact the well-being of the state. At the end of *Othello*, with the eponymous general dead, the state of Venice seems to be more vulnerable to Turkish invasion than before, while *Hamlet* closes with Fortinbras, the Prince of Norway, taking over Denmark. In transposing Shakespeare's plots to modern-day India, Bhardwaj negotiates this political dimension, even as he highlights the domestic elements of these tragedies. The domestic in fact becomes political in Bhardwaj's adaptations, with the central characters in each instance trying to find or return to an ideal home, only to find it torn apart by social and political turmoil. In both *Maqbool* and *Omkara*, the interlinked worlds of organized crime and political parties trap the eponymous protagonists and the women who love them, Nimmi and Dolly. When the women concerned dare to alter their domestic setup, they are each, directly or indirectly, punished. The final apotheosis of this thwarted quest for a home (and homeland) happens in *Haider*, where we find Kashmir caught in a terrible political bind between the Indian armed forces and insurgents.

All three Bhardwaj movies are situated in contested political or legal spaces – *Maqbool* in Mumbai's criminal underworld and *Omkara* in the ganglands of Uttar Pradesh, while *Haider* gets played out against terrorism in Kashmir. In these spaces, the women of Bhardwaj's adaptations most acutely bring out the tragic desire for a home, and their bodies bear the brunt of the failure to achieve this. For instance, in *Maqbool*, Nimmi, much like her counterpart Lady Macbeth in Shakespeare, urges Maqbool to murder Abba-ji (Duncan), but the principal motivation for this, as I have noted elsewhere (Sen 2009), is personal. Nimmi is Abba-ji's mistress and believes that she is about to be replaced by a new Bollywood starlet. With the younger and unattached Maqbool, on the other hand, she can imagine a more stable home, especially since she can no longer return to her parents' house after her long years in Abba-ji's concubinage. As the plot unfolds, we realize that the unholy criminal alliance among Mumbai politicians, Bollywood, and the underworld, which had prevented her from becoming an actress, now comes in the way of her securing a lasting home. Nimmi's madness coincides with the political turmoil in the state, with legislators being kidnapped and held for ransom by Maqbool's new foe, Guddu (Fleance). Maqbool, desperate to resolve the situation, makes matters worse by joining hands with arms smugglers and an international terrorist group. In what must be recognized as a frightening scenario in a post-9/11 world, Mumbai's underworld thus begins partnering with Islamic terrorists. This crisis also tragically distracts Maqbool from fully grasping Nimmi's descent into madness. Instead of providing her with the help she needs, he resorts to violence when, for instance, she says that she can hear her unborn child cry each night because they have killed its father. The results of this political crisis are catastrophic not only for Maqbool but also for Nimmi. She pays with her own life when, being stripped of all governmental protection, they have to go on the run and she is prematurely removed from the hospital where she was recuperating after a difficult childbirth.

Similarly, in *Omkara*, Dolly (Desdemona) dreams of a blissful married life with Omi (Othello). Here, too, Bhardwaj alters the Shakespearean plot: whereas in the play Othello and Desdemona are already married at the beginning, in the movie the marriage itself becomes a contentious issue when Omi, under the influence of Langda Tyagi (Iago), begins to doubt Dolly's fidelity. We are shown close-up scenes of Dolly in Omi's ancestral home, trying to make it her own domestic space. She is frequently reminded by Omi of his mother and the other wives who had once worn the traditional kamarbandh (waist ornament) and won the hearts of their husbands and extended families. The kamarbandh is Omi's gift to Dolly, and a pledge of his sincere intention to marry her. The ornament, much like the handkerchief in *Othello*, is thus tied to marital bliss, but the kamarbandh in the movie is also much more – it is an heirloom that has marked out the wives of this feudal family for generations. When Dolly loses it, the results are predictably catastrophic. Omi interrogates her as a hapless Dolly turns her neatly organized room upside down, searching for the missing ornament: "Haven't you kept the token of my love real carefully?! Maybe the chest gobbled it up or was it the famished almirah? A generations-old heirloom, and it takes you precisely three days to lose it! Sure you haven't gifted it away?" (Bhardwaj 2006). It is clear from Omi's insinuations that an ideal bride, one who would manage the household and her husband wisely and in accordance with patriarchal expectations, would not lose the kamarbandh so easily.

In *Omkara*, as in *Maqbool*, politics plays a key role in shattering domestic bliss. What causes Omi to begin doubting Dolly is, of course, Langda Tyagi's machinations after he gets passed over for the position of *bahubali* (chief henchman) during the necessary reshuffles in the lead up to state elections. What should have been a liberating democratic process therefore destroys Dolly's hopes for a home, even as the criminal violence with which Omi's gang supports their political party destroys the hope for a democracy that follows the rule of law. *Omkara* also pulls at other socio-political tensions that rip into the Indian subcontinent – notably its caste divisions. As Othello is the Moor, Omi is the darker-skinned man born to a Brahmin father and a lower-caste mother. He is constantly reminded of his "half-caste" status and that he is the "adha-Brahmin" who has dared to set his sights on the fairer, purebred Dolly. These tensions of caste politics get further aggravated once the electoral process kicks off, and Dolly's domestic desires get disrupted by a series of events leading to her tragic confrontation with Omi on their wedding night.

The first two films in Bhardwaj's trilogy, then, though set in vastly different geographical and demographic contexts, project a criminalized political nexus (where criminals contest and win elections even while they are in prison) that intrudes into and destroys the domestic spaces of the chief characters. Trapped, the women find their private desires pitted against larger political forces that ultimately come together to destroy their domestic hopes. In *Maqbool* as well as in *Omkara*, these personal, or rather domestic, crises drive the plot forward – crises that are aggravated by underlying political factors, and felt most acutely by the leading women in these adaptations. As a result, both women die trying to find this ideal domestic state – Nimmi in childbirth, and Dolly on the night of her ill-fated marriage.

HAIDER AND THE APOTHEOSIS OF THE DOMESTIC TRAGEDY

Bhardwaj's latest Shakespeare adaptation is set in Kashmir and continues with the theme of the political intruding into and disrupting the domestic space. It follows the story of Haider (Hamlet), the only son of Hilaal Meer (Hamlet Senior) and Ghazala (Gertrude). Khurram (Claudius), a lawyer who profits from the political disturbance in the state, makes use of the knowledge that his brother Hilaal has been helping the insurgents in his capacity as a doctor and gets him arrested during a raid by the armed forces. Haider returns to Kashmir, interrupting his studies at Aligarh University, and desperately tries to trace his father's whereabouts. For all practical purposes, Hilaal has joined the thousands of Kashmiri men who "disappeared" or went missing in the course of the army's routine interrogations. Haider is aided in his quest by Arshia (Ophelia), who is a journalist. Yet it is Haider's relationship with his mother, and not Arshia, that drives the movie forward and gives it much of its emotional urgency. The film goes much further than Shakespeare's play-text, with adolescent scenes of Haider applying perfume on Ghazala and anecdotes that are told by other characters about how, as a child, he wanted to marry his mother.

Haider, unsurprisingly, follows the pattern of Bhardwaj's previous films, with Ghazala (Gertrude) coming across as a much stronger character than her Shakespearean counterpart in voicing her sexual desires and her hopes for a stable domestic life with her son and new husband (Khurram). But the stakes in the film are also higher, for tied to Ghazala's dreams about her home is the fate of the Kashmiri homeland. Kashmir is, of course, claimed by both India and Pakistan, with the Line of Control dividing the territory, a division manifest in parallel political maps of the subcontinent. In 1947, as part of the final exit negotiations with the British Empire, Kashmir was left as an independent kingdom, but soon afterwards Hari Singh, the maharaja of Kashmir, faced with an incursion from its western neighbour, applied for military support from India (Sen 2018, 91). The region has since been subject to dispute, making it one of the most contentious issues between the nuclear neighbours Pakistan and India.

Compared to other Bollywood films, *Haider* goes far in its attempts to depict the crippling political realities of Kashmir – which brings us to the Hamlet-like question: to show or not to show, or rather, how much to show of the stark political state of Kashmir. In the film there is the mention of the AFSPA (Armed Forces Special Powers Act), which gave the Indian Army the power to enter and search and to detain suspects; and Ghazala is initially shown as "a half-widow" or the wife of a person who has "disappeared" during the army raids. At one point, we are told that, when two elephants fight, the grass must get crushed, highlighting the plight of the valley caught between feuding India and Pakistan. So *Haider* does not shy away from portraying the conflict zones of Kashmir. The question is, does it do enough? As historian Mridu Rai (2014) notes, Ghazala, Haider's mother, is "one of the most vacant characters this film could have produced. She keeps proclaiming she is a half-widow while she has the privilege of becoming, except for the minor religio-legal hurdle soon overcome, a full-fledged wife. The only other person ... she cares for ... is her son. And that son, unlike those of many mothers of the disappeared, is alive. How is one to derive sympathy for the half-widow, half-mother of Kashmir from what she represents?"

Part of the problem that Rai outlines here arises from the fact that, as in Bhardwaj's other adaptations of Shakespeare, the main action in *Haider* is restricted to the domestic space. Furthermore, as the plot unfolds, the Kashmiri setting becomes more and more incidental, for the murder of Doctor Hilaal (Haider's father) results from his brother Khurram's jealousy rather than from any separatist zeal (Sen 2018, 91). The film gives us glimpses of political unrest in Kashmir without fully knowing what to do with it. The film thus appears only to be checking off boxes, as Rai argues, and not fully acknowledging or exploring the stock figures it deploys – the missing men, half-widows, and stateless people. Perhaps most troubling are the messages included with the final credits, which, as Rai argues, "politically neutered [the] film." The first of these observes that "thousands of lives have been lost in the Kashmir conflict," without, as Rai observes, distinguishing between civilian and non-civilian deaths. The second message cheerfully announces the rising tourism in recent years, while the third celebrates the flood relief efforts of the Indian Army in 2014, ignoring the role of the Kashmiris themselves (Rai 2014).

Haider, however, fits in well with Bhardwaj's Shakespeare trilogy in the way that the domestic plot reveals and reflects the significance of the larger political world that disrupts and destroys it. While Bhardwaj's depiction of the political problems of the Indian state remains incomplete, the characters, particularly Ghazala, follow the usual arc. Her dreams of finding a stable home, much like those of Nimmi and Dolly, are dashed at the end. Unlike them, however, she is able to save a loved one, for Bhardwaj's Hamlet gets to live. Ghazala becomes the avenger: as a suicide bomber, she kills Khurram for his offences against both Hilaal Meer and her son, Haider. The climactic moment in the film is thus Ghazala's death. Similarly, in *Maqbool*, Nimmi's death – unlike Lady Macbeth's, which receives only passing mention – is shown on screen. The camera lingers as Maqbool clings to Nimmi's corpse and carefully covers her with a scarf. When the police arrive, they pause and take note of Nimmi's death. In *Omkara*, the camera returns repeatedly to Dolly's corpse in order to dramatize the full effects of the tragedy. She lies on a swing, fully dressed in her bridal finery, while Omi sits next to her, motionless. They are discovered by a distraught Indu (Emilia) and later by Langda Tyagi and Kesu Firangi (Cassio). In *Haider*, there is no corpse to mourn over, but Ghazala's disintegrated body, as surely as the visible ones of Nimmi and Dolly, marks the impossibility of securing stable futures for the women who inhabit India's marginal spaces. In tracing the dilemmas of these women, Bhardwaj turns Shakespeare's plots into Indian stories of private loss and political failure.

CONCLUSION

Bhardwaj's trilogy has a sense of continuity not only because the films share certain common themes such as violence in the political and domestic spheres, but also because the director casts some of India's best-known actors in the films. For instance, the critically acclaimed actor Naseeruddin Shah, who plays Inspector Purohit in *Maqbool*, also appears as the crime lord Bhaisaab (the Duke of Venice) in *Omkara*. Similarly, Irfan Khan is both Maqbool and Ruhdaar (Bhardwaj's twist on Hamlet's Father's Ghost). Most prominently, Tabu plays the roles of both Nimmi and Ghazala. Such a repetition, especially in the case of the characters based on Lady Macbeth and Gertrude, helps us better recognize the domestic tragedies that get played out in these adaptations – the shattered dreams of these women from the socially and politically marginalized spaces of India. In chronicling these lives, Bhardwaj's Shakespeare films stand out as highly acclaimed global adaptations.

NOTES

1 In April 2018, Bhardwaj announced his decision to create a second trilogy, this time based on Shakespeare's comedies. The first film in this series, tentatively titled *Chaudhvin Ki Raat*, is based on *Twelfth Night*. For more, see Sundaram (2018).

2 For more on the Parsi theatre and its contribution to the performance of Shakespeare on stage and on screen, see Verma (2005, 270–9).

REFERENCES

Bhardwaj, Vishal, dir. 2006. *Omkara*. Shemaroo Films.

– 2015. "I Am My Own Audience." Interview with Prashant Singh. *Hindustan Times*, 25 December. http://www.hindustantimes.com/bollywood/i-am-my-own-audience-vishal-bhardwaj/story-CbIQhAmX9yuREg8OqA75BO.html.

Chakravarti, Paromita. 2016. Review of *Haider* (film), dir. Vishal Bhardwaj. *Shakespeare Bulletin* 34 (1): 129–32.

Charry, Brinda, and Gitanjali Shahani. 2014. "The Global as Local / Othello as Omkara." In *Bollywood Shakespeares*, edited by Craig Dionne and Parmita Kapadia, 107–23. New York: Palgrave.

Heidenberg, Mike. 2014. "No Country for Young Women: Empowering Emilia in Vishal Bhardwaj's *Omkara*." In *Bollywood Shakespeares*, edited by Craig Dionne and Parmita Kapadia, 87–105. New York: Palgrave.

Huang, Alexa. 2009a. *Chinese Shakespeares: Two Centuries of Cultural Exchange*. New York: Columbia University Press.

– ed. 2009b. "Asian Shakespeares on Screen: Two Films in Perspective." Special section, *Borrowers and Lenders: The Journal of Shakespeare and Appropriation* 4 (2). http://www.borrowers.uga.edu/.

Lanier, Douglas. 2007. "Film Spin-Offs and Citations." In *Shakespeares After Shakespeare: An Encyclopedia of the Bard in Mass Media and Popular Culture*, vol. 1, edited by Richard Burt. 132–365. Westport: Greenwood Press.

Massai, Sonia, ed. 2005. *World-Wide Shakespeares: Local Appropriations in Film and Performance*. London: Routledge.

Rai, Mridu. 2014. "Haider: A Politically Neutered Film." DNA *India*, 11October.http://www.dnaindia.com/analysis/column-haider-a-politically-neutered-film-2025040.

Rodgers, Amy. 2016. "Vishal Bhardwaj." *Shakespeare Bulletin* 34 (3): 500–4.

Rothwell, Kenneth S. 2004. *A History of Shakespeare on Screen: A Century of Film and Television*. Cambridge: Cambridge University Press.

Sen, Amrita. 2009. "Maqbool and Bollywood Conventions." In "Asian Shakespeares on Screen: Two Films in Perspective," edited by Alexa Huang, special section, *Borrowers and Lenders: The Journal of Shakespeare and Appropriation* 4 (2). http://www.borrowers.uga.edu/.

– 2018. "Locating Hamlet in Kashmir: *Haider*, Terrorism, and

Shakespearean Transmission." In *Shakespeare's Hamlet in an Era of Textual Exhaustion*, edited by Sonya Freeman Loftis, Allison Kellar, and Lisa Ulevich, 87–100. New York: Routledge.

Senda, Akihiko. 1998. "The Rebirth of Shakespeare in Japan." In *Shakespeare and the Japanese Stage*, edited by Takashi Sasayama, J.R. Mulryne, and Margaret Shewring, 15–37. Cambridge: Cambridge University Press.

Singh, Jyotsna G., and Abdulhamit Arvas. 2015. "Global Shakespeares, Affective Histories, Cultural Memories." *Shakespeare Survey* 68: 183–96.

Sundaram, Lasyapriya. 2018. "Vishal Bhardwaj to Adapt Shakespeare's 'Twelfth Night' for the Big Screen." *Times of India*, 11 April. http://timesofindia.indiatimes.com/articleshow/63613008.cms.

Trivedi, Poonam. 2007. "'Filmi' Shakespeare." *Literature/Film Quarterly* 35 (2): 148–58.

– 2014. "Hamlets of India." *Indian Express*, 14 October. https://indianexpress.com/article/opinion/columns/hamlets-of-india/.

– 2018. "Woman as Avenger: 'Indianising' the Shakespearean Tragic in the Films of Vishal Bhardwaj." In *Shakespeare and Indian Cinemas: "Local Habitations,"* edited by Poonam Trivedi and Paromita Chakravarti, 23–44. New York: Routledge.

Verma, Rajiva. 2005. "Shakespeare in Hindi Cinema." In *India's Shakespeare: Translation, Interpretation and Performance*, edited by Poonam Trivedi and Dennis Bartholomeusz, 269–90. New Delhi: Pearson.

15

QUEERING WILL AND KIT

Slash and the Shakespeare Biopic

LISA S. STARKS

We seem to have an unquenchable curiosity about the lives of literary celebrities – especially the most iconic author of them all, Will Shakespeare. Numerous films with fictional takes on the Bard's life exploit this curiosity. They also fulfill other desires that we may have to connect with the famous writer. Shakespeare biopics speak directly to the way we perceive the author as both a historical person who lived in the past and a contemporary who lives among us now. First, the biopic genre forces filmmakers to grapple with making the past present, not just the narrative of Shakespeare's life but also the sights and sounds of the world in which he lived. Second, the biopics provide a rich history of the ways that we have understood Shakespeare as a historical person in a particular place in time – which, of course, is also always the present time. And, third, they showcase the cult of celebrity surrounding the iconic author, revealing cultural values invested in the myth of the Bard.

No matter the perspective, these biopics – as well as the earlier ones to which they respond – fabricate Will's personal life and focus on the interrelationships between gender, sexuality, and authorship. Because of Shakespeare's status as an icon, as well as controversies surrounding sexuality in his sonnets and some of his plays, these relationships are heightened in films about his life. Despite the many representations of male-male eroticism in his poems and plays, Shakespeare is constantly portrayed as heterosexual in biopics. At times, queer sexuality is completely rejected or effaced in television shows and films about

Shakespeare's life; most often, however, it is displaced or projected onto the character of Marlowe or the character identified as the fair youth of Shakespeare's sonnets. Shakespeare, the ultimate canonical author, thus remains consistently straight in these depictions.

Biopics since the late seventies have tended to focus on interrelationships between Will's masculinity, his sexuality, and his life as an author. Even though they share this common focus, they offer contrasting takes on it. Shakespeare is portrayed as a writer torn between an erotic rivalry with his patron and a "Dark Lady" who refuses to have sex with him in the 1978 BBC series *Will Shakespeare*; a would-be playwright suffering from writer's block and sexual impotence, until he finds his "muse," in the 1998 film *Shakespeare in Love*; an aging poet suffering from syphilis and betrayal in the 2005 BBC television film *A Waste of Shame*; a bumbling, illiterate stand-in for Edward de Vere, Earl of Oxford, who appears as the true "Bard" in the 2011 film *Anonymous*; a sexually repressed, middle-class father in the BBC television sitcom *Upstart Crow* (2016–); and a naive young man torn between love and other responsibilities, whose story is told alongside that of a magnetic Christopher ("Kit") Marlowe in the 2017 TNT series *Will*.

In the most recent of these examples, two television series – the drama *Will* and sitcom *Upstart Crow* – provide fascinating examples that respond to the earlier Shakespeare biopics' tendency to fetishize and romanticize the Bard. In each, Will is presented as a lacklustre figure, but in entirely different ways. *Will* presents a hipster Shakespeare whose story is overshadowed by that of an intense and captivating Marlowe; *Upstart Crow* presents the poet as an ineffectual, misunderstood "nerd." This sitcom, a popular BBC series that has been renewed for subsequent seasons, has inspired comic memes, such as the one in figure 15.1, and other social media blurbs that mock the image of the Bard, but not much beyond these circulated images and basic Internet advertising. *Will*, on the other hand, has developed a significant following on the Web, as discussed below. The show, cancelled after only one season, is seriously flawed – mainly because of its distracting, overblown subplot dealing with Catholic persecution and espionage, as well as its rather dull portrayal of Will himself. Nevertheless, the series is enjoying a rich, alternative afterlife on the Internet, exceeding the boundaries of the television show itself to flourish in virtual subcultures.

Figure 15.1 | Shakespeare meme, with David Mitchell from *Upstart Crow* as Will Shakespeare, 2018.

THE AUTHOR BIOPIC

This focus of Shakespeare biopics on gender, sexuality, and cultural myth is inherent in the biopic itself. Often treated as a lesser film genre in cinema studies, the biopic is a fictionalized depiction of a historical person, typically one whose life deserves or needs to be shown (Brown and Vidal 2014, 3), so as "to enter the biographical subject into the pantheon of cultural mythology, one way or another, and to show why he or she belongs there," as Dennis Bingham has noted (2010, 10). Of course, the biopic's main ingredient is the biographical subject, a person who has actually lived (Brown and Vidal 2014, 3). This character then embodies or furthers larger cultural views, events, or issues – such as norms of gender and sexuality.

Moreover, because it draws from various biographical materials in multiple ways, the biopic falls under the rubric of an adaptation. Biopics draw from multiple kinds of sources and media – a mix of biographies, letters, or other oral and/or visual artifacts – that

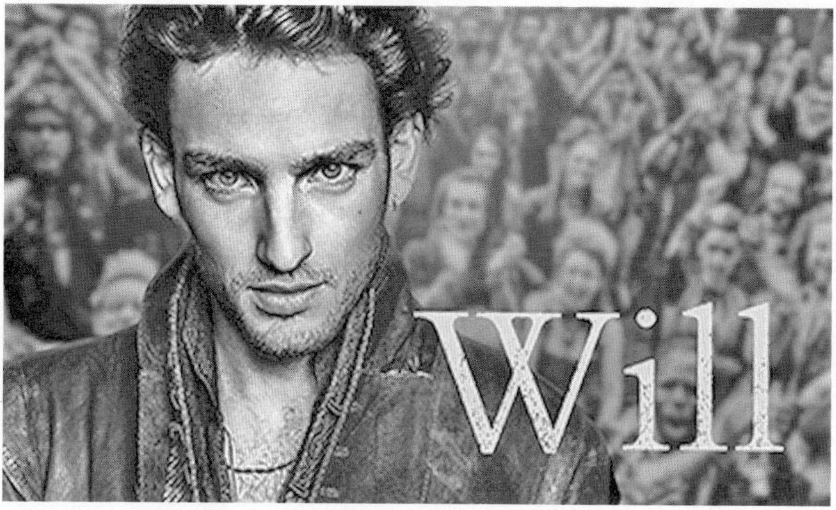

Figure 15.2 | Laurie Davidson as Will Shakespeare (*Will*, 2017).

are adapted, not simply presented, into a new cinematic narrative. A hybrid genre, the biopic may fall into more than one category, categorized as a drama, a musical, a romantic comedy, and so on – as in *Yankee Doodle Dandy*, the 1942 musical biopic of George M. Cohan (Brown and Vidal 2014, 17). Nevertheless, the biopic's subject – the *actual* person – is necessarily missing from the film's representations, which fail to fully grasp that person's whole being in any tangible way. Instead, the biopic offers a multitude of images to compensate for the lack of the actual subject's presence on screen (Brown and Vidal 2014, 16; Nichols 1993, 177).

THE "QUEER LITE" SHAKESPEARE BIOPIC

This lack of the subject's presence is especially felt in the Shakespeare biopics, as they address a historical person whose biographical information is scarce, and whose private life – the focus of a biopic – must therefore be, in a large part, fiction. This lack of source biographical material is complicated further by the author biopic genre, as it typically presents the author's *personal* story as one in which *heterosexual* relationships provide the source of the writer's genius and inspiration (Custen 1992, 75; North 2012, 102). Shakespeare biopics tend to embrace this convention in their treatment of the author's life and sexuality. They usually represent the writer's iconic status, the sources of genius, and the process of writing as linked to Will's heterosexuality and traditional masculine identity in one way or another.

The history of Shakespeare as a character on screen begins at the start of the twentieth century. From early cinema to current-day television and digital media, the iconic author has been a figure of fascination and a subject of multiple representations. Probably the earliest depiction of him as a character is his appearance in Georges Méliès' *La Mort de Jules César* in 1907. In this silent film, he appears struggling with writer's block, which is cured when he falls asleep and dreams of his characters. In the later twentieth century, Shakespeare becomes the main character in television series and feature films about his life – biopics, that is – which are adapted mostly from biographies, his sonnets and plays, and previous films about him. In general, as noted above, the biopic investigates the construction of an identity; in particular, the *author* biopic is deeply inflected with intersecting notions of gender, sexuality, and *literary genius*. Given their iconic subject matter, then, Shakespeare biopics engage in complex ways with the assumptions underlying the author biopic film genre and the cultural myths of literary genius they reaffirm. Shakespeare, as the ultimate canonical author, has thus become the prototypical subject of the author biopic.

Representations of Shakespeare in biopics suggest audiences' desires to see the author fetishized, romanticized, mocked – or, in the case of *Anonymous*, displaced onto a more elite figure. Shakespeare biopics exhibit the broad range of the male biopic and treat one of the big issues surrounding Shakespeare's life story – his sexuality – by maintaining that the Bard, like the traditional subject of the biopic genre, is straight. I call this standard the "queer lite" Shakespeare biopic – a film or show about Shakespeare's life that gestures toward his queer sexuality, while simultaneously denying it and/or displacing it onto other characters. The queer lite biopics insist that Shakespeare be heterosexual and, in most cases, "heteronormative" (i.e., fulfilling cultural norms of gender and sexuality that legitimize only heterosexual marriage and childrearing). In the queer lite Shakespeare biopic, even when non-normative sexualities are introduced or developed in some way, they are countered with elements that ensure that Will himself is portrayed in line with cultural norms of gender and sexuality. In that way, the myth of the

Bard and the source of his genius continue to be identified with heterosexuality and traditional masculinity.

Even the 2011 film *Anonymous* (dir. Roland Emmerich), which dramatizes the Oxfordian conspiracy theory that Edward de Vere, Earl of Oxford, penned Shakespeare's plays, represents the aristocratic Oxford (Rhys Ifans) – who takes on the role of the "true" Bard, as opposed to the bumbling, low-class, illiterate actor, William Shakespeare (Rafe Spall), who takes credit for Oxford's plays – as undeniably straight, albeit rather tragically so. As a young man (Jamie Campbell Bower, who also plays Kit in the TNT series *Will* discussed below), de Vere has a passionate affair with Elizabeth I, who secretly bears him a child later revealed to be Henry Wriothesley, Earl of Southampton (the figure who is often identified as the fair youth of *The Sonnets*). In Oedipal fashion, Oxford discovers later in life that the queen, the mother of his illegitimate son, is actually also his own biological mother. This Sophoclean twist notwithstanding, *Anonymous* is a conservative film whose agenda is to entrench, rather than challenge, established norms of gender, sexuality, and authorship. Because he is unaware of his true parentage, Oxford's desires, even when non-normative in having sexual relations with his mother, do not stray beyond the bounds of heterosexuality. The love scenes between the young Edward and Elizabeth are especially passionate and shot in typical Hollywood cinematic style. Moreover, the film neutralizes the homoeroticism in "Shakespeare's" *Sonnets*, for Oxford's relationship with Southampton (here portrayed as his illegitimate son) becomes a paternal rather than an erotic one. Thus, in *Anonymous*, as in many other Shakespeare biopics, gender and sexuality conform to the ideals of iconic authorship – even when the icon's identity is displaced from the low-born Shakespeare onto the high-born Oxford. As the "real" Bard, de Vere embodies the Romantic myth of the isolated genius who rises above the rabble and common folk – such as the likes of William Shakespeare from Stratford-upon-Avon (Lanier 2013).

SHAKESPEARE AS "FAMILY GUY" – *UPSTART CROW*

In contrast to the anti-Stratfordian *Anonymous*, more recent Shakespeare biopics have reinstated William Shakespeare as the author of his plays; but, like that film, they continue the tradition of previous biopics in depicting the Bard as sexually normative, even when

Figure 15.3 | Anne (Liza Tarbuck) and Will Shakespeare (*Upstart Crow*, 2016).

episodes contain queer plots or subtexts. The queer lite Shakespeare biopic has surfaced recently in a genre that contrasts with earlier examples, the television sitcom. Creator Ben Elton's current BBC show *Upstart Crow*, in its second season at the time of writing, draws a great deal from the humour of old BBC favourites – especially Elton's *Blackadder* – and jokes about the unreliability of mass transit in the contemporary United Kingdom. This sitcom biopic features Will (David Mitchell) as a misunderstood middle-class "family guy" who is loyal to wife and family, whom he visits often in Stratford.

Much of the show's humour revolves around others mocking Shakespeare for his "hoity-toity" plays and seemingly nonsensical language. The series projects a double-entanglement with feminism, including an "everyday-sitcom-mom" wife Anne (Liza Tarbuck), who talks back to her husband and has an uncanny sense about his writing, often predicting great moments in plays and their future uses; a moody and sarcastic daughter, Susannah; and a fictional character named Kate (Gemma Whelan), one of Will's servants in London, a smart young woman who wants to act on the stage. To counter these strong, quasi-feminist characters, others appear, such as a rather demeaning portrait of Emilia Bassano Lanyer

Figure 15.4 | Will and Kit (Tim Downie) (*Upstart Crow*, 2016).

(Montserrat Lombardas), the "Dark Lady" of the sonnets in this version, as a rather shallow woman (no mention of her own literary achievements), who is offended by Shakespeare's poems, preferring superficial flattery instead. Lanyer spurns Will and goes off with the flirtatious Kit Marlowe (Tim Downie), who rhymes her name "Emilia" with "I wanna feel ya."

Kit Marlowe is Will's "very cool" friend, who serves as a comic sidekick but not his erotic rival, romantic partner, or even collaborator in this series. Kit, apparently, is too busy spying to do his own writing. Desperate for Kit's approval, Will writes Kit's plays for him, so that the series comically responds to the authorship conspiracy theory that Marlowe wrote Shakespeare's plays by positing the reverse. Most importantly, however, in *Upstart Crow* there is not anything queer about Kit or his relationship with Will, not even sexual tension or erotic subtext. Kit resembles the prototypical "cool guy with all the chicks" in high school. It is Will, not Kit, who harbours non-normative (although closeted) sexual desires, even though the former never acts on them. Importantly, a great deal of humour results from Will's repressed desire. He is consistently teased for his homoerotic sonnets and early drafts of plays. His *Romeo and Julian*, for instance, leads to numerous "gay jokes" and defensive, sometimes homophobic responses from Will himself. Interestingly, Will's best writing seems to be associated with these closeted desires. He has a great deal of trouble getting the heterosexual lovers right, as when he struggles to draft the "straight" *Romeo and Juliet*; whereas he has no trouble depicting the homoerotic desire in his sonnets and other writing, which Will calls "experimental." The latter appears to be the heart of his inspiration.

Nevertheless, the series undercuts that point by deflecting it with homophobic humour, so that the portrait of Shakespeare as straight remains intact, in line with other queer lite biopics. For example, Lord Southampton (Adam Harley) – the idealized young man of *The Sonnets* in this version, as in John Mortimer's – reacts antagonistically when he discovers his portrayal in Will's sonnets. This Southampton becomes angry that, in Will's poems, the speaker desires the fair youth for his feminine beauty but refuses to have sex with his beloved because he is a man (figure 15.5). Southampton hurls a number of off-colour gay jokes (some drawn from contemporary "drag humour," such as "I'm a chick with a dick") at Will, but then chides the poet for his homophobia. Robert Greene (Mark Heap), the comic villain in the series, steals Will's sonnets and has him arrested for "incitement to hugger-buggery," or sodomy. Will is released because his buddy Kit convinces the Lord Inquisitor (John Sessions) that no one will read or understand *The Sonnets* anyway, so that the poems will more likely "incite" a "long nap" rather than "hugger-buggery." Thus, in queer lite fashion, the show brings in LGBTQ concerns but then neutralizes them, thereby disassociating Shakespeare from queer desires even as it aligns him with them. This series' double engagement with queer sexuality and its depiction of Will as family man, a generic requirement of the sitcom, promote a normative portrait of Shakespeare, one that mocks his literary celebrity status and his image as the ultimate iconic author.

WILL, OR QUEERING KIT

Airing concurrently with the UK's *Upstart Crow*, the US series *Will*, which premiered in July 2017, takes an approach to the character that contrasts with those of the British sitcom and previous Shakespeare biopics; but it, too, exhibits the characteristics of the queer lite biopic. Rather than an average, middle-aged family man, as in the UK series, Will (Laurie Davidson) is a sensitive young man who has come to London to follow his dream and to support his wife

Figure 15.5 | Southampton (Adam Harley) responds to Will's sonnets (*Upstart Crow*, 2016).

and children. This series, created by Craig Pearce (who has previously collaborated with Baz Luhrmann) and directed by Shekhar Kapur (the *Elizabeth* biopics), is a kind of punk version of *Shakespeare in Love.*

Like that film, the series includes an added female character, this one the actor Richard Burbage's fictional sister, Alice (Olivia DeJonge), who, like Gwyneth Paltrow in *Shakespeare in Love,* is young, pretty, white, blonde, spirited, independent, and intelligent. Indeed, there are many similarities between *Will* and *Shakespeare in Love*, especially in the love plots with Will and Viola or Alice. Similar to Viola, Alice becomes Will's true love interest, inserted into the plot to establish the playwright's heterosexuality. In both, the lovemaking scenes are highly conventional, the stuff of Hollywood romance. And, in both *Shakespeare in Love* and *Will*, the sonnets that Shakespeare addresses to the fair youth (1–126) are instead addressed to his female love interest (Sonnet 18 in the former, 29 and 116 in the latter), rather than to the aristocratic young man to whom the first 126 of the sonnets are generally addressed. In contrast to *Shakespeare in Love*, however, this Will does not suffer from writer's block per se, and certainly not one that is linked to his

Figure 15.6 | Alice (Olivia DeJonge) and Will collaborate (*Will*, 2017).

sexual virility, as it is in that film. Instead, rather than existing as his muse, Alice more actively collaborates with Will, providing him with most of his ideas and pointing him to sources for play plots. Will has to learn – from Alice – that all great artists borrow from sources and existing narratives, and then make them their own. The two literally steal a book from a street bookseller, further emphasizing this idea.

In this version, though, Will's fictional love interest does have to contend with a very real Anne Shakespeare, who in one episode comes to visit Will in London, children in tow. As opposed to the way that Anne is represented in previous biopics, such as Mortimer's *Will Shakespeare*, *A Waste of Shame*, and *Upstart Crow* (for different reasons), this Anne is treated the most sympathetically in *Will*. She struggles to deal with Will's infidelity and to become a part of his world; Will responds empathetically, offering for her and the children all to live as a family in London. However, Anne realizes that she will never be able to relate to her husband's passion, his writing, so she decides to move the family back home to Stratford. The couple separate, but with mutual respect and love, not animosity. This Anne is not weak, stupid, unattractive, or mean, as she is often depicted. She is just different from the man she married. Other female characters – such as Amilia Bassano (Jasmin Savoy Brown),

Figure 15.7 | Will and Kit (Jamie Campbell Bower) (*Will*, 2017).

Shakespeare's sophisticated female confidante, and Moll (Richard Burbage's friend, a fictional character, Abigail Hardingham) – are included in the series to provide strong female counterparts to male characters. Nevertheless, their depictions ultimately reinforce gender norms, such as that of the supportive woman helping prop up male genius. Alice fulfills this normative gender role, just as she serves to verify Will's heterosexual identity in the series, which offsets the erotic intensity between him and his foil, the charismatic and queer Kit Marlowe (Jamie Campbell Bower).

In this series, Kit Marlowe is a sexy, hip, cynical-yet-vulnerable, extremely cool, queer playwright/rock star of the theatre (often appearing shirtless and clad in very tight black pants). As noted above, in this series, it is *Marlowe* – not Shakespeare – who suffers from writer's block; Kit goes to tremendous lengths for inspiration, seeking both sexual and life-threatening thrills to spark his creativity. Much more of the series is devoted to the agonizing depths he undergoes to write *Doctor Faustus*, which he ends up imagining in a vision-like trance, than to Will's struggles as an author. Unlike Kit, Will is able to write easily once he finds a hook, or a purpose – as in penning *Richard III* to accuse the Catholic hunter-torturer Topcliffe (Ewen Bremner) of his crimes, referencing Hamlet's *Murder of Gonzago* with Claudius.

There is a marked difference between this Marlowe and the one from Mortimer's *Will Shakespeare*, which testifies to the cultural differences between 1978 in the United Kingdom and 2017 in the United States. In Mortimer's *Will Shakespeare*, Christopher Marlowe (Ian McShane) epitomizes the gay male stereotype that culminated in the seventies, especially ones from British films and television (as in the 1969 film *Staircase*, dir. Stanley Donen, and the BBC sitcom *Are You Being Served?*), of the homosexual as a narcissistic diva. This Marlowe ends up being betrayed by his male lover, Ingram Frizer (Simon Rouse), in a plot that suggests his death resulted from – and was a kind of punishment for – his vanity and homosexuality. Although Marlowe and Shakespeare (Tim Curry) are both rivals and collaborators in this series, there is no erotic component. Between the two, it is very clear who is gay and who is not.

Conversely, in the recent TNT series *Will*, Marlowe appears as openly gay or bisexual, without the negative stereotypes associated with Mortimer's characterization; as the actor who plays Will in the series, Laurie Davidson, describes Kit, he is "androgynous," "bisexual," and "smokin'" (2017). Nevertheless, in keeping with the queer lite script, only Kit, *not* Will, exhibits non-normative sexuality. Kit bears the full weight of that ideological burden, allowing Shakespeare as icon to remain heterosexual in the series. Despite some very tense and sexually charged exchanges between the two men – when Kit sneaks a kiss on the lips from Will, who recoils; and when Kit softly declares love for Will, for instance – this TNT series depicts a Shakespeare who is every bit as straight as he is in *Shakespeare in Love*. Unlike *Shakespeare in Love*, however, *Will* highlights and invests a great deal of energy in presenting a range of sexualities in the theatre world, as well as developing and championing a queer Marlowe.

Although Will is a bit lacklustre in this show, Kit is a fascinating character. Throughout most of the series, Kit searches for extreme stimulation and thrills: he is shown being caressed by a number of naked and aesthetically perfect men, who adore the playwright and linger in his hall; partaking in occult rituals; surviving a night of being "buried alive" to live on the edge of life and death; and dabbling with Catholicism. As the series develops, Marlowe's past comes to light. In Episode 5, Kit appears comforting his deathly ill older lover, an artist named Barrett (Barry) Emerson (Julian Sands), whom he affectionately refers to as "my king" – making this series

Figure 15.8 | Kit and Barrett (Julian Sands) (*Will*, 2017).

the only biopic, to my knowledge, that references Marlowe's *Edward II*, which centres on a king's love for his male minion. Barry refers to Kit as "my wasp," perhaps as a metaphor for the "sting" of their relationship. On his sick bed, Barrett urges Marlowe to repent for their "sinful" relationship. Lovingly, Kit replies, "We have nothing to repent," but Barrett counters with the comment, "We are both of us damned." Marlowe insists that they are not, that his lover will go to heaven; but the dying man refuses this comfort, replying that he "sold his soul to be with" Kit – a line that echoes Marlowe's *Doctor Faustus*. As Kit explains later, Barry had helped him become "Marlowe, the superstar," but then Kit got so wrapped up in his celebrity that he lost track of any kind of meaning or value in life or relationships. When his lover dies, Kit is devastated, and he exclaims, "Goodbye, my sage, sturdy king; if your love cost me my soul, then here's to damnation, darling; I shall see thee in Hell." Kit takes these moments to heart, repeatedly insisting that he's damned throughout the series and using this pain to inspire *Doctor Faustus*.

Meaningfully, however, the series itself does not share Barrett or Kit's self-condemnation of their relationship. Furthermore, Kit himself becomes a very positive character in the series. Ultimately, he is remarkably selfless, even after first appearing to be self-indulgent and selfish, an empty void who refuses to believe in anything. Once Kit reveals his vulnerability, he extends tenderness and kindness to Barrett, Tommy (his young lover), Will, and also Alice, whom he attempts to save from the clutches of Topcliffe, rebuking the torturer when rescuing her.

WILL AND KIT'S AFTERLIFE – SLASH AND FANFICTION

The queer lite depiction of a straight Shakespeare is clearly not the end of the biopic story. Audience reception of the depiction of queer sexuality (or lack of it) in these biopics exceeds the depiction of it in these films, especially on "fandom" (fiction that riffs off of literature, films, or shows) and "slash" websites, on which participants post written narratives, blogs, and videos that imagine "[a] same-sex romantic and/or sexual relationship between two characters who are not currently in such a relationship in the canon" (The Brat Queen 2018). This writer points out that the meaning of "slash" can be rather slippery, but most groups, movements, and/or posts that identify themselves as slash fit into this basic definition. On these slash websites, viewer responses from fandom and LGBTQ subcultures have enthusiastically tapped into already existing fanfiction narratives about Shakespeare to revise the erotic dynamic and open up the limited portrayal of Shakespeare's sexuality offered in mainstream biopics.

In particular, TNT's *Will* spurred a flurry of posts and comments on slash websites and blogs, as well as YouTube videos, in which Will and Kit form an intensely romantic relationship. These responses call for Will to be bisexual or gay, offering their own revised narratives and expressing disappointment at the show's unwillingness to depict a queer Shakespeare, as is evident on the Archive of Our Own slash website.[1] Comments on this website offer direct responses to particular episodes in that series. The posting entitled "Déjà Vu" (12 August 2017), for instance, articulates Kit's imagined desires for Will: "And oh how he'd live to see that gorgeous face of Will's amass the sea of writhing bodies he used to inspire his hand. But tonight he had different measures in mind. Tonight, he wanted to be completely alone with this skittish animal. He wanted to prey upon him, touch and caress every inch of him and watch as he shuddered away only to reach out for more." Another, entitled "Whose Deepness Doth Entice" (18 September 2017), illustrates a more romantic slash

Figure 15.9 | YouTube video screenshot.

scenario between Will and Kit: "The moment came when either of them could have broken the kiss – and should have, if it were going to be something that could be easily forgotten – and neither of them did." This entry contrasts with the rather blunt depiction of the two as lovers in one entitled "Chimes at Midnight" (31 July 2017): "William and Marlowe work together (on writing and also sex)." On YouTube, the slash fantasy of Will and Kit is also alive and kicking. There are several videos, including one posted by Little Sociopath (see figure 15.9), in which scenes are spliced together to create a union between Will and Kit that moves beyond the sexual attraction and brief kiss depicted in the series. In its afterlife, therefore, the TNT series most fully challenges the limits of the queer lite Shakespeare biopic.

These examples of slash bring to the light the tension between spectators' desires in these virtual/LGBTQ communities and the normative depictions of sexuality offered in mainstream popular culture. Shakespeare biopics are deeply entrenched and invested in the author's heterosexuality and masculinity, continually reinforcing the notion that the ultimate iconic author – Will Shakespeare – must not be seen to deviate from sexual and gender norms, at least not beyond a certain degree. To maintain this heterosexual Will, these films tend to repeat a similar strategy – that of the queer lite biopic – even if it is developed differently, with variations on the displacement and disavowal of a queer Will. In the process, the reception of Shakespeare biopics reveals a complex interrelationship concerning attitudes toward gender and sexuality. The biopics mostly reinforce the image of a straight and traditionally masculine Bard, thus demonstrating how invested our mainstream culture is in these norms, especially in relation to Shakespeare. Nevertheless, the response of subcultures like slash resist and overturn this agenda and provide alternative narratives that creatively queer Will and Kit, resisting and revising cultural notions of literary celebrity.

NOTES

Many thanks to Louise Geddes, Milton Wendland, Daniel Lauby, and Kenneth Graham for their helpful feedback on earlier stages of this chapter.

1 See Works in Christopher Marlowe / William Shakespeare on the Archive of Our Own website, https://archiveofourown.org/tags/Christopher%20Marlowe*s*William%20Shakespeare/works?page=1.

REFERENCES

Bingham, Dennis. 2010. *Whose Lives Are They Anyway? The Biopic as Contemporary Film Genre*. New Brunswick, NJ: Rutgers University Press.

The Brat Queen. 2018. "What Is Slash?" The Fanfic Symposium (website). http://trickster.org/symposium/symp139.html.

Brown, Tom, and Belén Vidal. 2014. "Introduction." *The Biopic in Contemporary Film Culture*, edited by Brown and Vidal, 1–32. New York: Routledge.

Custen, George F. 1992. *Bio/Pics: How Hollywood Constructed Public History*. New Brunswick, NJ: Rutgers University Press.

Davidson, Laurie. 2017. Interview. "Inside the Episode: 'Cowards Die Many Times.'" TNT on Demand Extras. TNT iPad App.

Lanier, Douglas M. 2013 "'There Won't Be Puppets, Will There?': 'Heroic' Authorship and the Cultural Politics of *Anonymous*." In *Shakespeare Beyond Doubt: Evidence, Argument, Controversy*, edited by Paul Edmonson and Stanley Wells, 215–24. Cambridge: Cambridge University Press.

Little Sociopath. 2017. "Will and Christopher//Hypnotic." Song by Zella Day. YouTube video. Posted 19 July 2017. https://www.youtube.com/watch?v=tpFshzkYBHo.

Nichols, Bill. 1993. "'Getting to Know You . . .': Knowledge, Power, and the Body." In *Theorizing Documentary*, edited by Michael Renov, 174–91. New York: Routledge.

North, Julian. 2012. "Jane Austen's Life on Page and Screen." In *Uses of Austen: Jane's Afterlives*, edited by Gillian Dow and C. Hanson, 92–114. London: Palgrave Macmillan.

Shakespeare in Love. (1998) 2014. Written by Marc Norman and Tom Stoppard. Directed by John Madden. Miramax; Lionsgate. DVD.

Upstart Crow. 2016. Written by Ben Elton. Directed by Richard Boden and Matt Lipsey. BBC Television; Amazon Prime Video. 2017. Streaming video.

A Waste of Shame: The Mystery of William Shakespeare's Sonnets. (2005) 2013. Written by William Boyd. Directed by John McKay. BBC Television; BFS Entertainment. DVD.

Will. (2017) 2018. Written by Craig Pearce et al. Directed by Shekhar Kapur et al. TNT Network; Amazon Prime Video. Streaming video.

Will Shakespeare. (1978) 2008. Written by John Mortimer. Directed by Peter Wood, Mark Cullingham, and Robert Knights. BBC Television; A&E Television Networks. DVD.

16

STAR TREK'S SHAKESPEARE PROBLEM

BRANDON CHRISTOPHER

It has been for some time a mystery to critics as to why James T. Kirk, captain of the *Starship Enterprise* in the television series *Star Trek* (1966–69) and *Star Trek: The Animated Series* (1973–74) and in the first six films in the *Star Trek* franchise (1979–91), claims Shakespeare as his favourite author. This assertion, writes Stephen Buhler, "comes as something of a surprise" (1995, 21). Jean Graham is similarly puzzled by the erudite Kirk, "whose literary knowledge has always been surprisingly extensive for a man who fights and sleeps his way through the galaxy" (2000, 24). Buhler's objection to the characterization of Captain Kirk as a Shakespeare fan is that "any of a number of other characters in" *Star Trek VI: The Undiscovered Country*, the most Shakespeare-saturated entry in the *Star Trek* canon, "would seem a far better candidate for claiming the poet as his or her favorite" (21). There are thus two interrelated aspects of objections to the Kirk-Shakespeare pairing. First, Kirk, womanizing and violent, is an inappropriate standard-bearer for Shakespeare in *Star Trek*'s imagined twenty-fourth century. In addition, the franchise provides a host of other, better candidates for the job.

But there is also, I believe, good reason for making Kirk a fan of Shakespeare. Kirk is, at least in terms of first-generation *Star Trek* characters, the hero. After all, it is Kirk who literally gives voice to the crew's mission at the beginning of each episode of the 1960s television series.[1] And it makes sense for Kirk, as hero, to embody the aspirations and values of both his society and the television series that portrays it.[2] Central among the markers of the series' aspirations and values is Shakespeare. Shakespeare and his works are cited repeatedly throughout the various series and films in the franchise, with thirteen episodes and one film deriving their titles from Shakespeare's plays; another handful of episodes loosely borrowing Shakespeare's plots; and characters repeatedly quoting from and acting out a number of scenes from Shakespeare. Add to this other paratextual associations between Shakespeare and *Star Trek*, especially Patrick Stewart's pre-*Trek* career with the Royal Shakespeare Company (1966–82), but also William Shatner's tenure at the Stratford, Ontario, Shakespeare Festival in the 1950s and early 1960s and Christopher Plummer's appearance in *The Undiscovered Country*, and a clear pattern of association between the franchise and Shakespeare emerges.

But what does it mean to send a ship full of (and created by) Shakespeare fans into space? What does Shakespeare mean for the franchise and for its characters? This chapter reads these various and persistent citations of Shakespeare as exemplars of the franchise's investment in and championing of a Western humanist philosophical ideal. Knowledge and, perhaps more importantly, comprehension of Shakespeare is used in the series as a sign of the purported superiority of a world view informed by European cultural traditions. Through its citations of Shakespeare, especially as they are used in a number of the franchise's celebratory assimilation narratives, *Star Trek* reveals itself as a fantasy of unending European expansion, the near-universal superiority of which marks the franchise's vision of the future as one dominated by an ethos of, if not white supremacy, then at least Anglo-American supremacy (if indeed the two concepts can be disentangled). The franchise thus serves, I argue, as an inadvertent warning about the potentially pernicious place that Shakespeare continues to occupy in the contemporary popular imagination.

THE NEVERENDING FRONTIER

From its initial conception as a reimagining of the television series *Wagon Train* set in space (Roddenberry 1964, 3), *Star Trek* has demonstrated a sustained interest in the dynamics of contact between humanity and other sentient species. The franchise's vision of inter-species contact is not, however, ideologically neutral. As Valerie Fulton (1994) notes, "The Federation's goals are both 'to seek out new civilizations' and 'to boldly go where no one has gone before' – missions that clearly contradict each other unless read through the lens of frontier ideology, which grants new civilizations existence only to the extent that the originary culture has 'found' them." Exploration, as it is imagined in the franchise, is "quasimilitaristic," and the series' "basic premises reify nineteenth-century notions of the relationships between the dominant and subordinate, between cultures that have evolved and those that have not" (McGeough 2016, 230, 231).

Crucial to the franchise's formulation of human-nonhuman relations is a fundamental and abiding belief in the superiority of humanity and of the human perspective. For *Star Trek*, this "human perspective" is inextricably linked to the world view of its creator, Gene Roddenberry, who, as Victor Grech argues, "imposed his humanist views on *Star Trek* with an iron hand" (2016, 15). It is thus not surprising that two of the franchise's series, *Star Trek: The Next Generation* (1987–94) and *Star Trek: Deep Space Nine* (1993–99), centre their premiere episodes ("Encounter at Farpoint" and "Emissary," respectively) on a spirited defence of humanity in the face of apparently omnipotent antagonists. In *The Next Generation*, the antagonist, an alien who is a member of the so-called Q Continuum, traps the *Enterprise* and demands that its captain, Jean-Luc Picard, defend humanity in light of its various historical atrocities. In *Deep Space Nine*, the station's newly minted commander, Benjamin Sisko, must explain the human experience to a race of alien beings that do not experience time linearly. In each case, the human protagonist successfully defends humanity, Picard through a demonstration of non-violent problem solving and Sisko by way of an extended analogy to baseball.

Deep Space Nine's use of baseball as analogous to the human experience is indicative of the extent to which the *Star Trek* franchise partakes in what Iain Robert Smith describes as the pervasive "Americentrism in science fiction narratives" (2008, 3). Indeed, the world view espoused by the franchise is profoundly indebted to post-Enlightenment, Anglo-American tradition. It is telling that, of the forty-six main cast members of the five different live-action series in the franchise, a total of two – Alexander Siddig and Linda Park – were born outside of North America or the United Kingdom, and even these two had been residents of the United Kingdom and the United States, respectively, since they were children. The portrait that the franchise thus paints of humanity is one in which the population of Earth has been assimilated to Anglo-American cultural practices and beliefs, "a pattern card of egalitarian homogeneity" (Hurd 1997, 23).

Indeed, Roddenberry's utopian commitment to secular humanism results in a pervasive trend within the franchise, in which nonhuman characters are repeatedly cast in celebratory assimilation narratives. In each of the later *Star Trek* television series, there is at least one nonhuman character whose assimilation into human culture is an ongoing concern of the series. Likely as a result of its setting on the fringes of Federation-controlled space, *Star Trek: Deep Space Nine* features assimilation narratives surrounding a number of characters, including Odo, the shapeshifting security chief; Nog, the Ferengi who eventually joins Starfleet, the Earth-based exploration and defence wing of the Federation; and Garak, the Cardassian tailor and former/current spy who remains after the occupying Cardassians relinquish the eponymous space station to Federation control. The latter seasons of *Star Trek: Voyager* (1995–2001) feature the re-assimilation narrative of Seven of Nine, who had been captured and assimilated into the Borg Collective, a hive-minded, human-machine hybrid race whose defining characteristic is the absorption and assimilation of other sentient species. One of the continuing plots of the prequel series, *Star Trek: Enterprise* (2001–05), is the slow assimilation of the initially antagonistic Vulcan first officer T'Pol.

SHAKESPEARE: THE EXPANSION OF THE HUMAN

If one of the abiding concerns of the *Star Trek* franchise is proselytizing a world view shaped by Roddenberry's postwar Anglo-American humanism through its repeated celebratory assimilation narratives, one of the key figures in that proselytization is Shakespeare. The pattern of implicating Shakespeare in the process of assimilation begins in "By Any Other Name," from the second season of the original series. In it, the aggressive, imperially minded aliens from the planet Kelvan abandon their to-that-point successful commandeering of the *Enterprise* when they realize that exposure to humans has corrupted their identities, undermining their powerful collectivity with an incipient individualism. The primary manifestation of this process is the growing attraction between Kirk and the alien Kelinda, an attraction that is inaugurated when Kirk recites the line from *Romeo and Juliet* that gives the episode its title. Kirk's decision to quote from *Romeo and Juliet* makes sense, given the resonance of the play's plot of boundary-crossing romance with the episode's narrative of inter-species attraction. That said, the content and narrative context of the quotation are only part of its function in the scene. As quotations from Shakespeare do so often in the *Star Trek* franchise, Kirk's citation of Shakespeare works in multiple ways here, simultaneously offering an analogue to the particular moment in the television series and an aesthetic and emotional justification for cross-cultural exchange. The Shakespearean text in this moment is not simply a valued cultural artifact but also a model for experiencing the world, for *feeling* like a human. Similarly, in *Deep Space Nine*, when Garak confronts his former commander, Enabran Tain (who is also, as it turns out, his secret father), his divorce from his Cardassian heritage is signalled by his quotation of *Julius Caesar*: "I'm afraid the fault, dear Tain, is not in our stars but in ourselves" ("The Die Is Cast"). The significance of the moment is signalled in the exchange between Garak and the station's chief medical officer, Julian Bashir, with which the previous episode opens:

GARAK: But I'm sorry, Doctor, I just don't see the value of this man's work.
BASHIR: Garak, Shakespeare is one of the giants of human literature.
GARAK: I knew Brutus was going to kill Caesar in the first act, but Caesar didn't figure it out until the knife is in his back.
BASHIR: That's what makes it a tragedy. Caesar couldn't conceive that his best friend would plot to kill him.
GARAK: Tragedy is not the word I'd use. Farce would be more appropriate. Supposedly, this man is supposed to be the leader of a great empire, a brilliant military tactician, and yet he can't see what's going on under his own nose. ("Improbable Cause")

As in "By Any Other Name," knowledge of Shakespeare is insufficient; it is an *understanding* of Shakespeare that marks the character's growing association with humanity.

This connection between humanity, emotions, and Shakespeare is most often evoked in the assimilation narrative of Data, the android officer in *The Next Generation*. From the first episode, in which Data declares, to Commander Riker, "I am superior, sir, in many ways, but I would gladly give it up to be human," for which Riker quickly nicknames him "Pinocchio" ("Encounter at Farpoint"), Data's quest to become human is one of the foundational narratives on which the series is built. "Data's appeal," argues Esther Rashkin, "comes, fundamentally, from his constant efforts to become more human-like" (2011, 322). Notably, these efforts manifest themselves repeatedly in the series by way of Data's ongoing attempts to engage with Shakespeare's works. In "The Measure of a Man," from the second season, in which Data's rights as an autonomous being are put on trial, one of the three items that Data chooses to keep as mementos of his time aboard the *Enterprise* is a book of Shakespeare, as revealed when the episode's antagonist, Commander Maddox, reads out the opening lines of Sonnet 29. The next season, in "The Defector," Data explores his incipient humanity by performing the lead role from *Henry V*. When Riker, temporarily imbued with god-like power, offers to transform Data into a human in the first-season episode "Hide and Q," Data quotes *Hamlet* to explain his refusal: "'This above all, to thine own self be true?' Sorry, Commander, I must decline" ("Hide and Q"). While this passage, on its surface, seems to mark Shakespeare as an impediment to Data's quest to become human, its significance, like Garak's quotation of *Julius Caesar*, lies in his comprehension of it. At this early stage in his assimilation ("Hide and Q" is only the tenth episode in the series), Data uses the quotation from Shakespeare as a metric of assessment, judging his "own self" to be, at that moment, insufficiently human to justify the proffered transformation. Ironically, the very comprehension of Shakespeare that would mark his successful assimilation functions here to mark his failure to have fully achieved his goal.

As David Reinheimer notes, "The most extended series of Shakespearean allusions centers around Commander Data" (1995, 46). But it is worth taking a look at what, or rather who, is just barely off-centre in each of these scenes. That is, while Data's is undoubtedly the most prominent assimilation narrative in the series, and that narrative depends on repeated associations of humanness with Shakespeare's works, I would argue that the most striking assimilation story in the series, in that it is the most fully achieved, is that of the *Enterprise*'s predominant fan of Shakespeare, Captain Picard.

ONE OF THE CAPTAIN'S FAVOURITE AUTHORS

In virtually every instance of Data's use of Shakespeare as a tool to understand humanity, his apprehension of the text is mediated by Captain Picard. While Data plays Henry in the holographically reconstructed camp at Agincourt, Picard stands watching, in full uniform, silently mouthing his lines. It is Picard who gives voice to the place of Shakespeare in Data's assimilation process: "Data, you're here to learn about the human condition and there is no better way of doing that than by embracing Shakespeare" ("The Defector"). The book of Shakespeare that Data rates as one of his three most prized possessions is, we are told, a gift from Picard. And, again, when Data quotes *Hamlet* to decline his magical transformation into a human, he identifies the author of the play not as Shakespeare but as "one of the Captain's favourite authors" ("Hide and Q"). Another edition of Shakespeare appears in "The Most Toys," where it is taken from Data's quarters after his apparent death. Picking up the book, Picard opens it and reveals it to be *Hamlet* (or at least to contain *Hamlet*). In each case, though the allusions to Shakespeare indisputably reflect on Data's story, they also mark Picard as Data's mentor in the double, and apparently inextricable, processes of learning Shakespeare and learning humanness.

Indeed, Picard, the first and most persistent quoter of Shakespeare in the series, is undoubtedly the inheritor of Captain Kirk's Shakespeare connoisseurship. In the pilot episode, faced with a replica of a violent twenty-first-century tribunal, Picard's immediate reaction is to quote from *Henry VI, Part 2*: "I recognise this court system as the one that agreed with that line from Shakespeare. 'Kill all the lawyers'" ("Encounter at Farpoint"). Throughout virtually the entire series, a collected works of Shakespeare is visible behind glass in Picard's ready room. When "Q" – while reading Picard's Shakespeare – quotes first *As You Like It* and then *Macbeth* as a means of denigrating humanity, Picard responds by quoting *Hamlet*: "Oh, no. I know *Hamlet*. And what he might say with irony, I say with conviction: 'What a piece of work is man! How noble in reason. How infinite in faculty. In form, in moving, how express and admirable. In action, how like an angel. In apprehension, how like a god'" ("Hide and Q"). When "Q" leaves the conversation in disgust, Picard's victory in his defence of humanity is marked by his having regained possession of his copy of *The Globe Illustrated Shakespeare*, around which he wraps his hands protectively (figure 16.1).

Given that Patrick Stewart, who plays Picard, spent the better part of his pre–*Star Trek* acting career as a member of the Royal Shakespeare Company, it makes sense that he should be given ample opportunities to demonstrate his facility with the plays. But Patrick Stewart is not captain of the *Enterprise*; Jean-Luc Picard is.

Figure 16.1 | Jean-Luc Picard (Patrick Stewart) clutches *The Globe Illustrated Shakespeare.*

And, accent notwithstanding, Picard is not English, he is French – his brother Robert continues to live in rural France on the family vineyard ("Family"). It might then make more sense if, instead of from Shakespeare's collected works, Picard derived his lessons about humanity from the plays of Molière or the essays of Montaigne. This, however, cannot be, as the French language has, by the time period of the series, become "an obscure language" ("Code of Honor"). However, the disappearance of French is mentioned only briefly, and nothing is made of it other than Picard's mildly indignant declaration that "the French language for centuries on Earth represented civilization" ("Code of Honor"). Furthermore, despite this one-time celebration of his French heritage, Picard is apparently a committed anglophile. In addition to his encyclopedic knowledge of Shakespeare, he is a devoted consumer of Earl Grey tea and is familiar with the music of Gilbert and Sullivan (*Star Trek: Insurrection*). Indeed, it is in his transcending his roots that Picard demonstrates his suitability for the role of captain of a starship: "Sipping Earl Grey tea and writing articles about the archaeological past of the various cultures that he encounters, Picard is a fantasy vision of nineteenth-century British imperialism being enacted nobly and bloodlessly where no one has gone before. Despite (or because of) his amateurism, Picard in the guise of the idealised British colonialist is the proper mediator of any planet's history" (McGeough 2016, 236). Divorced from his roots, advocating powerfully for the dominant culture into which his heritage has been absorbed, Picard is the model of the assimilated subject turned assimilator. In this, he represents the culmination of the humanist fantasy that animates the *Star Trek* franchise, a fantasy of Anglo-American hegemony that is most clearly and repeatedly focalized through the series' advocacy of Shakespeare connoisseurship as a conduit to humanness. As Mark Houlahan puts it, Shakespeare's "texts are a crucial part of Federation cultural capital, a guarantor of their 'universal humanity'" (1995, 30).

If *Star Trek*'s utopian universalism makes it problematic, it is because of its formulation of that universalism as a galaxy-wide dissemination of mid-to-late twentieth-century Anglo-American culture. It is telling that the Collected Works that Picard holds in "Hide and Q" is not a replica of the First Folio, or of another seventeenth-century edition of the plays, but is rather the 1986 edition of *The Globe Illustrated Shakespeare*, which was itself based almost entirely on Howard Staunton's three-volume *The Plays of Shakespeare*, published in 1860. The book thus serves as a near-perfect synecdoche for the series' deployment of Shakespeare more generally. That is, "Shakespeare" for *Star Trek* should be understood not simply as a collection of culturally valued texts but as emblematic of a nineteenth-century ethos of Anglo-American world dominance repackaged for a 1980s audience. To commit oneself to Shakespeare, the franchise tells us, is to submit willingly and happily to that dominance. Failure to do so is nothing less than a failure to be human, which, in the universe of *Star Trek*, is to be a failure, period.

NOTES

1 In the interest of precision, it should be noted that Kirk does not speak the famous "where no man has gone before" introduction at the beginning of two early episodes of the series, "The Cage," the failed pilot episode of the series, which did not feature Kirk, and the subsequent successful pilot, "Where No Man Has Gone Before."

2 A number of critics have characterized the series as creator Gene Roddenberry's utopian vision of humanity's future. Given this reading of the series, it does not seem like a stretch to ascribe the values of the society depicted to the series itself.

REFERENCES

Buhler, Stephen M. 1995. "'Who Calls Me Villain?' Blank Verse and the Black Hat." *Extrapolation: A Journal of Science Fiction and Fantasy* 36 (1): 18–27.

Fulton, Valerie. 1994. "An Other Frontier: Voyaging West with Mark Twain and Star Trek's Imperial Subject." *Postmodern Culture: An Electronic Journal of Interdisciplinary Criticism* 4 (3). https://muse.jhu.edu/issue/1596.

Graham, Jean E. 2000. "Holodeck Masquing: Early Modern Genre Meets *Star Trek*." *Journal of Popular Culture* 34 (2): 21–7.

Grech, Victor. 2016. "Deicide in Star Trek: The Ultimate Expression of Humanism?" *Foundation: The International Review of Science Fiction* 45 (123): 14–23.

Houlahan, Mark. 1995. "Cosmic Hamlets? Contesting Shakespeare in Federation Space." *Extrapolation: A Journal of Science Fiction and Fantasy* 36 (1): 28–37.

Hurd, Denise Alessandria. 1997. "The Monster Inside: 19th Century Racial Constructs in the 24th Century Mythos of Star Trek." *Journal of Popular Culture* 31 (1): 23–35.

McGeough, Kevin M. 2016. "Victorian Archaeologies, Anthropologies and Adventures in the Final Frontier: Modes of Nineteenth-Century Scientific Exploration and Display in *Star Trek*." *Science Fiction Film and Television* 9 (2): 229–52.

Rashkin, Esther. 2011. "Data Learns to Dance: *Star Trek* and the Quest to Be Human." *American Imago* 68 (2): 321–46.

Reinheimer, David. 1995. "Ontological and Ethical Allusion: Shakespeare in *The Next Generation*." *Extrapolation: A Journal of Science Fiction and Fantasy* 36 (1): 46–54.

Roddenberry, Gene. 1964. *Star Trek*. Series Outline. 11 March. http://leethomson.myzen.co.uk/Star_Trek/1_Original_Series/Star_Trek_Pitch.pdf.

Smith, Iain Robert. 2008. "'Beam Me up, Ömer': Transnational Media Flow and the Cultural Politics of the Turkish *Star Trek* Remake." *Velvet Light Trap* 61: 3–13.

Star Trek Episodes, Series, and Movies Referenced

"By Any Other Name." *Star Trek*, season 2, episode 22, 23 February 1968. *Netflix*, https://www.netflix.com/watch/70178535?.

"Code of Honor." *Star Trek: The Next Generation*, season 1, episode 4, 12 October 1987. *Netflix*, https://www.netflix.com/watch/70177866?.

"The Defector." *Star Trek: The Next Generation*, season 3, episode 10, 1 January 1990. *Netflix*, https://www.netflix.com/watch/70177920?.

"The Die Is Cast." *Star Trek: Deep Space Nine*, season 3, episode 21, 1 May 1995. *Netflix*, https://www.netflix.com/watch/70205872?.

"Emissary." *Star Trek: Deep Space Nine*, season 1, episodes 1 and 2, 3 January 1993. *Netflix*, https://www.netflix.com/watch/70205806?.

"Encounter at Farpoint." *Star Trek: The Next Generation*, season 1, episodes 1 and 2, 28 September 1987. *Netflix*, https://www.netflix.com/watch/70177863?.

"Family." *Star Trek: The Next Generation*, season 4, episode 2, 1 October 1990. *Netflix*, https://www.netflix.com/watch/70177938?.

"Hide and Q." *Star Trek: The Next Generation*, season 1, episode 10, 30 November 1987. *Netflix*, https://www.netflix.com/watch/70177872?.

"Improbable Cause." *Star Trek: Deep Space Nine*, season 3, episode 20, 24 April 1995. *Netflix*, https://www.netflix.com/watch/70205871?.

"The Measure of a Man." *Star Trek: The Next Generation*, season 3, episode 9, 13 February 1989. *Netflix*, https://www.netflix.com/watch/70177897?.

"The Most Toys." *Star Trek: The Next Generation*, season 3, episode 22, 7 May 1990. *Netflix*, https://www.netflix.com/watch/70177932?.

Star Trek. Desilu Productions and Paramount Television, 1966–69.

Star Trek: The Animated Series. Filmation, Norway Productions, and Paramount Television Service, 1973–74.

Star Trek: Deep Space Nine. Paramount Domestic Television, 1993–99.

Star Trek: Enterprise. Paramount Television, Braga Productions, and Rick Berman Productions, 2001–5.

Star Trek: Insurrection. Directed by Jonathan Frakes, Paramount Pictures, 1998.

Star Trek: The Next Generation. Paramount Domestic Television, 1987–94.

Star Trek VI: The Undiscovered Country. Directed by Nicholas Meyer, Paramount Pictures, 1991.

Star Trek: Voyager. Paramount Network Television, 1995–2001.

17

RETELLING *MACBETH* FOR THE DIGITAL AGE

The Multimodal Poetics of Sleep No More

JACOB CLAFLIN

Sleep No More, an adaptation of *Macbeth*, is an immersive performance event that engages all five senses, from the smell of dirt in the graveyard to the taste of the chocolate in the candy shop. It tells *Macbeth*'s story from multiple viewpoints, all without a single spoken word from Shakespeare's play. In this chapter, I argue that, through its use of a variety of performative and communicative modes, *Sleep No More* engages its audience in a new way. If, as Lauren Eriks Cline argues in her chapter in this volume, theatre audiences can normally be understood to write the meanings of the productions they witness, then *Sleep No More* challenges and complicates this norm, inviting interactive engagement while mediating the interaction in a way that shapes the audience's ability to determine a meaning from the production.

To build my case, I draw on an approach that I call multimodal poetics. Based on social semiotic multimodality, multimodal poetics offers a way to analyze a text that uses more than words. Multimodal poetics works on the level of modes (basically forms of communication) – for example, writing, speaking, images, colour, gesture, and costume. Multimodality itself is not new, and all theatre is inherently multimodal, but the approach I am using reframes the work of the social semioticians as a tool for analyzing theatre, among other media.

Sleep No More is a promenade-style performance created by the performance company Punchdrunk. The original production ran for a short time in London in 2003, then again in Boston in 2009. In 2011, Punchdrunk reinvented *Sleep No More*, teaming up with the production company Emursive (founded specifically to bring *Sleep No More* to Manhattan) for its New York debut. The performance, originally conceived as a limited run, has been extended indefinitely. In *Sleep No More*, each audience member can choose where they go in the playing space. The cast members take special care to separate groups, attempting to ensure that each person wanders the space alone. This presents an interesting challenge in discussing the production, as my experience in the playing space, which Punchdrunk calls the McKittrick Hotel, in June 2014 was a unique experience that no one else will ever have. There simply is no way to take in all of *Sleep No More* in a single trip.

The story of *Sleep No More* takes only an hour but resets over the course of the three-hour performance for a total of three runs of the story. The price of a ticket dictates when an audience member can enter the performance; in my case, I entered with about two hours remaining. Although there is a set end time for the performance, audience members can leave at any time they choose. As they enter, the audience members are handed white masks and sent out, via the elevator operator, into the "hotel" to explore the installation. There are many different rooms, including a candy shop, a taxidermy shop, and a detective agency, some connected by a street. There are several bedrooms, a ballroom, a graveyard, a forest, a sanitarium, an alchemist's shop, even a dilapidated bar. Rooms are filled with props, all appropriate to the setting of late 1930s America. Music and sounds play all through the installation, and each room is lit in a way that suggests a noir-style film with a constant haze. The complexity of this set is far beyond anything I have personally encountered at any production of a Shakespeare play.

Once an audience member crosses the threshold into the playing space, the primary modes of the performance are distinctly non-verbal, comprising the complex set, props, lighting, and dances. What makes this performance so compelling is the level of detail with which it uses these non-verbal modes. The dances use the language of modern dance to communicate the emotions of the characters as well as the physical interaction between the characters, such as murder, rape, and intimacy. The set and props help to refine the broad strokes of the dancing by establishing place, but also by creating an emotional ambiance. Some rooms are filled with tarnished and decaying props or with props that have connections to death, while others are filled with books and comfortable chairs. The props, set, lighting, and dance are all part of the language of *Sleep No More*.

Throughout this elaborate set, the twenty-five or so performers interact with each other and, on rare occasions, with the audience; the performers include the staff of the Manderley Bar, who talk with audience members as they wait to be called to the elevator. Most performers portray characters from the story of *Macbeth*, including Macbeth, Lady Macbeth, Duncan, Malcom, Macduff, Lady Macduff, Hecate, and the witches. A few portray new characters, such as Agnes Naismith, who is searching for her sister (who I believe is Lady Macduff), and Nurse Shaw in the sanitarium, who takes the place of the Scottish doctor caring for the sleepwalking Lady Macbeth and is driven insane by the witches. All of the performers are dressed in 1930s noir-style costumes, with the men in suits and tuxedos and the women in elegant evening gowns.

Before they enter the performance, audience members are asked not to talk, use their phones, or take their masks off. The performers tell their stories though dance, gesture, body position, and facial expression accompanied by music. As Sivan Grunfeld (2013) points out, "Finding a cohesive story within the maelstrom of *Sleep No More* was impossible … Eventually, I stopped trying [to find a cohesive narrative] and began to create my own narrative." The nature of the performance in fact offers the audience a choice in how they interpret the show because they can chose how they interact with the production. Audience members can watch a given performance or move away and explore the set. Some choose to follow a single character (I did this once I'd identified the Macbeth character by stumbling into the rave that stands in for Macbeth's second meeting with the witches). Others stay in a single location to view the performances there. Even without any direct interaction with the actors, the audience's movement in the space can create a great deal of action. Members of the audience often follow performers who dash out to another part of the massive set, sometimes up several flights of stairs at speed. Audience members often vie for position as they run along. The experience is visceral, exhilarating, and exhausting.

While vying for position with other audience members, one can feel the stonework of a building, sit in the chair at a desk, taste the bonbons in a candy store, or smell a stuffed bird. One of the key features of *Sleep No More*'s playing space is the ability of audience members to choose. They can choose to eat a bonbon or not. They can choose where they are in relation to the actors in a given moment. The ability to choose is how Punchdrunk invites a sense of interaction with the performance.

This ability accesses ideas from a more modern medium: video games. Although the first iteration of *Sleep No More* in 2003 predated the 2007 release of 2K Games' *Bioshock* video game, the current reimagined New York production of *Sleep No More* has a great deal in common with the game. *Bioshock* is a story about a man who seemingly stumbles onto a vast underwater city named Rapture that was established as a kind of utopia in the 1950s. By the time he arrives, that utopia has become a dystopia. Despite the fact that the city is ruined, the setting still has strong art deco and noir elements throughout. The theme of ambition is an important part of the story of *Bioshock,* as it is for *Macbeth,* but *Bioshock* is not an adaptation of *Macbeth*. The strong connection to *Sleep No More* comes through in the interaction of the player character with the environment, which the current *Sleep No More* emulates.

Bioshock is a first-person shooter videogame, meaning that players experience the city of Rapture through the eyes of Jack, the character they control. Players can see Jack's hands or, later in the game, the weapon he is holding. Although there is a structure to the game and players are limited in where they can go, they have free rein within a given level to explore it however they wish. Throughout the game, Jack must discover the secrets of Rapture to understand what happened in the city and his place within it. In *Sleep No More*, audience members are encouraged to be curious and pick things up, and they are told there is a mystery to solve. Once they are off the elevator, their experience mirrors that of *Bioshock*, to a point. In Gallows Green, the town *Sleep No More* is set in, the audience member is not an active part of the story, but a voyeuristic, anonymous observer. Still, the experience of walking through a number of rooms with specific props laid out to encourage the audience member to look through things is much like that of *Bioshock* or other first-person shooter games. The biggest difference is, of course, that *Bioshock* takes place on a screen, while *Sleep No More* is tangible, not limited by screen size.[1]

Although both *Bioshock* and *Sleep No More* present the option to interact with the environment, they both refuse to allow the audience to influence the story through this interaction. In *Bioshock*, the player must sort out how to survive on each level, but nearly every moment tied directly to the overarching story is scripted. For example, in one pivotal moment in the story, the character has no choice but to kill Andrew Ryan, the Ayn Rand–inspired character who built Rapture. The game forces the player to enter the room, then takes over, showing Jack's murder of Ryan; the player at that moment has no control, not even a choice of how to kill Ryan. *Sleep No More*, similarly, has moments where the production limits the audience's ability to choose. At about the halfway point in the story, the ushers who lurk in the playing space begin herding the audience into the main ballroom. There the audience watches a reception for Duncan as all the characters interact. The same thing happens at the end of the story, when the audience is herded into the ballroom to watch the final banquet, where Macbeth's crimes are revealed and punished. As with *Bioshock*, the audience at *Sleep No More* has no way to influence the main story events.

Both *Bioshock* and *Sleep No More* create a kind of paradox where audience members feel as if they are free to act, yet simultaneously realize they have no ability to influence the story in any way. As Myrto Koumarianos and Cassandra Silver comment with respect to *Sleep No More*:

> The sense of autonomy cultivated by [our] gradual entry into the performance contributed significantly to the ease with which we were drawn into the fiction of the action. Our sense of almost unlimited agency resulted in higher stakes for our own participation and performance – our implication in the action begged our accountability to ourselves, to our fellow spectators, and to the performers. We remained autonomous, accountable, "real" in some sense inside the space; yet we were simultaneously drawn into an identically faced and therefore faceless community, into a fiction over which we ultimately had no control. (2013, 168)

Sean Bartley (2013) and Colette Gordon (2013) also address this paradox between the freedom to roam and interact and the inability to influence the story itself. This paradox of freedom and powerlessness is present in both *Sleep No More* and *Bioshock*, but what separates *Sleep No More* from games like *Bioshock* is that, in the performance, the audience are simply faceless observers, not the focus of the story like they are in the game, even if the player character has no way to influence the story itself. In *Sleep No More*, just like in the majority of theatrical performance arenas, the audience does not talk, and they usually do not touch the actors (this seems to be an unspoken rule, though there are a few instances where it is allowable). Unlike a more traditional theatre performance arena, there is a noticeable sense of voyeurism in *Sleep No More*. The nature of the space allows you to get as close to or as far from the actors as you want. Although they will react to the audience at certain times, the bulk of the performers ignore the audience, making them feel like little more than faceless observers.

The inability to change the story still does not ensure that every audience member sees the same story, as happens in more traditional theatre. An audience member following Macbeth will encounter a different story than one following Agnes Naismith, for example. But what *Sleep No More* does do is ensure that the story each audience member encounters will contain similar elements of suspense, horror, and the gothic. This happens due to the designers' deft manipulation of the modes of costume, set, props, lighting, and music. The themes in *Macbeth* permeate all the modes of *Sleep No More*, ensuring that all audience members will encounter stories of ambition, power, and murder, even if they encounter Macbeth himself only in the two group scenes.

The theatrical modes of *Sleep No More*, such as lighting, set, costume, and props, work the same way in the McKittrick Hotel as they do on any other stage. There is therefore a significant continuity in the way *Sleep No More* and conventional stage productions of *Macbeth* engage an audience. For example, W.B. Worthen (2012, 2014) argues that, despite the immersive quality of the performance, an audience interprets *Sleep No More* in much the same way they would interpret a more traditional performance. He states: "In performance, *Sleep No More* models a vision of theatrical 'cognition' surprisingly dependent on a familiar, literary *Macbeth*, in effect marking the persistence of a 'poetic' dramatic logic even in the 'immersive' dynamics of theatrical production" (2014, 123). However, the lack of spoken language in *Sleep No More* sets it crucially apart from Macbeth, requiring modes such as lighting, set, and props to carry the bulk of the semiotic load.

Because *Sleep No More* uses no spoken language, Punchdrunk essentially replaces Shakespeare's language with a brilliantly designed physical playing space for the actors to perform in. This playing space creates a feeling of suspense and horror in the audience from the moment the elevator operator pushes them off. The language of

Macbeth creates an eerie and suspenseful ambiance. A large part of this ambiance comes from the complex imagery of the play. In her classic work on Shakespeare's imagery, Caroline Spurgeon states: "The imagery in *Macbeth* appears to me to be more rich and varied, more highly imaginative, more unapproachable by any other writer, than that of any other single play" (1977, 13). To Spurgeon, "an appreciable part of the emotions we feel throughout of pity, fear, and horror, is due to the subtle but definite and repeated action of this imagery upon our minds, of which, in our preoccupation with the main theme, we remain often largely unconscious" (21). Productions of *Macbeth* often use set, costume, lighting, and sound to accentuate these images and draw out the gothic ambiance. With *Sleep No More*, this idea is taken to an extreme. Props and set details embody the imagery in the language of *Macbeth*, creating an ambiance that is unique, and yet familiar to those who know the play.

Perhaps the most prevalent image from *Macbeth* and *Sleep No More* concerns birds. The text of *Macbeth* is filled with birds: "as sparrows eagles, or the hare the lion"; "The raven himself is hoarse"; "The temple-haunting martlet"; "it was the owl that shrieked"; "A falcon, tow'ring in her pride of place, / Was by a mousing owl hawked at and killed"; "Augurs and understood relations have / by maggot-pies and choughs and rooks brought forth / The secret'st man of blood"; "O hell-kite! All? / What my pretty chickens and their dam / At one fell swoop?" (Shakespeare 1997, 1.2.35; 1.5.37; 1.6.4; 2.2.3; 2.4.12–13; 3.4.123–4; 4.3.218–20). Birds permeate the text. The imagery accesses ideas about birds, specifically the idea of birds as omens. A number of these references are obvious. The cawing raven is a well-known sign that death is on its way, the house martin (martlet) in the castle was supposed to be a good omen (it is ironic in *Macbeth*), and of course Macbeth himself comments on the prophetic nature of birds in the lines about magpies, choughs, and rooks. Even when a specific bird is not directly acting as an omen, the reference reinforces the theme of prophesy that is integral to *Macbeth*.

The designers of *Sleep No More* recall this bird imagery in the set and props. The space is filled with stuffed birds of all kinds. Most of the ones I encountered were game birds and small songbirds. In the alchemist's shop there were not only stuffed birds, but wings, feathers, and empty bird cages. In several locations I saw eggs, including in the dark room of the detective office, where there were also bird claws and even taxonomy charts and Audubon-style paintings of birds on the walls. Hecate carries a peacock fan, and when Macbeth smothers Duncan with a feather pillow, the feathers spill out over the audience (de Winter n.d.). Even the masks that all the audience members wear have beak-shaped noses.

While *Sleep No More*'s preponderance of birds echoes themes in *Macbeth*, some of those themes differ from Shakespeare's. More than *Macbeth*, *Sleep No More* uses the birds as a reminder of the victims of Macbeth's actions. The number of stuffed game birds changes the nature of the birds for *Sleep No More*. In *Macbeth*, the most common birds mentioned are raptors – eagles, hawks, kites, buzzards, owls – which are linked to the predations of Macbeth and others, and corvids – ravens, crows, rooks, choughs, magpies – linked more to the themes of prophesy and death. Only a few songbirds and game birds are referenced. This keeps the focus on the predatory nature of birds, as well as their connection to death and prophesy. The shift to game birds and songbirds, at least in my experience of *Sleep No More*, brings out the few references to the victims in *Macbeth*: the martlet that falsely comforts Duncan upon entering Macbeth's castle, Macduff calling his wife and children a hen and chicks, Macbeth calling the messenger he abuses a goose and a loon. *Sleep No More* shifts the focus from the Macbeths to their victims, as well as the extra characters that Punchdrunk added, most of whom are also victims, though not always of the Macbeths.

Punchdrunk adapts the birds and other imagery of *Macbeth* into its set and lighting by emulating media that modern audiences associate with the horror and suspense that *Macbeth's* imagery elicits. Primarily the sets recall film noir as well as Hitchcock's films, specifically *Vertigo* (the "theatre" is called the McKittrick Hotel, which is the hotel from *Vertigo*) and *Rebecca* (the bar in the McKittrick is the Manderley, the name of the de Winter estate in *Rebecca*). As Glenn Ricci (2013) points out, a good deal of the music also comes from Bernard Hermann's scores for three of Hitchcock's movies: *The Man Who Knew Too Much*, *Vertigo*, and *Psycho*. The costumes and the sets reflect those in some of Hitchcock's films: men in tuxedoes, trench coats, and fedoras, women in elegant evening wear or crisp white nurse uniforms.

This connection between *Sleep No More* and Hitchcock appropriates a distinct *mise en scène* from some of Hitchcock's films and other noir films to create a feeling of suspense and horror in the McKittrick. The dark lighting borrowed from noir films brings out the darkness of the play itself – "Stars, hide your fires"; "Come, thick night"; "There's husbandry in heaven, / Their candles are all out"; "Light thickens, and the crow / Makes wing to th' rooky wood" (Shakespeare 1997, 1.4.50, 1.5.49, 2.1.4–5, 3.2.51–2). The music and references to Hitchcock films bring out the elements of suspense Hitchcock was famous for and put them to work in this new text. The *Sleep No More* designers make use of texts that shaped a modern cultural idea of what a suspense or classic horror film looks like to bring that cultural idea into their performance space.

This choice acts as a kind of frame, which both excludes things outside of it and focuses the viewer toward the things within it. Using a noir/Hitchcock *mise en scène* allows Punchdrunk to guide the audience toward a meaning tied to horror and suspense, and not, for example, comedy or romance. The designers exclude elements in the *mise en scène* that would signal to the audience a mood other than suspense, horror, and supernatural thriller. At the same time the prevalence of Hitchcock/noir-like elements in every room of the performance space constantly reinforces the themes of ambition, power, and supernatural influence that also dominate *Macbeth*. The audience simply cannot escape these visual themes; they have no choice, despite their freedom to move about the installation.

The paradoxes of *Sleep No More*'s performance space are an integral part of how the text conveys meaning. The distance provided by the masks creates a kind of anonymity, the same that sitting in a darkened auditorium grants. The masks also create a voyeuristic feeling similar to social media, where someone can experience the (mediated) life of a friend through what they post on Facebook or Twitter. As with social media, the audience does not have all the facts. Often, they may not even have that specific character's full narrative. They must make inferences to interpret what they experienced into a cohesive narrative. The limits set by the bellhop and the ushers, the visual motifs such as the birds, and the Hitchcock/noir-style *mise en scène* keep the audience member from wandering too far from the plot that the creators intend, no matter how much the elevator operator encourages an audience member to be bold.

Sleep No More is a daring Shakespeare adaptation. Its multiple modes create an entirely different kind of performance, one that accesses ideas from film and video games. Much like video games, it presents a paradox of choice and control, where audience members are encouraged to interact directly with the set but cannot influence the story through their interaction, and are limited in what meaning they can create from the experience by the very set they are encouraged to interact with. Despite this paradox, *Sleep No More* remains a truly unique adaptation of Shakespeare, one that pushes the boundaries of conventional theatre by bringing a new kind of interaction to theatre-goers.

NOTE

1 In 2011–12, Punchdrunk collaborated with the MIT media lab to create an online version of *Sleep No More* where the users were interfaced with audience members at the site in New York. The masks transmitted the experience back to those on the computer and allowed them to interact with the participant in New York. The effect was much like a video game for the online audience. The project garnered some interesting attention, and there are several articles about it, but it seems that it was simply an experiment and not something a user can now access.

REFERENCES

Bartley, Sean. 2013. "Punchdrunk: Performance, Permission, Paradox." In Kozusko 2013.

de Winter, Maximilian (pseudonym). n.d. "Bird-Watching at the McKittrick, Part Two: *Sleep No More.*" *Back to Manderley* (blog). Accessed 12 February 2015. http://paisleysweets.tumblr.com/post/38116712522/bird-watching-at-the-mckittrick-part-two-sleep.

Gordon, Colette. 2013. "Touching the Spectator: Intimacy, Immersion, and the Theatre of the Velvet Rope." In Kozusko 2013.

Grunfeld, Sivan. 2013. "Fractured Realities: A Receptive Review of Punchdrunk's *Sleep No More.*" In Kozusko 2013.

Hutcheon, Linda, and Siobhan O'Flynn. 2013. *A Theory of Adaptation.* 2nd ed. London: Routledge.

Koumarianos, Myrto, and Cassandra Silver. 2013. "Dashing at a Nightmare: Haunting Macbeth in *Sleep No More.*" *TDR: The Drama Review* 57 (1 [T 217]): 167–75.

Kozusko, Matt, ed. 2013. "Site, Space, and Intimacy: *Sleep No More's* Immersive Intertext." Special section, *Borrowers and Lenders: The Journal of Shakespeare and Appropriation* 7 (2). http://www.borrowers.uga.edu/.

Ricci, Glenn. 2013. "Tracking the Scottish Play: The Sounds of *Sleep No More*." In Kozusko 2013.

Shakespeare, William. 1997. *Macbeth*. In *The Norton Shakespeare*. Edited by Stephen Greenblatt. New York: Norton.

Spurgeon, Caroline F. 1977. "Shakespeare's Imagery in *Macbeth*." In *Twentieth Century Interpretations of Macbeth: A Collection of Critical Essays*, edited by Terence Hawkes, 13–21. Englewood Cliffs, NJ: Prentice-Hall.

Worthen, W.B. 2012. "'The Written Troubles of the Brain': *Sleep No More* and the Space of Character." *Theatre Journal* 64 (1): 79–97.

– 2014. *Shakespeare Performance Studies*. Cambridge: Cambridge University Press.

18

SQUARE BRACKETS AND PERFORMANCE CHOICES

Considering the Shakespearean Stage Direction

GINA HAUSKNECHT

The stage directions in a favourite volume of Shakespeare offer a powerful means for students and other readers to explore Shakespeare's plays simultaneously as performance, the original form for which they were created, and as text, made for us by centuries of editorial intervention. In a significant sense, Shakespeare did not write the book we read, and even when we return to the early printed texts, as Alan Dessen reminds us, "We are eavesdropping on the early stages of a conversation conducted in a language we only partly understand" (1995, 174). Reading from our modern editions, we are likely to speed past the square brackets enclosing text – scene divisions or locations, characters' names, or stage directions – that did not appear in the original printed versions of the plays: the quartos or First Folio. Yet, closely considered, the square brackets in most of our reading and teaching texts challenge some of our dearest and stickiest assumptions about the play we encounter in class or on the shelf. In the popular imagination, Shakespeare is a mostly solitary genius, bent over his quill pen, and the play is a direct, mostly unmediated transmission of Shakespeare's art from him to us. But *our* book of Shakespeare's plays didn't come straight from that quill. My students are intrigued by how the book in front of them was shaped by people other than Shakespeare, and they are energized by the invitation to think like an editor and to examine the editor's decisions. For example, they respond passionately to Leah Marcus's case for "unediting" *The Tempest* and rally to her call for editors to be more upfront about their attempts to bring fixed meaning to ambiguous words and phrases. Those reading Shakespeare outside of the classroom, too, can readily consider the editor's impact on their experience of the plays by paying attention to those square brackets.

The stage direction in particular illustrates the editor's control over the text in an immediate and sometimes startling way. Students are typically surprised that many of the stage directions in our classroom editions were written or directly influenced by the first Shakespeare editor, Nicholas Rowe, in the early eighteenth century. Their imaginations light up when they are released from the dictates of those stage directions and given responsibility for thinking out their own staging choices. Once attuned to the square brackets that indicate some kind of editorial intervention, my students are prepared to engage, and indeed argue, with the editorial tradition. They have gotten mad about the editorial stage direction in *Much Ado About Nothing* when Claudio "hands" Hero to Leonato and about the absence of a stage direction in Bevington's *Hamlet* when Polonius declares that Claudius should "take this from this, if this be otherwise" (Shakespeare 2014, 243; 1113). Having claimed the authority to make critical judgments about the printed page, they are then ready to think like directors. Meticulous close reading ensues as they test their own imaginations against the demands of the dialogue.

For years, the teaching magic of the editorial stage direction informed my classroom practice in a relatively casual way. The square bracket was one among many tools in a performance pedagogy toolkit. I used critical questioning of an editorial stage direction alongside other formal considerations in discussions of a given scene (for example, "Why is Richard II touching the ground here? How would you know he is, from the text itself, leaving the stage direction aside? What could this look like?"). I found, though, that the more attention I gave the editorial stage direction, the more deeply my students processed how much the editor has intervened in their understanding of the text. Shock is not too strong a term for my students' reaction to the discovery that there is not a single stable text of a beloved play, fairly closely resembling what Shakespeare penned. For those familiar with *Hamlet*, say, appreciation or a sense of mastery over this most canonical of texts has been part of their self-definition as a reader and student. That sense of the ground giving way beneath their feet, sometimes tinged with a little healthy grief, is generally followed by awe at the editor's command over the reading experience: "I always assumed that editors made small and slight additions to plays … but it's the exact opposite. I found this very interesting because having an editor is, narrative-wise, like having a second author work on the piece. The power of the editor is so grand that it shapes the reader's experience with the story" (McClure 2018). In response, I began to formalize my classroom stage-direction exercises into a more deliberative approach to teaching the plays as both performance texts and editorial constructs. I developed an instructional website and a research assignment, both of which ask students to explore the long editorial history of a single stage direction, examine editorial choices, and, finally, consider the implications of those choices for performance.

As a way to engage students directly with a variety of approaches editors have taken to stage directions, I created an interactive online learning tool, *All the World's a Stage Direction* (ATWASD), which asks its users to look closely at a set of passages from Shakespeare plays to which modern editors have added stage directions (Hausknecht 2013). For each passage, there are several questions to which the user responds by highlighting or clicking text; the tool then responds to the user's selection with further information. The questions ask what evidence in the text has led an editor to insert a given stage direction; whether that stage direction is necessary, elucidating an otherwise opaque or invisible action; and, finally, whether and how an interpolated stage direction may influence our perception of the scene. Each exercise concludes with a series of performance questions about the passage in which the stage direction appears. Two examples follow.

I had long taught the famous staging crux in Act 3, Scene 3 of *Othello* with its seemingly simple question, often answered so compellingly on stage, "How does Iago get the handkerchief from Emilia?" The exercise on ATWASD begins by asking users to identify the *last* line of dialogue in this passage that confirms that Emilia still has the handkerchief (Emilia's "Look, here 'tis") and the *first* line that indicates unambiguously that Iago has taken possession of it (Emilia's "Give't me again"). It then asks users to consider where in the five-line gap between these two phrases they think the transfer should occur and to see if they can identify either or both of the two places where editors have traditionally inserted a stage direction specifying the handkerchief changing hands. Next, the exercise encourages comparison of three different versions of the stage direction that appear most often in modern teaching editions: "Snatching it," a frequent choice and one that dates back to Rowe (2014, 1179; 1709, 2604); "He takes the napkin" (2008, 473); and the even simpler "Takes it" (1963, 104). The next question is whether there even needs to be a stage direction. George Steevens, alone among the eighteenth-century editors, left it out, but almost all modern editors put one in; the exercise asks users to consider why.

There are a host of interpretive questions here: What difference does the location of the stage direction make to our understanding of the emotional rhythm of the passage? How do these different stage direction phrasings shape and direct our understanding of what's happening between Iago and Emilia? What should this action look like and what does *that* choice imply for the marriage of Iago and Emilia, and for the character of each? Finally, to ask whether the scene needs a stage direction is to ask for whom the stage direction is provided: Can a *reader* understand what's going on in the scene without a stage direction explaining where and how the handkerchief moves from Iago to Emilia? Does a stage direction provide useful information for an *actor* making a performance decision? Alternately, although we are used to stage directions inserted directly into the text and dictating a specific movement at a specific moment, Margaret Jane Kidnie proposes that printing stage directions in the margins, which allows for more of the interpretative possibilities inherent in the dialogue, "cultivates the reader's active engagement with the script" (2004, 175).

Richard III provides another compelling instance of an editorial stage direction driving our understanding of a critical encounter, the wooing of Lady Anne. Samuel Johnson's 1765 edition is the first to insert a stage direction at the point in this scene where Richard, improbably, produces a ring. Johnson's edition reads "She puts on the ring" (1765, 242), and almost every edition follows suit until the twentieth century. (Three years after Johnson, Edward Capell's stage direction reads "putting it on," but, as is frequently the case, Capell's stage direction is roundly ignored and Johnson's is the one that sticks.) Modern editions, however, mostly favour the phrase "slips the ring on her finger," with variants on whether the subject is specified as "He," "Richard," or "Gloucester" (respectively, 2014, 654; 2002, 915; 1974, 716). The ATWASD exercise asks the user first to determine where it makes sense for the stage direction to appear and then, once again, to consider whether the stage direction is necessary, and, finally, how to understand the implications of the different wordings. Here the stage direction – the articulation of an action that the dialogue insists upon without describing – necessarily produces an interpretation, making either Anne or Richard the principal agent of the exchange. The user is then referred to John Jowett's discussion of what is at stake in this case:

> A conservative editor will let the text speak for itself in such an instance, but an editorial stage direction will undoubtedly clarify the action. Once an editor has decided that an intervention is justified, the question arises as to the precise nature of the [editorial stage direction]. Should the direction stipulate that Richard gives the ring or that Anne takes it? Is "To take" an active or passive action, to take hold of or to receive? Does the action take place before or after Anne's line? Such questions are critical, for, as the play unfolds, it emerges that to take is indeed to give: Anne not only gives her hand in marriage but loses her life as a result. (2007, 154–5)

The ATWASD website exercises explore stage directions that I have found to be productively problematic in class. To put students themselves in charge of this exploration, I also designed a research project that allows them to do original investigations into a stage direction of their own choosing. The starting point for this assignment is any interpolated stage direction in Bevington's *Complete Works* (2014) that suggests to them an interpretative gesture by the editorial hand. Using online editions, they research the history of the stage direction, first by confirming its absence in the Folio and, as applicable, quarto printings; then by checking Rowe; and then moving on to other eighteenth-century, nineteenth-century, and early twentieth-century editions before looking at a number of modern teaching editions. From this comparison of multiple editions, they develop an argument about the impact or import of the variations.

The resulting papers have been sensitive to a range of nuances triggered by a given stage direction. Many of my students have been especially interested in stage directions that they regard as impinging on or amplifying female autonomy. One examined the differences in how and where Isabella is escorted off the stage in the final scene of *Measure for Measure*, having discovered that the stage direction introduced by Lewis Theobald in 1733, "Isabella is carried off, guarded" (388), is sometimes replaced in modern editions by one of a number of variants of "Exit Isabella, guarded" (2015, 1312) and is sometimes augmented by "Isabella is placed under guard" (2011, 826), and, further, that the timing of Isabella's exit shifts from edition to edition. This student proposed that in the Theobald-derived stage directions, Isabella is constrained and diminished:

> This is not only because she is being acted upon rather than being the actor, but also because the connotation of being carried suggests an invasion of space and body and a more forceful removal than simply exiting with guards … The earlier she exits, the more objectified she is. She has no opportunity to be an active part of the scene where her virtues are being discussed if she is removed immediately after the Duke says she should go to prison … Similarly, the stage directions that place Isabella under guard before removing her from the stage show that she is a threat to the power systems that allow Angelo to abuse his position, break the law, and threaten her body. (Remund Wiger 2017)

Another student hypothesized different kinds of marriages implied by how Imogen and Posthumus exchange ring and bracelet in the first scene of *Cymbeline*. Rowe, she found, introduced the stage direction "Putting on the ring" at Posthumus's line "Remain, remain thou here" without specifying Imogen's action of giving him the ring, her mother's diamond, a half-dozen lines earlier. Next, Rowe adds "Putting the Bracelet on her arm" after Posthumus's "It is a Manacle of Love, I'll place it" (1709, 2753). This student discovered numerous minor variants on these stage directions rippling throughout the next three hundred years of editions, but her significant finding was exemplified by the Norton second edition, which, in contrast to Rowe and his inheritors, places three stage directions in the passage: "She gives him a ring … He puts on the ring … He gives her a bracelet" (2008, 1243). For her, the difference between "putting" and "giving" suggests different degrees of intimacy and mutuality and influences how the reader understands Posthumus's later actions and their reunion in the final scene (Tollefsrud 2017).

Other discoveries have operated at the level of theme and genre. One student worked out the resonances of a stage direction written in by Theobald, but not widely adopted, at the revelation of Sebastian and Viola's twinship at the end of *Twelfth Night*. Immediately before

Sebastian, bursting onto stage, stops short to remark, "You throw a strange regard upon me," Theobald wrote in "All stand in amaze" (1733, 531). Using the *Oxford English Dictionary* to better conceptualize how both "strange" and "amaze" would have sounded to Shakespeare and Theobald's audiences, she argued that Theobald's stage direction emphasizes the difference between how the characters and the audience have experienced disguise and illusion, an irony that structures comedy and highlights "a transformative moment of wonder" (Mills 2017).

Central to many of these studies is the critical question of whether the governing purpose of a stage direction is to clarify a physical motion without which the words won't make sense to the casual reader or, more interpretively, to express an image or idea about what's happening. Frequently, students feel emboldened by their increased ability to spot implicit stage directions on their own and reject the need for what come to seem like excessive stage directions. A student who integrated into a performance history of *Much Ado About Nothing* the variations in the stage direction dictating how Hero reacts to Claudio's accusation in Act 4, Scene 1 – either fainting, swooning, or falling to the ground (2015, 646; 2014, 244; 2008, 1452) – also revelled in finding that even distinguished scholars can be as snarky as undergrads. She rushed into class one day with this footnote from Furness's Variorum *Much Ado*: "No dramatist needs stage directions, in the text, less than Shakespeare; he leaves nothing to conjecture, he tells us everything. When Beatrice exclaims in terror 'Why, how now, Cousin! Wherefore you sink down!' whosoever needs to be told, in a stage direction, that 'Hero swoons' ought to have the word 'says' inserted in the text, for his better comprehension, before every speech" (1899, 201; Steffensmeier 2017). In other cases, the editor's guiding hand is welcomed, as in this discussion of editorial stage directions in the lovers' fight in Act 3, Scene 2 of *A Midsummer Night's Dream*: "To the actor poring over the pages of this play, studying each and every line for a clue to aid in their portrayal, these stage directions may seem redundant and unnecessary. However, they aid in the understanding of the average reader, and add to the sense of urgency, chaos, and emotion that underlie the scene and the play itself" (Bekebrede 2017). These papers have made possible genuinely original Shakespearean research by undergraduates in a mid-level course without access to a non-virtual archive, awakening scholarly creativity in a wide range of my students.

For me, the chief value of this way of teaching and reading Shakespeare is that it transforms our understanding of what a Shakespeare play is, giving us more of a sense of the historical texture from which modern texts and performances emerge. It unfixes some of my students' certainties about an object previously defined for them by its permanence. For years I've observed, both in and outside of the classroom, that the most powerful draw and most formidable obstacle to experiencing Shakespeare directly is his canonicity. I am invited to talk to groups who are wrestling with a play they admire and don't understand very well, sometimes in advance of attending a local performance, feeling they need help with work of this stature. Similarly, students come to my Shakespeare class out of reverence for the master playwright, and with an appetite for the cultural capital associated with appreciating him. Yet it's that same perception of remote, unalloyed genius that ordinary people can't enjoy that keeps most students away, as far as possible, from my Shakespeare class – and that limits the audience for that local performance. Eric Spencer argues in the next chapter that the question of Shakespearean "translation," that is, modern language versions of the plays, drives to the heart of what makes Shakespeare valuable: is it universal themes, characters, and dilemmas in which we can recognize ourselves, or is the special value embedded in the unique, often obscure language itself? As he observes, some argue that modernizing Shakespeare's language removes a barrier to his text and promotes engagement with the riches of his stories. Paying attention to editorial stage directions and other interventions signalled by the square brackets gives readers another way to engage with these hallowed old plays. It shows us that, rather than a static work of art, the Shakespeare play we read and see on stage or film is always a collaborative venture. Identifying the editor's presence on the page allows us access to the modern Shakespeare text precisely as a modern Shakespeare text: made by living editors, with guidance from three hundred years of editors before them, and brought to dramatic life only by the painstaking decisions of living theatre artists and the theatrical imagination of the willing reader.

REFERENCES

Bekebrede, Dana. 2017. "Comedy in Chaos: The Lovers' Actions in *A Midsummer Night's Dream*." Undergraduate student essay, Coe College.

Dessen, Alan C. 1995. *Recovering Shakespeare's Theatrical Vocabulary*. Cambridge: Cambridge University Press.

Hausknecht, Gina. 2013. *All The World's A Stage Direction: An Interactive Learning Tool* (website). http://shakespearestagedirections.coe.edu.

Jowett, John. 2007. *Shakespeare and Text*. Oxford: Oxford University Press.

Kidnie, Margaret Jane. 2004. "The Staging of Shakespeare's Drama in Print Editions." In *Textual Performances: The Modern Reproduction of Shakespeare's Drama*, edited by Lukas Erne and Margaret Jane Kidnie, 158–77. Cambridge: Cambridge University Press.

Marcus, Leah. 2009. "The Blue-Eyed Witch." In *The Tempest: A Case Study in Critical Controversy*, 2nd ed., edited by Gerald Graff and James Phelan, 244–64. Boston: Bedford / St Martin's.

McClure, Alizé. 2018. Undergraduate student journal entry, Coe College.

Mills, Laura. 2017. "Revelation and Dramatic Structure in Shakespeare's Twelfth Night." Undergraduate student essay, Coe College.

Remund Wiger, Ella. 2017. "Chastity, Autonomy, and Exiting Guarded in *Measure for Measure*." Undergraduate student essay, Coe College.

Shakespeare, William. 1709. *The Works of Mr William Shakespeare*. Edited by Nicholas Rowe. London.

– 1733. *The Works of Shakespeare*. Edited by Lewis Theobald. London.

– 1765. *The Plays of William Shakespeare, with the Corrections and Illustrations of Various Commentators*. Edited by Samuel Johnson. London.

– 1766. *Twenty of the plays of Shakespeare*. Edited by George Steevens. London.

– 1768. *Mr William Shakespeare his comedies, histories, and tragedies*. Edited by Edward Capell. London.

– 1899. *A New Variorum Edition of Shakespeare*. Edited by Horace Howard Furness. Philadelphia.

– 1963. *The Tragedy of Othello, The Moor of Venice. The Signet Classic Shakespeare*. Edited by Alvin Kernan. New York: New American Library.

– 1974. *The Riverside Shakespeare*. Edited by G. Blakemore Evans. Boston: Houghton Mifflin.

– 2002. *The Complete Pelican Shakespeare*. Edited by Stephen Orgel and A.R. Braunmuller. New York: Penguin.
– 2005. *The Oxford Shakespeare*. 2nd ed. Edited by Stanley Wells and Gary Taylor. Oxford: Clarendon Press.
– 2008. *The Norton Shakespeare*. 2nd ed. Edited by Stephen Greenblatt. New York: W.W. Norton.
– 2011. *The Arden Shakespeare Complete Works*. Edited by Richard Proudfoot, Ann Thompson, and David Scott Kastan. London: Methuen.
– 2014. *The Complete Works of Shakespeare*. 7th ed. Edited by David Bevington. Boston: Pearson.
– 2015. *The Bedford Shakespeare*. Edited by Russ McDonald and Lena Cowen Orlin. Boston: Bedford / St Martin's.
Steffensmeier, Sophie. 2017. "A 'Fallen' Hero: A Look at Stage Direction and Tone." Undergraduate student essay, Coe College.
Tollefsrud, Claire. 2017. "The Ring, the Bracelet, and the Ambiguity of Shakespeare." Undergraduate student essay, Coe College.

19

"NOR UNDERSTOOD NONE NEITHER"

Why It Might Be Time to Think Seriously about Shakespeare in Modern English

ERIC SPENCER

You may recognize in my title a moment of audience incomprehension from *Love's Labour's Lost.* The pedantic schoolmaster Holofernes and the linguistically extravagant Spaniard Don Armado have just planned out, with much self-indulgent verbal display, a pageant of the Nine Worthies. Holofernes turns to Constable Dull, who has been on stage, silent, throughout the scene, and says, "Goodman Dull, thou hast spoken no word all this while." "Nor understood none neither," Dull replies (Shakespeare 2002, 5.1.139–41). The joke is partly on the aptly named Dull, of course, but like so many rejoinders from Shakespeare's clowns, Dull's reply may also call attention to the needless impenetrability of his elitist superiors.

The present chapter originated in my (admittedly unsubstantiated) worry that contemporary audiences and readers sometimes experience Shakespeare the way Dull experiences Holofernes – as an intimidating and incomprehensible representative of high culture, to whom deference, rather than respect or love, is owed. For similar reasons, over the past twenty years, the American linguist John McWhorter has been championing modern English translations of Shakespeare. Despite being an avid theatre-goer and a highly educated expert on language, McWhorter confesses that he struggles to understand Shakespeare's language in real time during performance. He suspects that many theatre-goers struggle just as much or more. So while he concedes the obvious – that "translated Shakespeare is no longer Shakespeare in the strictest sense" – he also asks us whether we are "satisfied with Shakespeare's being genuinely meaningful only to an elite few unless edited to death or carefully excerpted, with most of the rest of us genuflecting in the name of 'culture' and keeping our confusion to ourselves?" (2015). We might therefore consider modern English translations of Shakespeare, McWhorter concludes, at least for the stage, lest we doom Shakespeare to becoming a status symbol and not an artist who might speak to us.

Apparently thinking along similar lines, the Oregon Shakespeare Festival (OSF) announced, in the fall of 2015, its *Play On! Shakespeare Translation/Adaptation Project*. This project (in fact already under way before 2012) involves commissioning accomplished playwrights to translate the entire Shakespeare canon, and then staging the translated plays, while also continuing to mount productions using the original texts.

Perhaps it is not too soon, then, to take a long hard look at the case for Shakespeare in modern English. Now, what follows is *not* that long hard look, but rather an argument for taking it, because I have been troubled by the tone and the content of the translation discussion to date (especially but not exclusively on the anti-translation side), and equally troubled by how little discussion there's been. Even after the OSF announcement, professional Shakespeareans have had almost nothing to say about the matter. The flagship Shakespeare journals ignore it. What little discussion there has been appears mostly in brief editorials, commentaries, and op-ed pieces, not in thorough, full-dress scholarly efforts. When prominent Shakespeareans have weighed in, their eagerness to discourage translation has permitted them to leave incompatible assumptions about the sources of Shakespeare's value unexamined, compromising their arguments against translation. The matter, I submit, deserves more thoughtful, sustained attention.

But some of you may already be thinking that the matter has provoked little discussion because it merits none. If so, you're not alone. The linguist David Crystal, perhaps the most persistent published opponent of translating Shakespeare, makes a representative anti-translation case in a 2002 essay titled "To Modernize or Not to Modernize: There Is No Question." The title alone dismisses intralingual translation of Shakespeare as not worth asking about. (It is also an example of how the debate generates cheesy titles.) Crystal writes, "I see the question of 'modernizing' Shakespeare has reared its head again" (Crystal 2002). As this weary "reared its head again" suggests, Crystal treats the debate like a game of Whack-a-Mole;

proponents of translation are identical, persistent, and mindless, to be bludgeoned back into their burrows repeatedly with the same hammer. And sure enough, Crystal repeated his 2002 case (sometimes with long passages repeated verbatim) in 2008's *Think on My Words: Exploring Shakespeare's Language* and in a 2011 exchange with McWhorter (who, to be fair, also recycles old material) in *Voice and Speech Review*. Crystal's admittedly plausible case boils down to this: Shakespeare's English is simply not different enough from contemporary English to seriously impede comprehension. "Rather than modernize Shakespeare," Crystal concludes, "all our effort should be devoted to making people more fluent in 'Shakespearian,' by devising appropriately graded EME [Early Modern English] syllabuses and writing carefully graded introductions, phrase books, and other materials – just as one would in the real foreign-language teaching world" (Crystal 2002, 17). Because "dissociating authors from the language they have carefully chosen to use hits deeply at their identity," translation should be only "a last resort" (ibid.). (He does not suggest how we might know when recourse to that last resort is called for.) Case closed, if the silly moles would only listen.

Unfortunately for Crystal, what should be a last resort isn't. High school and college students already rely on the paraphrases at *No Fear Shakespeare*, *GradeSaver*, and other websites. Meanwhile, a retired Long Beach State professor of critical thinking and linguistics named Kent Richmond is energetically marketing his verse translations online; the back cover of his *Romeo and Juliet* asserts, with breathtaking confidence, that his version "Captures the original's tone, complexity, and poetry," "Preserves the work's literary integrity," "Reveals subtlety and richness without notes or glosses," and is "Ready for serious, faithful stage performance" (Delabastita 2016, 204). McWhorter has praised Richmond (perhaps too enthusiastically); the community of professional Shakespeareans has ignored him. But whether the profession recognizes it or not, translated Shakespeare is already here, in spades – and that's leaving aside to what degree modern editors and directors might be said to "translate" the plays. The question for professional Shakespeareans, then, really isn't "to modernize or not to modernize" – that train has left the station. The question is instead whether to encourage high-quality literary translation, as we would for any foreign-language author we value, or to cede that burgeoning market, with all its pedagogical stakes, to the *GradeSaver*s and Richmonds.

After all, comprehension may not always be as easy as Crystal suggests. Even he recommends that we provide students with materials like those used "in the real foreign-language teaching world," although he adds that students of Early Modern English will have a much easier time of it than foreign-language learners. This doesn't sound unreasonable, but we might pause to consider that the Chaucerian Mark H. Liddell, in an 1898 *Atlantic Monthly* article, similarly recommended that students receive instruction in Early Modern English (to replace instruction in Greek and Latin), allowing them to read Shakespeare profitably without resort to notes, dictionaries, or translation (Delabastita 2016, 197). As Dirk Delabastita notes, Liddell's proposal closely resembles Crystal's call to make people "more fluent in Shakespearian." But if the problem of comprehension was acute enough in 1898 to prompt Liddell's proposal, is it likely to be so obviously negligible now as Crystal argues? Delabastita concludes that "if scholars have written dictionaries of Shakespearean English intended for native speakers of English, and if those native speakers are also being told that they should perhaps learn Shakespearean English in the way of a classical or foreign language, could we not take the next step and regard 'Shakespearean' as a 'different' language that requires 'translation'?" (2016, 198).

Well, I'm not sure. (Nor, apparently, is Delabastita, judging from all those scare quotes.) It might help if we knew exactly how much audiences and readers actually understand, or even how to measure such understanding. Unfortunately, the crucial question of audience comprehension remains on both sides a matter of unsubstantiated anecdote. In her 2001 call for translation, the linguist and translation scholar Susan Bassnett cites her bored children as representative of a generation that doesn't have Shakespeare and the King James Version in their heads like her generation did, and for whom Shakespeare's original words, she concludes rather boldly, "might as well be Tibetan" (2001, 3). Similarly, in his contribution to the *Voice and Speech Review* debate with David and Ben Crystal (titled, tritely, "The Real Shakespearean Tragedy"), McWhorter cites his own play-going experience as evidence that, for anyone but experts, "the language of Shakespeare remains lovely in snippets, but downright tiresome as the vehicle of an evening-length presentation" (McWhorter, Crystal, and Crystal 2011, 38). David Crystal counters by citing inner-city teenagers he saw excitedly engaged at a production of *King Lear* (ibid). In a 2015 op-ed piece for the *New*

York Times deploring the Oregon Shakespeare Festival's translation project, James Shapiro similarly points to "deeply engrossed" Rikers Island inmates he saw at a ninety-minute, original language *Much Ado*. Though there's probably some truth to what both sides suggest about audience experiences, such diametrically opposed anecdotes – all imputing emotions to subjects whose minds the writer has no access to – can decide nothing. Popular opinion may be similarly inconclusive: in an essay for the 2004 Arden Shakespeare collection *Shakespeare and the Language of Translation*, Bassnett notes that "discussions on local and national radio, considerable correspondence from members of the public, debates in schools, a debate ... at the Shakespeare Birthplace Trust in Stratford and ... at the Roundhouse" yielded the following result: "some 40 per cent in favour of modern versions and (the more vociferous) 60 per cent rejecting translation entirely" (2004, 57). A 60–40 split may mean an electoral landslide, but it hardly suggests that truth lies self-evidently with the majority. It might suggest, however, that something complex and substantial – something more than a game of Whack-a-Mole – is at stake.

But the audience comprehension question *does* lead, I think, to a central, under-addressed problem in the translation debate – namely, the coexistence of incompatible and apparently non-negotiable assumptions about what makes Shakespeare valuable. On the one hand, we are told that Shakespeare's value derives from his universality, as evidenced by the duration and extent of his appeal – hence the stories of enthusiasm for Shakespeare from even the least likely anglophone audiences, like Shapiro's inmates. Who needs translation when audiences already dig it so much? We might call this the "easy" Shakespeare, available to all without preparation, presumably because of his uncanny grasp of human nature. Neither Crystal nor Shapiro, however, asks whether their unlikely Shakespeare lovers understood the language, or just enjoyed the charismatic power of actors in live performance. That power is very important, but it is not an argument against translation. Who says they wouldn't have enjoyed even more the same actors performing a translated text?

On the other hand, while they celebrate Shakespeare's accessibility, opponents of translation also celebrate the irreplaceable complexity, resonance, and profundity – in short, the laudable *difficulty* – of Shakespeare's language. "Shakespeare in other words isn't Shakespeare," says Russ McDonald in his *Bedford Companion to Shakespeare* (1996, 180). Bassnett, even while recommending translation, says "the essence of Shakespeare is language" (2001, 3). In a 2009 reply to McWhorter in the *New Republic* (revealingly titled "The Untouchable"), Antoni Cimolino, artistic director of the venerable Stratford Festival in Ontario, argues that problems understanding Shakespeare arise not because of the passage of time but because the plays were meant to be "dense, complex, and profoundly non-naturalistic dramatic poems"; translating Shakespeare is misguided, then, because by "trying to nail down meaning, we reduce it." Besides, Cimolino continues, Shakespeare knew that "context and intuition would carry his audiences through the more difficult passages." So, instead of allowing those passages "to frustrate us and make us yearn to replace his plays with simpler ones, we should be patient, enjoy what we can, and return again and again to this inexhaustible well of meaning" (2009, 4–5). Shapiro (2015) similarly insists that "Shakespeare's use of resonance and ambiguity, defining features of his language, is ... lost in translation," and this loss is fatal since the "only thing Shakespearean about his plays *is* the language." Indeed, even the OSF tries not to let translation transgress on the sanctity of the original language. In its commission to Kenneth Cavender to translate *Timon of Athens*, it stipulates what is, for purists, the impossible: Cavender's text should be "faithful to the meaning, poetry, and dramatic intent of the original" but also "absolutely intelligible to contemporary audiences" (Kaiser 2012, 3).

As a professional Shakespearean, I'm predisposed to find such respect for Shakespeare's irreproducible language compelling. I've probably said such things in class. And yet I'm troubled. If Shakespeare in other words isn't Shakespeare, as McDonald claims, then have non-anglophone audiences and readers of Shakespeare been experiencing something that isn't Shakespeare *at all*? If Shakespeare's language is "untouchable," as Cimolino claims, then how does he justify the cuts and rearrangements he has made as a director staging the plays? Or how does he justify not mounting all his productions in original pronunciation, since sound after all contributes crucially to the effect of "dense ... dramatic poems"? And if "context and intuition" will get us through the more difficult passages – which suggests that understanding *all* of the original language in its full complexity *isn't* a mandatory part of experiencing Shakespeare – then why declare that language "untouchable"?

More broadly, does it make sense to insist on making Shakespeare universally available through education and performance – on the assumption that the plays offer something of unique value to anyone who encounters them – and at the same time to insist that this unique value is wrapped up in a language so subtle and difficult that legions of salaried scholars cannot agree about what it means, and for whom such disagreement is celebrated as evidence of Shakespeare's transcendent inexhaustibility? Shapiro (2015) seems to be trying to solve this problem – that is, the problem of making profundity accessible without diluting its accompanying difficulty – when he argues that audiences don't need to understand "exactly what Macbeth says" as long as they "grasp what Macbeth feels," and this they can do "only if the actor knows exactly what the character's words mean." He then claims, with surprising anti-theatrical vitriol, that contemporary actors almost never do know what the words mean, and *that's* why audiences struggle to understand. But if he's right that audiences need understand only what a character feels, he seems to be saying that the real value of Shakespeare lies *not* in the language but in the *emotional experience* of the character toward which the language points, such that actors *translate* the language into the experience through performance (though admittedly Shapiro doesn't use the word "translation" for this process). If reformulating the language in this way is acceptable to Shapiro, why not in others?

These arguments, then, seemingly try to assert both ease *and* difficulty – a popular, universal Shakespeare *and* an elite, difficult Shakespeare – and then to pretend there's no tension between them. For easy accessibility implies that, even when we can't follow the language exactly, we can identify the crucial ideas or feelings it expresses, and that in turn implies that we can name those ideas or feelings, define them, formulate them in words other than those used by Shakespeare – in short, translate them. If, by contrast, the language is so suggestive and resonant, so resistant to translation because every nuance potentially leads to hitherto unnoticed semantic possibilities, then it can't also be easily accessible. Trying to have it both ways – to claim that Shakespeare's irreproducibly polyvalent language constitutes his greatness and cannot therefore be translated, but also that audiences can experience the real Shakespeare with little or no help – repeatedly produces, at least for me, incoherent claims. Thus, David Crystal says Shakespeare's not hard, but we need manuals and graded syllabi; he also recommends that people circumnavigate occasional "islands of difficulty" by seeing a play before and after reading it (McWhorter, Crystal, and Crystal 2011, 44). But I have trouble imagining anyone outside a tiny coterie of aficionados who would regularly sandwich their study of a play with live performances. Meanwhile his son, the Shakespearean actor Ben Crystal, boasts that he won a bet with a fellow actor by speaking the most gnarled passage the latter could find to a full house at the reconstructed Globe such that there were "no comprehension problems," but he also insists that "audiences must learn to work a little bit" – after all, who said that "Shakespeare, one of the greatest dramatists, who often deals with *incredibly complex ideas*, should be easy?" (ibid., 50, my emphasis). Ralph Alan Cohen (2015) of the American Shakespeare Center conveniently concludes that Shakespeare isn't "*too* hard. But it is just the right kind of hard." Maybe so, but this Goldilocks principle also makes it easy to eat your elitist Shakespearean cake and still have it in populist, Shakespeare-speaks-to-everyone form.

Such devotion to Shakespeare as the source of an authoritative (even sacred and untouchable) text, among accomplished and innovative directors like Cimolino and Cohen, paradoxically threatens the power and vitality of performance. As the editors of the Routledge *Adaptations of Shakespeare* anthology point out, "Every drama text is an incomplete entity that must be 'translated' by being put on stage. Adaptation is ... only an extreme version of the reworking that takes place in any theatrical production. Theatre does things to the drama text that cannot be justified as acts of fidelity, and yet are necessary for any production to take place" (Fischlin and Fortier 2000, 7). In other words, things are lost in the translation to performance, no less than in translation to another language, but that is part of what gives performance its beauty and power; the alternative is no performance at all. Only when we refuse to acknowledge that vital performance *requires* infidelity in this way, argues W.B. Worthen in *Shakespeare and the Authority of Performance*, does performing recognized classics "[threaten] to become an act of transgression" (1997, 191). For Worthen, such refusal produces, in contemporary discussion of stage performance, gestures of allegiance to Shakespeare that protest a little too much, because they try to reconcile incompatible goals. On the one hand, in order to avoid turning Shakespeare into museum theatre, companies design performances that will speak to modern audiences. On the other hand, they insist that such accommodation to modern sensibilities channels the real, original Shakespeare without distortion or compromise. Worthen suspects that the latter impulse unnecessarily hems in the former, so that, by treating Shakespeare as "sacred text," we "impoverish the work of our own performances, and the work of the plays in *our* making of the world" (ibid., my emphasis).

I suppose I'm suggesting, then, that discomfort at the prospect of a violated taboo may give opponents of translation their peremptory and impatient tone, and proponents of it their tendency to offer conciliatory qualifications. Now, let me be clear: I don't for a moment imagine that translation, in any form, doesn't involve loss. Given my druthers, I would have the original texts (or the closest thing we have to them) performed, read, and taught. Nor, for that matter, do I underestimate the difficulty of producing a good intralingual translation of Shakespeare. Translation between relatively similar versions of the same language poses special and intricate challenges; Shakespeare's verbal genius and intimidating canonicity will only intensify those challenges. But I would like to see the debate carried out in a way that acknowledges, even embraces, the inevitability of loss and change in any vital cultural tradition, while at the same resisting irresponsible ignorance of or indifference to the sovereign otherness of the past. I suspect perfect solutions exist here no more than they do elsewhere. We cannot have an untouchable original and at the same time do the cultural work of the present, yet both impulses are valuable. As a result, we might spend a little more time thoughtfully *dwelling* in this contradiction, not simply denying it or resigning ourselves to it.

I don't know whether such dwelling in contradiction is best accomplished by promoting translation or resisting it. But we might at least consider what many translators and translation scholars have long argued – that translation need not be only a poor, apologetic substitute for linguistic access to an original, a kind of remedial prosthesis. It can also be (and has been) a source of invigorating creative opportunity. Thus, for example, Ton Hoenselaars (2013) laments the "extraordinary level of rigidity" in the debate over modernizing Shakespeare, in particular the lack of "awareness ... that such intra-lingual Shakespeare ... which is emphatically not 'Shakespeare for Dummies'... may provide a boost to the creativity of the English language" (216). Similarly, Delabastita points out that intralingual translation may occur when comprehension is not an issue, as in some recent translations of *Macbeth* into Scots, the purpose of which was not to modernize Shakespeare for bewildered contemporary audiences but to lift Scots "above the status of a dialect or bastard offshoot of English and [make] it a 'real' language that accommodates Shakespeare's tragedy as comfortably as English" (2004, 39). In introducing his own Scottish translation of *Macbeth*, David Purves (1992) suggests that because "performances of this great play have in modern times become ritualized, the use of Scots serves to restore meaning to important passages which have tended to become worn-out and hackneyed." I suppose, then, that we might at least try the route of high-quality literary translation – after all, doing so will not suddenly deprive us of well-edited "original" texts – and we might encourage Shakespeareans to treat the question, with its considerable intricacies and implications, as more than a game of Whack-a-Mole.

REFERENCES

Bassnett, Susan. 2001. "Shakespeare's in Danger: We Have to Act Now to Avoid a Great Tragedy." *Independent*, 14 November. https://www.independent.co.uk/news/education/education-news/shakespeares-in-danger-we-have-to-act-now-to-avoid-a-great-tragedy-9159195.html.

– 2004. "Engendering Anew: Shakespeare, Gender, and Translation." In *Shakespeare and the Language of Translation*, edited by A.J. Hoenselaars, 53–67. London: Arden Shakespeare.

Cimolino, Antoni. 2009. "The Untouchables." *New Republic*, 14 July. https://newrepublic.com/article/62201/disputations-the-untouchables.

Cohen, Ralph Alan. 2015. "American Shakespeare Center Director of Mission's Response to the Shakespeare Translation Project." Online posting. *Shaksper: The Global Electronic Shakespeare Conference*, 9 October. http://shaksper.net/archive/2015/362-october/31101-a-facelift-for-shakespeare-6.

Crystal, David. 2002. "To Modernize or Not to Modernize? There Is No Question." *Around the Globe* 21 (2002): 15–17. www.davidcrystal.com/books-and-articles/shakespeare.

– 2008. *Think on My Words: Exploring Shakespeare's Language*. Cambridge: Cambridge University Press.

Delabastita, Dirk. 2004. "'If I Know the Letters and the Language': Translation as a Dramatic Device in Shakespeare's Plays." In

Shakespeare and the Language of Translation, edited by A.J. Hoenselaars, 31–52. London: Arden Shakespeare.

– 2016. "'He Shall Signify from Time to Time': *Romeo and Juliet* in Modern English." *Perspectives: Studies in Translation Theory and Practice* 25 (2): 189–213. https://www.tandfonline.com/doi/abs/10.1080/0907676X.2016.1234491.

Fischlin, Daniel, and Mark Fortier. 2000. "General Introduction." *Adaptations of Shakespeare*, 1–22. New York: Routledge.

Hoenselaars, Ton. 2013. "Shakespeare and the Cultures of Translation." *Shakespeare Survey* 66: 206–19.

Kaiser, Scott. 2012. "Translating Timon: The Oregon Shakespeare Festival's *Shakespeare Translation/Adaptation Project*." Scottkaisershakespeare.com (website). https://scottkaisershakespeare.com/pdf/essays/kaiser-translating-timon.pdf.

McDonald, Russ. 1996. *The Bedford Companion to Shakespeare*. Boston and New York: Bedford / St Martin's.

McWhorter, John. 2015. "A Facelift for Shakespeare." *Wall Street Journal*, 25 September.

McWhorter, John, David Crystal, and Ben Crystal. 2011. "Translating Shakespeare into English: A Debate." *Voice and Speech Review* 7 (1): 38–51. https://www.tandfonline.com/doi/full/10.1080/23268263.2011.10739518.

Purves, David. 1992. "Translator's Note." *The Tragedie o Macbeth*. Edinburgh: Rob Roy Press. www.scottishcorpus.ac.uk/document/?documentid=1672.

Shakespeare, William. 2002. *The Complete Works*. Edited by Stephen Orgel and A.R. Braunmuller. New York: Penguin.

Shapiro, James. 2015. "Shakespeare in Modern English?" *New York Times*, 7 October. http://www.nytimes.com/2015/10/07/opinion/shakespeare-in-modern-english.html?_r=0.

Worthen, W.B. 1997. *Shakespeare and the Authority of Performance*. Cambridge: Cambridge University Press.

CONTRIBUTORS

RUSSELL J. BODI is professor of English at Owens State Community College in Toledo, Ohio, where he is also director of the Honors Program. He presently serves as the chair of the Ohio Shakespeare Conference, an annual venue for Shakespeare scholarship.

CHRISTIE CARSON is reader in Shakespeare and performance in the Department of English at Royal Holloway University of London. She is the co-editor of four collections of essays for Cambridge University Press: *Shakespeare's Globe: A Theatrical Experiment*, with Farah Karim-Cooper; *Shakespeare in Stages: New Theatre Histories*, with Christine Dymkowski; *Shakespeare Beyond English*, with Susan Bennett; and *Shakespeare and the Digital World*, with Peter Kirwan.

BRANDON CHRISTOPHER is associate professor and chair of the Department of English at the University of Winnipeg. His research and teaching focus on early modern drama (especially Shakespeare), adaptations of Shakespeare and his works in contemporary culture, and comics and graphic narratives. He is currently at work on a book tentatively titled "Shakespeare and Comics / Comics and Shakespeare: Adaptation, Reciprocity, and the Contingency of Cultural Value."

ANTONI CIMOLINO, artistic director of the Stratford Festival, began his Stratford career as an actor, most notably playing Romeo opposite Megan Follows's Juliet. Throughout his thirty-one seasons, he has held a number of leadership roles, including general manager, general director, and executive director. Since being appointed artistic director in 2013, he and Anita Gaffney, the festival's executive director, have introduced The Forum, The Laboratory, and Stratford HD, and have launched a $100-million campaign to build the new Tom Patterson Theatre. He has directed dozens of plays, including such recent Stratford productions as *Cymbeline*, *Mary Stuart*, *Macbeth*, and *King Lear*.

JACOB CLAFLIN, a graduate of the Mary Baldwin University Shakespeare and performance master's program, defended his dissertation on multimodal poetics and Shakespeare at Idaho State University in 2017. He is currently a full-time instructor at the College of Eastern Idaho, a new community college where he is working to develop a robust English program including an Introduction to Shakespeare course. Jake has a keen interest in Shakespeare on stage and screen and in comic book adaptations and appropriations of Shakespeare.

LAUREN ERIKS CLINE is assistant professor of English at Hampden-Sydney College. Her research examines the intersections of performance, spectatorship, and narrative in audience and actor accounts of theatre-going. Her work has appeared in *Nineteenth Century Theatre and Film*, *Victorian Literature and Culture*, and *The Oxford Handbook of Shakespeare and Embodiment* and is forthcoming from *Shakespeare Studies* and *Theatre Survey*.

DAVID B. GOLDSTEIN is associate professor of English at York University, in Toronto. His first monograph, *Eating and Ethics in Shakespeare's England*, shared the Shakespeare's Globe Book Award. He has also published two books of poetry and two essay collections, *Culinary Shakespeare* (with Amy Tigner) and *Shakespeare and Hospitality* (with Julia Reinhard Lupton). His essays on early modern literature, Emmanuel Levinas, food studies, ecology, and contemporary poetry have appeared in *Studies in English Literature*, *Shakespeare Studies*, *Gastronomica*, and numerous other journals and collections. He is currently co-director of the Folger Shakespeare Library's Mellon-funded collaborative research project *Before "Farm to Table": Early Modern Foodways and Cultures*.

KENNETH GRAHAM is professor of English at the University of Waterloo, where he teaches Shakespeare and English Renaissance literature. His publications include *The Performance of Conviction: Plainness and Rhetoric in the Early English Renaissance*, *Disciplinary Measures from the Metrical Psalms to Milton*, and *Shakespeare and Religious Change* (co-edited with Philip Collington). He recently published "Shakespearean Comedy and Early Modern Religious Culture" in *The Oxford Handbook of Shakespearean Comedy*, and his essay on *Measure for Measure* will appear in *Religion and Literature*. He is now writing about Shakespeare's religious language.

GINA HAUSKNECHT, John William King Professor of Literature and Creative Writing and associate dean for student academics at Coe College in Iowa, teaches early modern British literature, including Shakespeare, British Renaissance poetry, and Milton. Her publications include articles on seventeenth-century literature and culture, intersections of gender and political theory, and pedagogy and higher education. Her research on the textual history of stage directions in editions of Shakespeare is reflected in the interactive online learning tool *All the World's a Stage Direction*.

PETER HOLLAND is McMeel Family Professor in Shakespeare Studies in the Department of Film, Television and Theatre and associate dean for the arts at the University of Notre Dame, in Indiana. He was editor of *Shakespeare Survey* for nineteen years and is co–general editor for *Oxford Shakespeare Topics*, *Great Shakespeareans*, *Arden Shakespeare in the Theatre*, and the *Arden Shakespeare 4th Series*. He has edited many Shakespeare plays including *A Midsummer Night's Dream* (Oxford) and *Coriolanus* (Arden 3rd series). He is chair of the International Shakespeare Association. Current projects include a monograph, *Shakespeare and Forgetting*, and editing *King Lear* for Arden 4.

R.W. JONES is a PhD candidate at the University of Texas, and is currently working on a dissertation examining the influence of contemporary theatre conventions on the "original practices" movement. He has served as assistant director of Shakespeare studies at the university, as well as assistant director of the Shakespeare at

Winedale program. In addition, he owns an MFA in Shakespeare and performance from Mary Baldwin University in Virginia, and has previously published on connections between *Antony and Cleopatra* and the York Crucifixion play. He has also worked as a professional actor and director in both Virginia and Texas.

ALYSIA KOLENTSIS is associate professor of English at St Jerome's University in the University of Waterloo. Her research focuses on early modern drama and poetry, with a particular focus on Shakespeare and language. She has published essays in *Shakespeare Survey*, *Exemplaria*, and *Genre*, and has contributed chapters to the *Oxford Handbook of Shakespeare's Poetry*, *Shakespeare in Our Time*, and the forthcoming *Cambridge Companion to Shakespeare's Language*. Her book project, *Shakespeare's Common Language*, is a study of Shakespeare's easily overlooked words.

CHRISTINA LUCKYJ is professor of English at Dalhousie University in Halifax, Nova Scotia, where she specializes in early modern literature. She is the author of *"A Moving Rhetoricke:" Gender and Silence in Early Modern England*, editor of *The Duchess of Malfi: A Critical Guide*, and co-editor (with Niamh J. O'Leary) of *The Politics of Female Alliance in Early Modern England.* She recently provided a new introduction and commentary for the New Cambridge *Othello* and is completing a study of the politics of the female voice in early modern England.

JULIA REINHARD LUPTON is professor of English at the University of California, Irvine, where she has taught since 1989. She is the author or co-author of five books on Shakespeare, including *Shakespeare Dwelling*, *Thinking with Shakespeare*, and *Citizen-Saints*. She is the co-editor of several volumes, including *Shakespeare and Hospitality*, with David Goldstein; *Political Theology and Early Modernity*, with Graham Hammill; and *Face to Face in Shakespearean Drama*, with Matthew J. Smith. She is a former Guggenheim and ACLS fellow.

LINDA MCJANNET is professor of English and media studies (emerita) at Bentley University in Waltham, Massachusetts. She is the author of two monographs, *The Sultan Speaks: Dialogue in English Plays and Histories about the Ottoman Turks* and *The Voice of English Stage Directions: The Evolution of a Theatrical Code.* Her articles have appeared in *Shakespeare Quarterly*, *English Literary Renaissance*, *Borrowers and Lenders*, and *Dance Chronicle*, among others. A chapter on physical theatre and Shakespeare is forthcoming in *The Oxford Handbook of Shakespeare and Dance*. In 2013, with Emily Winerock and Amy Rodgers, she co-founded the Shakespeare and Dance Project (www.shakespeareandance.com).

RODERICK H. MCKEOWN earned his PhD at the University of Toronto in 2013, where his thesis won the Clifford Leech Prize for the best dissertation on drama, reading early modern plays through a prism of sociolinguistics, classical rhetoric, and speech act theory. His chapter in this volume is an early part of a project on diverse casting in contemporary productions of early modern drama. He works in academic administration at the University of Toronto's School of Graduate Studies, and has lectured in English literature at the university and in Innis College's writing and rhetoric program.

HAYLEY O'MALLEY is an English PhD candidate at the University of Michigan and has a master's in film aesthetics from Oxford University. She works on African-American cultural production, twentieth- and twenty-first-century literature and visual culture, and film adaptation, especially of Shakespeare. Her dissertation-in-progress, "Dreaming Black Cinema: The Making of African American Literature and Film after Civil Rights," explores how African-American writers were influenced by and in turn influenced the rise of independent black film from the late 1960s to the early 1990s.

AMRITA SEN is associate professor and deputy director, UGC–Human Resource Development Centre, University of Calcutta. She has published on East India Company women, Bollywood Shakespeares, and early modern ethnography. She has co-edited, with Julia Schleck, a special issue entitled "Alternative Histories of the East India Company" for the *Journal of Early Modern Cultural Studies*, and is co-editing, with J. Caitlin Finlayson, *Civic Performance: Pageantry and Entertainments in Early Modern London*.

ERIC SPENCER is professor of English at the College of Idaho, where he has taught Shakespeare, early modern literature, and composition for twenty-five years. Since receiving his doctorate from the University of California, Berkeley, he has concentrated on anthropological and philosophical approaches to literature, and has published a number of essays on money and justice in *Measure for Measure*, *The Merchant of Venice*, and *Henry IV, Part One*. He has also written many volumes' worth of marginal comments on student essays, and is second author of a twenty-three-year-old son.

LISA S. STARKS is professor of English at the University of South Florida, St Petersburg. She has published several essays, edited special issues of journals, and co-edited book collections on topics related to film, Shakespeare, and Renaissance drama, including the monograph *Violence, Trauma, and* Virtus *in Shakespeare's Roman Poems and Plays: Transforming Ovid*. She is currently working on two new projects: a book collection entitled *Ovid and Adaptation in Early Modern English Theater* and a monograph on Levinas, Shakespeare, and adaptation studies.

JEFFREY R. WILSON is a faculty member in the writing program at Harvard University, where he teaches the "Why Shakespeare?" section of the first-year writing course. Focused on intersections of Renaissance literature and modern sociology, his work has appeared in academic journals such as *Shakespeare*, *Genre*, *Medieval and Renaissance Drama in England*, *Law and the Humanities*, and *Crime, Media, Culture*, as well as public venues such as National Public Radio, the *Chronicle of Higher Education*, *Academe*, *The Smart Set*, and *CounterPunch*. He holds a PhD in English from the University of California, Irvine.

INDEX

Page numbers in *italics* denote photographs.